Dr Ben Robinson is a British archaeologist and television presenter.

Ben grew up in a Cambridgeshire fenland village, within a farming family. He has worked as a field archaeologist, an archaeological planning adviser, and once enjoyed the grand-sounding job title 'Inspector of Ancient Monuments'.

Ben joined cult archaeological TV show *Time Team* for several series and has presented regional BBC TV features on heritage subjects from Roman treasure to Victorian rubbish. He has taken to the skies as 'The Flying Archaeologist', traced King John's final ill-fated journey and tracked the path of Zeppelin raids for BBC Four. Latterly, Ben has joined Alice Roberts as 'the eye in the sky' for three series of Channel 4's *Britain's Most Historic Towns*, presented village archaeology and history series *Pubs, Ponds and Power: The Story of the Village*, and now fronts *Villages by the Sea* for BBC Two.

ENGLAND'S VILLAGES

AN EXTRAORDINARY
JOURNEY THROUGH TIME

BEN ROBINSON

BLINK

bringing you closer

First published in the UK by Blink Publishing
An imprint of Bonnier Books UK
4th Floor, Victoria House, Bloomsbury Square, London, WC1B 4DA
Owned by Bonnier Books
Sveavägen 56, Stockholm, Sweden

Paperback – 978–1–788704–60–1
Hardback – 978–1–786580–91–7
Ebook – 978–1–786580–97–9
Audio Digital Download – 978–1–786581–01–3

A CIP catalogue of this book is available from the British Library.

Designed and set by seagulls.net
Illustrations © Jitesh Patel, 2021
All images © Ben Robinson unless otherwise stated.
Printed and bound by Clays Ltd, Elcograf S.p.A

1 3 5 7 9 10 8 6 4 2

First published in hardback by Blink publishing in 2021
This edition published in paperback by Blink publishing in 2022

Blink Publishing is an imprint of Bonnier Books UK
www.bonnierbooks.co.uk

To Wilfie, Jo, Mary, Peter and Chloe.
Families make villages.

CONTENTS

INTRODUCTION

The past is all around us, not only as vague, ghostly impressions of long-gone activity, but firmly embedded in the structure and character of places we inhabit today. The history of a place is often disguised and goes unseen, or is simply accepted as a natural inheritance without questioning its meaning. However, a little curiosity can open up entire lost worlds for deeper exploration, and enrich our appreciation of the environments our predecessors have shaped for us. Even apparently familiar places have remarkable stories to tell.

English villages have been a defining characteristic of England and the English for a long time. They are familiar, and we have grown used to them. We can take them for granted. Many appear to have stood in effortless serenity for thousands of years, barely changing as the world moved on around them. But England's villages have a dynamic and often turbulent history, which belies the sleepy image that many people associate with them today.

There were villages before there were towns. Villages provided the solid social and economic backbone of the country for centuries. They were also centres of innovation and catalysts for change. English villages in all their diversity, prettiness and grittiness have rich stories to tell, not only about their own pasts, but also about the nation and its people. The history of England is in large part a history of its villages. It is a mistake, however, to think that today's villages are simply remnants from a lost past. Village roles have changed over time and they continue to change, but their influence on the national character remains. They are as relevant today as they ever were.

Villages have much more to offer than first meets the eye, but often you have to do a little work to uncover their secrets. Early photographs and films illuminate a village past that looks vaguely familiar, albeit one that is often rendered in grey and beige. Village fêtes, pageants and holidays seem to figure heavily in the footage, and when village work is featured, it invariably appears as wholesome and leisurely as the village entertainment: summer haymaking, harvests, picking fruit in orchards, a blacksmith shoeing a horse.

We are presented with pictures of quaint places that seem to have been populated by people with a mania for hats, who walked and danced in jerky movements to the accompaniment of a scratchy soundtrack. Documents written a long time before photographs and film were invented take us back far beyond the familiar village to a more remote history. It is thrilling to read the words written on parchment or paper by a person who lived several hundred years ago, and try to get to know them and their world.

The further back in time we go, the less material there is to work with. Written records for most English villages are very sparse indeed until well after medieval times. Until the late nineteenth century, not many historians were interested in investigating individual village histories. Village life was often considered far too mundane to record and far too familiar to have to document and explain. Written records help us to connect with past people and past places, but they only take us so far.

Thankfully we have other direct links to the past, and other ways of understanding how our own world has been formed. We are surrounded by the buildings and infrastructure of the past and merely looking around us can reveal much about the history of a village. Archaeology allows us to take our physical interaction with the village past to another level, or rather greater depths. Not only does archaeology take us back well beyond written history, but it both challenges and complements written accounts. Archaeology, by its very nature, is about opening up revealing things we didn't know. It is a very rewarding way to explore the past of any place.

For me there is nothing quite like being in a place, standing where history was made, and trying to work out how things have changed over time. If not quite a grand search for origins and the meaning of life, it is at least asking the question: 'How have we arrived at the point we are now?' I have been lucky to be able to explore the history of many villages through archaeological excavations, surveys, reading lots of other people's research, making

TV programmes, or simply looking at them as I wander through or fly over them. I hope that anybody interested in the history of villages will find something in this book that will help them enjoy making their own discoveries and asking their own questions.

WHAT IS A VILLAGE?

What exactly is a village, and what sets villages apart from other types of settlement? Dictionary definitions don't help much. The digital *Concise Oxford English Dictionary* definition is representative of many other dictionary definitions I have seen. It describes a village as a 'group of houses situated in a rural area, larger than a hamlet and smaller than a town'. A hamlet is defined as a small village, especially one without a church, and a town is a built-up area within defined boundaries, with its own local government, and larger than a village (but smaller than a city).

Surely there is more to it than that? Many of us probably have our own mental portrait of a traditional English village: old cottages, some thatched, clustered around a green, a market place, a church, or strung along a main street, and surrounded by open countryside. Most rural English villages now relate to a parish, a defined administrative area containing the village and its surrounding land, most of which will be farmed in one way or another. But there is a problem. The second clause of the *Concise Oxford English Dictionary* definition of a village embraces 'a self-contained district or community within a town or city' and even references the Olympic Village.

You will not find these nuances in earlier dictionaries. The definition of a village has changed over time, just as villages have changed over time. We cannot define a prehistoric, Roman or early Anglo-Saxon village in quite the same terms as we define a nineteenth-century industrial village. In those early periods we can't easily distinguish villages from hamlets using the presence or absence of a church as a determining factor. There were no parish churches. Even many sizeable villages that developed after the medieval period did not have their own parish church.

Size of population is relevant to distinguishing villages from hamlets and towns, but this has to be set in the context of the times. The prehistoric population of the British Isles probably grew to more than 1 million people before the Romans arrived, but the population of England was probably still under 2 million in 1086. In 1801, it was around 8 million. Today it's around 60 million. The nation's towns and villages generally had smaller populations in the past.

Early villages were products of societies that were organised very differently to our own, and yet there is still much in common between them and today's villages. Much about what makes a village now and in the past is as dependent on its community as it is on built structure. Most villages can be viewed, broadly, as the coming together of a previously dispersed community of households within a settlement based around a focus; or more than one focus, but nevertheless forming an identifiable larger cluster of homes and other buildings. A village can be deliberately and formally planned, or grow more 'organically' or haphazardly. It can develop slowly over centuries or quickly over a few years.

Time-depth, however, is important. A village does not need to have been around for hundreds of years to deserve the label. It may have been created relatively recently in one distinct episode, but there should be at least some aspiration for permanence or longevity. A village must also have some form of self-determination and governance. If it is not physically separated from other places, it should have an identity and characteristics that set it apart from adjacent places. A village can have a population of a few dozen, or several thousand. Though most villages have some things in common, the defining characteristics of a village will shift over the course of history as living patterns change and more archaeological information becomes available.

Modern retail, however, has given us the perfect example of a 'village' that is, in fact, anything but. Bicester Village was built on the outskirts of the ancient town of Bicester in Oxfordshire in the 1990s. It is a renowned shopping destination, but shoppers in Bicester Village do not walk along real village streets, in a real community. There are no residents, it is all private property and the shops are the same fashion chain stores that you can find in shopping centres all over the world.

Rather than the more usual indoor shopping mall arrangement, with retail outlets all enclosed in a gigantic monolithic multi-storey box, it has open-air parades of shop units. These are built in a synthetic, transatlantic vernacular style, a distant echo of south-east England, and New England weatherboarded village buildings. Apart from having open-air 'streets', there is nothing really 'villagey' about Bicester Village, but it has been a hugely successful commercial venture in a way that an ordinary covered shopping centre in a provincial town would not have been.

It is said to rank second only to Buckingham Palace among Britain's must-see destinations for Chinese tourists. Bicester Village doesn't fool them; they don't think it is a real English village, they just love the shopping experience it provides. There are reports of coach parties of Chinese shoppers being driven around the locality in order get a more realistic view of village England. Good for them.

Clarks Village, built on the site of a former rug and shoe factory, is of similar vintage and layout. It is situated in the countryside, almost in the shadow of Glastonbury Tor, but you will not find very much that reflects old Somerset in this shopping centre. Braintree Village in Essex is owned by the same company. There are shopping villages based on the Bicester Village model as far afield as Dublin, Madrid, Munich and Shanghai. What these places have in common, and what they borrow from villages, is that they are built on a more human scale than vast, urban shopping precincts.

The 'retail village' places attempt to invoke a more intimate, bespoke, homely experience. In addition to retail villages, there are holiday villages, retirement villages, sports villages; there is a new Olympic Village every four years. None of these are really villages in any meaningful sense of the word: they are too one-dimensional. So why have they borrowed the title?

Undoubtedly there is a misty-eyed nostalgia for a type of village and way of village life that we like to believe existed sometime over the last few hundred years or so, and it is exactly this that these 'villages' trade on. Many people draw comfort from the apparent immunity and indifference of villages to the frenetic pace of modern life, with its ever-changing fads and fashions, which churns away in the larger towns and cities. English villages are widely celebrated as blithely carrying on in their timeless, bucolic bubbles, untouched by the sort of troubles that seem to afflict urban areas.

This reassuring image is a great marketing tool. Stick a scene that looks vaguely like a pre-1950s English village on a product (anything from bread or a packet of biscuits to a newly built home) and it will sell comfort, ease, tradition, stability, authenticity, quality. Television dramas and films featuring images of bygone village life that never really existed remain extremely popular. The retired, second home owners and tourists seek out the most authentic and 'unspoilt' villages, trying to capture a piece of something intangible that will help to suspend time for a while, or at least belie the relentless march to a less certain future.

There is another take on this vision of village life, one that is not wholly positive, but is equally non-threatening and comforting. There has long been a widespread perception that there is something a bit homespun, home-made, folksy, amateurish even, about villages. Villages are tucked away out in 'the sticks', away from the buzz, sophistication and excellence of cities. Perceptions like these can lead to condescending humour.

Sports fans are infamous for enjoying their own witty observations on players' performances, and inventing special terms for the purpose. Cricket is full of it. Many times I have heard a sub-standard or comedic passage of play (such as a huge error in shot selection that sees a batsman's stumps shattered, fielders fumbling dropped catches, or poor captaincy tactics) greeted disparagingly with one word: 'village'. The critic means 'village cricket'; there is no need for further explanation or analysis.

They are referencing the sort of amateurish show that a small village with more enthusiasm than talent, and few finely honed athletes to draw on, would put out on a Sunday afternoon. A wild heave by a batsman is a 'mow', or 'a bit agricultural', and a ball thumped over midwicket on the leg side (rather than elegantly stroked through the cultured off side) has been despatched to 'cow corner'.

These phrases are not heard as much these days, especially since most batsmen now play this way in limited overs cricket. But there are plenty of other insults that draw on the association of the English countryside, and its villages in particular, with something a bit bumbling, backward and comedic. People behave like 'village idiots'; supposedly august institutions act like 'parish councils'. Like most jibes, these are crude caricatures, but they are clearly influenced by certain impressions of what the word village represents in many people's minds.

I think it is only fair that perceptions of villages and village life should be informed by some understanding and appreciation of their origins and history.

CHAPTER 1

IN SEARCH OF
VILLAGE ORIGINS

One summer, long ago, as a friend and I returned from one of our cycling expeditions around our home parish, I noticed a man with a metal detector slowly meandering across a field. Occasionally he paused, stooped and scooped out some soil with something that looked like an elongated gardening trowel. He then broke the clods of earth apart and examined them closely. I was nine or ten years old and it was the first time I had seen a metal detector, though its form and the basic principles of its use were familiar from war films and plastic soldiers wielding mine detectors.

Curiosity aroused, my friend and I put down our bikes and hesitantly approached. The detectorist did not want to be distracted by a couple of kids, but without ceasing his sweeps, he told us that he was looking for treasure dropped or buried by people who used to live here. 'But it's just an empty cow field, nobody has lived here, Sutton is over there,' I pointed out to him, in what I thought was a helpful bit of landscape orientation.

'Yes, I know, but villages can move about. Sometimes they are in one place, then somewhere else, maybe somewhere else again, before ending up where they are now.' He paused, contemplating his day's efforts. 'I know one thing, the bugger wasn't here.'

As we biked home I remember saying to my friend that the detectorist was daft. 'No wonder he hasn't found anything in that field. Sutton has always been in the same place,' I told him. 'It's got an old church, a post office and everything.' Years later I understood that the hapless metal detectorist was offering some abbreviated landscape history in order to explain himself to his young interrogators. He was right; villages can wander around throughout their history. Their focus can shift, they can shrink and expand again, or dwindle away until they disappear entirely, sometimes to be reborn in a different form, sometimes never to return. He also knew that even if all visible traces of a village had apparently long gone, artefacts plucked from the soil could indicate its former location.

Working out why villages formed in the first place, and then how they might have moved or vanished entirely requires an understanding of the changing character and wider pattern of human settlement in the British Isles. We can then start to explore the dynamic influences on village origins and development. The history of villages is not one of straightforward, linear evolution from a single starting point, but one marked by fractures, divergence and mutation.

BEFORE VILLAGES

People have lived in England, or to be technically accurate the land mass that came to be called England, for a very long time.

The earliest evidence of human activity comes from discarded stone tools, which have been found in places such as Pakefield in Suffolk and Happisburgh (pronounced *Haze-bruh*) on the Norfolk coast. Incredibly, it has actually been possible to walk in the footsteps of these ancient ancestors at Happisburgh; trails of their footprints have been exposed on eroding mud flats. Only Africa, the cradle of human evolution, has produced older human footprints. The small group of adults and children that strode out across the mud of an estuary nearly 1 million years ago are the first known Britons, but we can't also call them the first Norfolk villagers.

They were part of a sparsely distributed society of nomadic peoples, who were able to roam across Britain and the Continent without being impeded by the English Channel, which did not exist at the time. Over the next several hundred thousand years, people came and went as the land bridge with Europe persisted and then eroded, and the British climate fluctuated between being hot enough for lions and hippos and then too cold for woolly mammoths. Finally, around 8000 to 9000 years ago, rising sea levels prevented easy movement on foot between Britain and the Continent. Despite the fact that freedom to roam was now somewhat more limited, the people who remained on the British Isles still moved around within the territories available to them.

Even this mobile way of life relied on getting some shelter from the worst of the climate. That didn't exclusively mean cave dwellings, as the popular image of Stone Age people suggests, but it did not involve building villages either. In fact, the appearance of houses, permanent settlements and villages come along very late in the story of people in the English landscape. However, when the first villages develop, they come hand in hand with some of the most radical changes in human society.

Nomadic hunter-gatherer groups of the Mesolithic period (around 9600 to 4000 BC) set up temporary camps and homes that allowed them to follow food around and to cope with the challenges of the seasons. Scatters of flint tools and flakes of flint waste produced by tool-making Mesolithic people can be found across the English countryside. Nevertheless, except perhaps for temporary tent-like shelters and enigmatic, monumental timber structures (of which only faint archaeological traces remain), these people did not seem to invest much effort in building; or that's what we once thought.

In the year 2000, archaeologists began excavating a scatter of Mesolithic worked flints eroding from the cliffs along the Northumbrian coast near the village of Howick. Finally, traces of a building were revealed. The archaeological evidence shows that it was based on a circular hollow, six metres in diameter, with a superstructure supported by an arrangement of stout wooden posts with lesser timbers in-between. These would have formed a small, circular timber building with a conical thatched roof.

The building had a hearth for warmth and cooking that, along the building's floor, had been renewed several times. These successive floors were littered with food waste of animal bone and nutshells. The latter provided a sequence of radiocarbon dates, which established that not only did the building date from around 7800 BC, well back into the

Mesolithic period, but it had been occupied over a period of a hundred years or so. The Howick building, together with a similar structure later identified at the already well-known Mesolithic site at Star Carr in Yorkshire, are England's oldest known built homes.

There is growing evidence that in the warmer post-Ice Age climate, certain places with a ready year-round supply of food, like Howick, may have attracted some Mesolithic nomads to settle down permanently. It is tempting to extrapolate from the discoveries of Howick and Star Carr towards the possibility of finding clusters of similar houses that formed early villages. That is going to be very difficult to test; the Mesolithic period is such a long time ago and so much has happened to the English landscape since then. However, nothing yet suggests that anything like a permanent village was established this early in prehistory.

PUTTING DOWN ROOTS

Mesolithic people modified their environments to produce better grazing and hunting land, chiefly by simply setting fire to it when it got overgrown and then letting it grow back, but in England the arrival of farming is associated with the following Neolithic period (around 4000 to 2500 BC).

The introduction of arable agriculture provoked the need for permanent settlement. Sowing, tending, harvesting, processing and storing crops demands that people maintain their attention on one place in the landscape all year round. To become farmers, prehistoric people had to modify their hunter-gatherer lifestyles. You can't wander off for a few weeks to hunt migrating *aurochs* (intimidatingly large prehistoric wild cattle, now extinct), or move to the seaside for the fishing and shellfish seasons, and expect to find your crops to be doing just fine when you come back.

However, despite this more settled lifestyle, only a handful of Neolithic structures revealed by archaeological excavations across the country have been interpreted as houses. Even this interpretation remains doubtful in several cases, because some of these house-like buildings may not have had a domestic purpose at all. Some are associated with special objects (such as rare, highly polished axes) and places (such as windswept hilltops) that seem to have more symbolic and sacred meanings, rather than indicating domestic practicality and comfort.

The remains of the few Neolithic house-like buildings comprise arrays of soil-filled pits that mark where structural wooden posts were once driven into the ground, or slots where beams once lay. Just like the Howick house, the timbers themselves have long since rotted away. Unlike the Howick house, these Neolithic buildings tend to be rectangular or square. It is surprising that Neolithic society in England has not produced much more compelling and widespread evidence of permanent homes and settlement; this can't be to do with lack of population, materials or construction know-how.

Neolithic people transformed and marked the landscape in ways that had not been attempted before and were not paralleled afterwards. They were accomplished engineers and built truly astounding monuments that must have had great spiritual power, but generally these were not great places to live. Neolithic communities constructed huge burial mounds (long barrows) with monumental stone-built entrances, passages and chambers to house the dead. The living periodically congregated in *causewayed enclosures*, large oval compounds defined by segmental ditches and earth banks. They processed along *cursus* monuments, linear earthworks which cut across miles of landscape. They gathered for ceremonies in amphitheatre-like circular earthworks, now known as henges, which were adorned with settings of great timber posts, or huge stones. Neolithic people built Stonehenge.

Durrington Walls, around two miles from Stonehenge, has long been known as an important archaeological site. It is a vast, near circular earthwork henge monument, 1640 feet (500 metres) in diameter, which has been called a 'Superhenge'. It was clearly a very special place, but before the henge banks were constructed, Neolithic people had built something there that was even more remarkable. It may explain how and why Stonehenge and many of the other fascinating monuments in the region were built there in the first place.

Archaeological excavations between 2004 and 2007 revealed Neolithic buildings. They had been constructed in timber, with wattle and daub or chalky earth providing wall infill. They were square in plan and only two or three metres in width, with central hearths for fires, and floors made from a sort of chalk plaster. Internal slots for timber beams indicated the positions of internal partitions or fixed furnishings.

Only nine buildings were excavated, but their distribution suggested dense settlement over a larger area. It is possible that there were as many as 300 buildings in the vicinity, or even 1000 buildings if the entire area of the Durrington Walls site had been used. This implies a population of anywhere between several hundred and a few thousand people. All of which immediately raises the question: was this evidence of the first known English village, a permanently settled community of many families, living together on one site?

The answer is not straightforward. The periodic renewal of the buildings' floors and hearths, bracketed by a sequence of radiocarbon dates, suggests occupation of the site spanned a period of no more than half a century and possibly as little as seven years. Some of the buildings were probably not houses; they lacked debris from habitation and seem to have been open on one side. Perhaps they were sheds, shelters or had some religious purpose.

However, several of the buildings were associated with rubbish deposits (middens) containing broken pottery, flints, hearth sweepings and animal bone. This material gave a fascinating glimpse of life in the settlement. Almost all of the bone was from domesticated pigs and cattle; only a small percentage was from wild species such as deer and aurochs. This was not a hunter-gatherer community. Nevertheless, a closer analysis of the animal bone assemblage has shown that it doesn't quite match the sort of animal husbandry, slaughter and butchery patterns usually seen in settled prehistoric farming communities either.

The evidence suggests that the Durrington Walls community was not concerned about careful day-to-day subsistence throughout the year, but instead enjoyed spectacular consumption of the choicest cuts during seasonal feasting. The settlement was more Glastonbury Festival than Glastonbury town.

The ephemeral nature of the Durrington Walls Neolithic settlement contrasts with the stone-built permanence of the famous Neolithic village at Skara Brae on Orkney, which was occupied for 600 years until its abandonment around 2500 BC. Though 5000 years old, its clustered houses look as substantial and comfortable as nineteenth-century crofters' cottages. They have inbuilt box beds, hearths and cupboards constructed of stone.

It is the similarity in the traces of structures within the Neolithic houses at Durrington Walls with the layout of stone features at Skara Brae that has led to the interpretation that the Durrington Walls folk had similar furnishings, though built in timber.

The Skara Brae village and the settlement at Durrington Walls are special in different ways, and probably not representative of the way most Neolithic people usually lived. Given the general lack of archaeological evidence for permanent Neolithic homes across England, we probably have to conclude that most people lived in slight, temporary shelters and houses most of the time, little different from those used in the Mesolithic period. Apart from a few exceptional places and instances, Neolithic communities would have been dispersed across the landscape, and not concentrated in villages. The next era, the Bronze Age, however, provides much clearer evidence for the development of villages.

PREHISTORIC VILLAGES IN THEIR LANDSCAPES

As the Neolithic period gave way to the Bronze Age (around 2500 to 800 BC), people seemed to become much less enthusiastic about building huge, elaborate monuments. Instead, they chose to alter the English landscape in different, but equally dramatic, ways.

On Dartmoor, the earth and stone boundary banks of prehistoric fields (there known as *reaves)* stand out in the moorland landscape. They were long thought to be medieval, because of the extent and sophistication of the agricultural management they represent. Archaeologists simply could not believe that prehistoric society was capable of implementing, or actually needed, this sort of intensive farming. Across much of England, similar prehistoric remains have long been levelled by ploughing and buried beneath the soil, so are far more difficult to find. However, recent research has demonstrated lowland landscapes from the Lincolnshire and Cambridgeshire Fens to the Thames Valley and Norfolk Broads were carved up into fields in the middle Bronze Age. The fields were linked by droves and lanes and enclosed by ditches and banks. It was a campaign of landscape enclosure that would not be matched, in some instances, until the 19th century. Surely intensive farming had to be accompanied by a more intensive form of settlement; permanent villages?

At Grimspound, on Dartmoor, you can visit the remains of a Bronze Age village that was occupied from around 1500 to 700 BC. It was first excavated at the end of the nineteenth century. Twenty or so roundhouses with stone rubble walls are enclosed in a large circular, stone-walled compound about 150 metres in diameter. Several more individual house sites are scattered among the surrounding stone-banked field system. A much more recent discovery has provided an unparalleled view of life in a Bronze Age settlement.

In 1999, archaeologist Martin Redding found a few decayed upright posts sticking out of the side of an old quarry at a place called Must Farm near Peterborough. The quarry had filled with water after clay extraction had finished many years previously, but when the water levels temporarily dropped, the posts were exposed. I went down to see the site with him one day, not long after his discovery. We scraped a little soil away and confirmed that the posts were substantial and deeply buried. The tops of the posts were very decayed, but they were better preserved the deeper we dug. They looked ancient. Very ancient. We thought we might be looking at a timber causeway, but eventually excavations by Cambridge University's archaeological unit revealed an astounding Bronze Age settlement.

On dry land archaeological sites, most of the organic material of everyday life has decayed long ago. Only the most resilient material such as pot sherds, animal bone, flint and metal usually survive. However, sites like the one that Martin had found at Must Farm are exceptional. Buried wet sites can be sufficiently stifled of oxygen to prevent fragile organic materials being eaten away. This means that a whole array of things that usually crumble away to dust can survive for thousands of years.

The Must Farm settlement didn't dwindle away in any sense. It was cut off in its prime by a catastrophic fire. The houses were suspended above a stream channel, and as they burnt and collapsed, their charred contents were irretrievably lost to their owners beneath smouldering timbers, water and mud. It must have been a shocking and utterly devastating sight at the time. Everything gone in an instant.

This is the sort of circumstance that sets archaeologists' hearts racing. It has been called the 'Pompeii premise' after the town that was frozen in time by the sudden cataclysmic eruption of Mount Vesuvius in AD 79. Pompeii is a world famous archaeological site, celebrated for the special insights it lends to life in the Roman period. Here, on the edge of a brick pit near Peterborough, was a soggier, English, prehistoric rural equivalent.

The quality of preservation at the Must Farm site was mind-blowing. Bronze axe heads were still attached to their wooden hafts. The charred remains of woven textile garments were found along with bobbins of yarn and thread, ready for loom and sewing sessions that never came. Instead of the sherds of smashed, discarded pottery that are usually found on dry Bronze Age settlements, there were whole pots, comprising complete sets of cookware, tableware and storage containers stacked together. Some of these pots even contained the remains of meals that were being eaten or prepared as the fire struck. One clay pot still had a wooden spoon embedded in the charred remains of a last meal.

Four large roundhouses were identified in the excavations along with a smaller square structure, which was probably a storage building. The buildings sat within an enclosure formed by a timber palisade. A walkway of woven wooden panels (hurdles) ran around the inside of the palisade, like the wall walk on the inside of a castle's battlements. Similar walkways linked the houses. We don't know the full extent of the Must Farm settlement. Tragically, at least half of it, probably more, had been quarried away previously. However, it was more than simply the farmstead of a single household.

Must Farm was occupied for a relatively short period of time, perhaps only for a matter of months between around 1100 and 800 BC, right at the end of the Bronze Age. It was in effect a brand-new settlement when it burnt down, but clearly it had been built to last.

Both Must Farm and Grimspound signal the step change that took place during the later Bronze Age from single, dispersed households to small communities living permanently in clusters of houses. Villages were forming in the English landscape, and they were already diverse in character.

The scale and diversity of villages increased throughout the following Iron Age (800 BC to AD 43). In a field near Glastonbury in Somerset, the full extent of an Iron Age village was revealed over a period of fifteen years, from 1892 onwards. Around ninety house sites were excavated. Not all of these were occupied at the same time, but at its peak around 200 people lived there. This village, like Must Farm, was a wetland settlement.

Glastonbury Lake Village should be more accurately described as a 'swamp village'. It sat within an environment that would have changed with the seasons and fluctuations in the climate from open water and running streams, to marsh and squelchy grassland. Clusters of roundhouses had been rebuilt on the same sites over and over again to form mounds over a period spanning the second century BC until around AD 50.

Two other 'lake villages' were discovered at Meare, only a few miles from the Glastonbury Lake Village. These were different in that there was much less evidence for permanent, year-round habitation. The Meare sites seem to have been occupied only seasonally, and perhaps operated as markets. Unlike Grimspound, prehistoric settlers had deliberately sought out wetland environments at Must Farm and the later Somerset lake villages. It seems like a precarious and uncomfortable existence to us, but to prehistoric people, wetlands offered advantages. They were very rich in natural resources for both people and their livestock, with abundant fish, wild-fowl and lush natural water meadows for grazing. Reeds and marginal woodland and scrub supplied useful building materials; areas of open water and deep marsh provided some protection against attack. Not that these communities were cut off. At a time when networks of unpaved tracks made for unreliable travel across country, waterways were often a much more effective means of getting around. Boats were invaluable. Eight log boats were found at Must Farm.

The excavated evidence shows that the Glastonbury Lake Village and Must Farm communities also had good access to the usual dry land staples of the period: sheep, cattle, pigs and cereal crops. These were wetland settlements, but the difference between them and dry land sites is a matter of emphasis, rather than radical departure from the norms of the periods concerned. We can confidently say that these settlements represent much of the character of prehistoric settlements right across the country.

The Somerset lake villages and Must Farm have provided extraordinarily vivid pictures of later prehistoric life; not least glimpses into the types of houses that would have formed the heart of farmsteads and villages across the country. Round-houses offered quite a large living space and a comfortable environment, although one that would take time for us to get used to now. Imagine a central fire continually going, something always cooking, smoke rising gently to the rafters or wafting around when disturbed, people chatting and working on what they could in the best of the light, or sleeping in the shadows. Mothers, fathers, babies, toddlers, older children and elders all living together. There was only one door and probably no windows. A few of the more vulnerable and less hardy animals, such as lambs and calves would be inside with the family in pens. Dogs would be cuddling up to their owners and waiting for scraps for food. It was a dimly lit, fuggy, smelly environment, but cosy and welcoming, especially at night and in the worst weather. Clusters of households like these, sometimes in defended compounds, sometimes on open sites, formed farmsteads, hamlets and villages.

The place of villages in later Bronze Age and Iron Age settlement patterns will become much clearer as further archaeological excavations take place and further discoveries are made. For now, we can say that villages were established in these periods and that they played significant roles in very different environments. But how did villages develop as England became part of the Roman world?

ROMAN BRITAIN

Southern England had trading contact with Gaul and the Roman world in the first century BC and this increased in the years following Julius Caesar's half-hearted invasions of 55 BC and 54 BC. Some well-off Brits imported Roman wine and other goods, but not architectural plans or kits for Roman houses and blueprints for Roman towns. Only after the Claudian invasion of AD 43, and then only gradually, would Britons adopt lifestyles and architecture favoured by Roman citizens.

Roman writers provide glimpses of late Iron Age society in Britain, but it is a fragmentary and biased picture. They noted that Britain was divided into tribal kingdoms (some of which did not get on with each other at all), and that it was a well-managed and agriculturally productive place, despite the wretched weather. They remarked that the southern English culture was similar to that of its nearest Continental neighbours, whose lands the Roman Empire had occupied for some time; people lived in houses like those of the Gauls (French), and people and houses were notably numerous.

Native strongholds and fortifications were mentioned during the early years of the conquest, and some of these were not only temporary refuges. Roman writers were keen to mention that many *oppida* were taken during the conquest of Britain. To the Romans, strictly speaking, an *oppidum* was a defended town, but these places did not look like Roman towns and would not look like towns to us today.

Oppida were tribal centres, and generally more rural in character and spread out in form than the Romans' own towns and later English towns. Rather than a circuit of town walls enclosing a compact urban area, *oppida* in Britain were bounded by a network of banks and ditches, which defined an area that might comprise several discrete villages and farmsteads. *Oppida* could sprawl over huge areas of countryside; landscape features such as woodland, marsh and rivers were integral to their layout, providing additional boundaries, natural camouflage and security.

Most *oppida* were situated in the southern half of England and flourished from the late second century BC to the first decades of the first century AD. The earthworks of *oppida* ditches and banks can be seen at places such as Colchester (*Camulodunum,* which was successively controlled by the tribe named the *Trinovantes* and then by the *Catuvellauni*) and Stanwick in North Yorkshire (in *Brigantes* territory).

It is likely that the Roman definition of *oppida* in the British context also embraced another type of site: hill forts. These are a type of monument that came to dominate early archaeological perceptions of the Iron Age and Iron Age settlement. Hundreds of hill forts survive across England, though there are fewer in the flatter lands along the eastern side of the country. Some hill forts originated as earlier enclosures, sometimes way back in the Bronze Age or even Neolithic period, but these places were then remodelled on a grand scale in the Iron Age.

Many hill forts are vast constructions with one or more circuits of massive banks and ditches, either following the contours of a hill top or approximating a circle; wooden palisades and revetments, gate towers and maze-like entrances provided formidable defences. These were intimidating centres of power that, like the more sprawling *oppida*, could only be built and maintained by sizeable communities. It was once thought that hill forts were a bit like medieval castles, centres for elites and their followers, which were only densely populated temporarily in times of trouble. This may be partly true, but excavation has shown that substantial, village-sized communities lived permanently in many of them. The residents of *oppida* at Colchester, St Albans and Stanwick undoubtedly thought of themselves as living in especially important and exceptional centres of population when most settlements of the time were much smaller. Some archaeologists have described *oppida* as 'proto-towns', but that actually means they are not really towns, just a step towards the evolution of towns. In many respects these places share the characteristics of all rural settlements of the time. Archaeologically, they look like big villages or clusters of villages.

TOWNS, VILLAS AND VILLAGES

You can read a lot of books about Roman Britain and find copious references to forts, villas and towns, even 'small towns' and 'roadside settlements', but seldom will you find references to villages. However, villages did exist in Roman times and they played a significant part in the fabric of society, even if their presence has been masked. It is often difficult to make a clear distinction between a village and a small town of this period, and whether at some stage one became the other.

There were no true towns in prehistoric Britain. The Romans brought the idea of urban living and developed towns across England, but this did not happen overnight. As Roman control extended across the country in the decades following their arrival on the south coast, gradually they were able to bring ways of living modelled on Rome and their Mediterranean heartlands into this far-flung province. Towns with many of the same types of centralised amenities, functions, institutions, buildings and planned layouts, which are familiar in our towns today, had existed for centuries in the Greek and Roman world.

Many Roman towns in Britain were built to administer pre-existing tribal areas, and in some cases were situated on or near the old Iron Age tribal centres they replaced. The new Roman towns at Colchester (*Camulodunum*) and Dorchester (*Durnovaria*) near Maiden Castle did exactly this. Roman towns were often laid out on a grid pattern of streets, from which property plots were laid out; and houses, shops, public buildings and leisure facilities crowded along street fronts. Town walls that physically enclosed, defined and defended the core of the urban population were built and strengthened over time. Some towns grew from forts and others developed more haphazardly from villages strung out along the main Roman roads.

Any ancient urban Romano-Briton brought back to life would recognise some of their own world in England's modern road system and many of its towns and cities. In fact, from Canterbury to Chester, from Exeter to York and many places in-between, they would be able to see the remains of buildings and walk along streets that had been constructed in their time. They would call these places by their Roman names (*Durovernum Cantiacorum*, *Deva*, *Isca Dumnoniorum*, *Eboracum*) and we would know to which cities they were referring. Nevertheless, many towns founded in the Roman period were later abandoned and remain only as archaeological sites.

Our resurrected Roman citizen would also recognise some characteristics of today's village life, but only a few English villages would bring back even the vaguest recollections of places that had actually existed in Roman times. Places such as the village of Ancaster in Lincolnshire. First a fort, then a civilian settlement developed at this spot on Ermine Street, the main Roman road from London to York. Eventually in the middle of the third century AD, a circuit of ditches and walls, complete with towers, was built around what had become a small town.

The earthwork remnants of these substantial defences can still be seen in paddocks at the southern end of the village today. Archaeological excavations have revealed evidence of dense Romano-British occupation and the graves of its citizens. However, apart from the ruler-straight Ermine Street, which is still Ancaster's main street, the structure of the present village does not follow the pattern laid out by the Romans. The area enclosed by former town defences was abandoned and then largely ignored by the later village's development to the north.

Ancaster was once tentatively identified with a place called *Causennae*, which is mentioned in a famous Roman travel directory, the *Antonine Itinerary*, but a better candidate for that place has been found a few miles further south along Ermine Street. Ancaster cannot confidently be identified with any place in Britain named by Roman writers. The 'caster' part of the village's name reflects the presence of ancient fortifications, but Ancaster is not a Roman name, it is an Anglo-Saxon name.

The same sort of fractured developmental path from Roman towns to present-day villages can be seen in many other places across England. The Roman town of *Calleva Atrebatum* was a big deal. A tribal centre of the *Atrebates* before the conquest, it then became a very civilised Roman town; its substantial remains, still visible today, include a complete circuit of masonry town walls and an amphitheatre. A medieval parish church, manor and a handful of later buildings are tucked inside the town walls at the former east gate, but the rest of the Roman town site is completely deserted. The most substantial settlement in the locality, the village of Silchester in Hampshire, developed a mile away, completely shunning this illustrious Roman town.

Wroxeter in Shropshire, or rather *Viroconium Cornoviorum* as the Romans knew it, was the fourth largest town in Roman Britain. It was almost as big as Pompeii. Wroxeter village, though charming and interesting in its own way, is tiny. It is barely a pimple on the periphery of the former Roman metropolis. The villages now associated with these former Roman towns were definitely not part of the Roman urban ambition. These are not Roman villages, but later villages that happen to have developed on or near Roman sites.

So what were villages like in Roman Britain and have any survived? The Romans were here to control and exploit the rich resources of their conquered province, but they were never here in sufficient numbers to eradicate the existing prehistoric society. If they wanted to steal, trade and tax, to build Roman towns and fund Roman amenities, and create wealth and prestige for the Empire, they needed functioning, productive native rural communities. For much of the time, that meant leaving ancient farms and villages to carry on doing what they had been doing perfectly successfully for thousands of years, and creaming off the profits.

Out in the Romano-British countryside, especially in the parts of the country that were more remote from the secure Roman heartlands in the south of England and the Midlands, life in many Iron Age settlements simply carried on in prehistoric fashion after the Conquest, almost completely indifferent to changing lifestyles elsewhere. Old Iron Age buildings were renewed in an ages-old form, or rebuilt in distinctly non-Roman form. The villages at Chys-auster and at Carn Euny in Cornwall, for example, had been established deep in Iron Age times, but these places persisted late into the Roman period, possibly right until the end of the Roman occupation in the early fifth century AD, in the case of Carn Euny.

At both places it is still possible to walk among the remarkably preserved Romano-British village buildings. Their thatched roofs may be long gone, but their stone walls survive. It is an extraordinary feeling to step over the thresholds of these ancient homes, into the same spaces occupied by families who essentially lived a prehistoric life, albeit in Roman times. Both villages have a distinctive form of housing that was finally expressed in stone construction during the Roman period, but it is not a Roman form. It is a type of building particularly associated with the south-west of Britain at this time.

The covered circular and oval rooms of each house in these villages were arranged around a central open courtyard. There are at least ten such 'courtyard houses' at both villages, and their arrangement indicates peak populations of perhaps seventy people. There is evidence of village planning at Chysauster, which has houses arranged in rows. The houses have gardens and the village is set within its own field system defined by stone walls and terraces. The sites of other dispersed prehistoric and Romano-British roundhouses have been found in the vicinity.

Excavations up and down the country have shown, as at Chysauster, that native-style British farmsteads and villages previously assumed to have been abandoned or replaced under Roman rule in fact persisted and thrived well into Roman times. Only as the Roman period progressed did many native-style farms and villages, especially in the lowland areas, gradually take on a more Romanised character, seemingly as a matter of choice and preference by their owners.

In archaeological terms, the 'material culture' of the sites changed. Roman coins appear, and Roman pottery, dress items and tools replace the old prehistoric styles; even the structure of the places is different. Not only were old-style roundhouses replaced by rectangular ones, although usually these were still timber-framed and thatched, but the plan form of the farmsteads and villages also became more regular. Rectangular houses were set in garden plots, surrounded by paddocks and fields formed of straight boundaries and angles, and settlements were linked by lanes lined by drainage ditches. As a very general guide, the plan forms of Iron Age farmsteads and villages and their surrounding fields are all circles and curves. Their Romanised equivalents tend to be based on straight lines and angles.

In the more Romanised, lowland areas of England, another distinctive form of settlement and building type, long established in the Roman world, was on its way to Britain. Nothing remotely like a Roman villa had been seen in Britain prior to Roman rule. Villas were not simply grand houses built in the Roman style to impress the natives and entertain friends, but were the centres of working farm estates. They were owned by Roman officials and settlers, and also by wealthy and influential Britons who had fully embraced a Roman lifestyle.

Villas were constructed in the Roman style on rectangular plans, sometimes with wings or ancillary buildings arranged around a courtyard. Most seem to have been constructed from plastered timber frame on masonry footings, rather than being of masonry construction throughout, but they often had tiled roofs rather than thatched roofs, internal plastered walls, and floors made of small ceramic tiles (*tesserae*). The most lavishly decorated villas had wall paintings of vibrant colours and elaborate mosaic floors. They also had under-floor and in-wall heating systems (*hypocausts*) and heated bath suites, and many were set within gardens.

The buildings in a villa complex might include stables and barns for animals, crop processing and storage, and occasionally workshops for a smithy or other crafts and trades. Each villa was surrounded by its farmland and other territory, and this estate may have also included outlying farmsteads. Nevertheless, the main house was usually rela-tively isolated and occupied by a single household, along with some slaves and servants if the household was rich enough to have them.

Some Roman villas were palatial, some relatively modest, but they represented the higher end of the Roman property market and social scale. The small roundhouse farmsteads that persisted, differing little from their prehistoric prede-cessors except for the introduction of some Roman-style crockery, were definitely at the bottom of the less fashion-able and 'affordable' sector.

The word 'village' derives from the Latin word *villa*, via old French, but Roman villas were not villages, nor did they give rise to villages. *Villa* means country house, and the grandest Roman villas were the equivalent of the English country houses and 'Downton Abbey' style stately homes, with their surrounding estates, that can be seen across the country today.

In Roman Britain there may have been no officially recognised term directly equivalent to the word 'village', but the Roman term *vicus* is associated with villages. It had a specific administrative meaning to describe certain settlements that did not have the status of a provincial capital (*colonia*) or tribal capital (*civitas*), or were otherwise a fully incorporated town of Roman citizens, but nevertheless were officially recognised as significant places.

The term *vicus* could embrace town-sized places, districts within towns, and also village-sized settlements. *Vici,* civilian villages, grew outside the gates of Roman forts, such as Housesteads and Vindolanda on the Hadrian's Wall frontier. They offered a range of services and goods to the garrison, not least food, wine and beer. We can imagine people setting up various businesses to rake in any spare cash the troops cared to splash around. The *vici* alongside forts were a bit like today's garrison towns and villages, such as Aldershot and Catterick. Perhaps they were as 'lively' on Saturday nights.

Many village-sized civilian settlements also grew along the main Roman roads between the major towns and forts. They offered a range of services to travellers, and some of these roadside ribbon developments had a *mansio*, an official posting station and inn. Roadside temples and shrines were also common at such places; travellers could ask for a safe journey with offerings, or give thanks for a successful trip.

There is evidence that the Roman Empire sponsored, or at least encouraged, development of other specialised village-like settlements in some regions. In the Fens of East Anglia, the development of livestock farms and salt production centres may have been promoted under direct imperial control from the early second century AD onwards. Hadrian himself was interested in draining and developing marshland and would have seen the potential of this region.

In contrast to the surrounding regions, this was not a landscape of private villa estates during the Roman period, but was instead characterised by the development of hundreds of farmsteads and many nucleated villages. These comprised clusters of low status (peasant) houses, linked by tracks and surrounded by extensive networks of paddocks and fields. During the Roman period, salt production centres were also developed at Droitwich in Worcestershire and at Nantwich, Northwich and Middlewich in Cheshire.

Salt was an immensely important commodity, not just as a flavouring, but as a crucial preservative before refrigeration existed. All these English sources of salt had been discovered and exploited in prehistoric times, but the Romans were able to totally control production, expand the industrial settlements, and grow the industry for the benefit of the province and Empire. These places are the ancestors of the greater variety of specialist industrial villages and towns that developed later.

The Roman hold on Britain ceased in the early fifth century AD and any serious imperial interest in its affairs disappeared.

What remained of the Romano-British administration no doubt tried to soldier on at a regional level, but it did not take very long for all Roman institutions and the Roman way of life to dwindle away, or be swept away, by a tide of invaders and settlers from across the North Sea. Roman villas, towns and villages also declined, with little sign of Roman life, or any substantial occupation by the incomers.

Within the next century, the character of settlements in most parts of England changed again completely. The new, post-Roman, Anglo-Saxon era was a crucial one for the development of English life and English villages. It gave rise to many villages that thrive today, but tracing a direct evolutionary line from the earliest Anglo-Saxon settlements to present-day villages is not straightforward.

THE ENGLISH SETTLE IN BRITAIN

The people who came to be known collectively as the Anglo-Saxons were a disparate population of invaders and migrants from different north-west European homelands. They first began arriving in the south and east of England before the effective end of Roman rule in AD 410, but came in much greater numbers and swept further across the country during the next century or so. The Saxons came from north-west Germany, where the state of Lower Saxony still exists. The Angles are named from a north German territory, where there is still a district called Angeln. The Jutes came from Jutland, the land historically fought over by Germany and Denmark. Frisians (north-west Germany and the Netherlands) can also be thrown into this mix.

Saxons lend their name to southern English counties and regions (Sussex, South Saxons; Essex, East Saxons; Wessex, West Saxons), while the east side of England extending to Scotland was dominated by Angles. The Jutes settled in Kent.

This was not a nationally coordinated, politically motivated conquering force like the Roman Empire had deployed in Britain. The Romans ruled with the classic colonial aim of administering and milking a well-ordered province that could be shaped in their own image. The Anglo-Saxon pattern of occupation and settlement displayed none of the totalitarian control freakishness of the Romans. The early Anglo-Saxons (around AD 400 to 650) were not centrally organised or motivated enough to seize total control of the entire Roman system of governance. They did not develop nor even successfully maintain Roman towns, though occasionally they made use of the ruins as strongholds.

Urban life simply did not make sense to the new settlers; intensive and resource-hungry towns required sophisticated administration, authority over a hinterland, and control over extensive supply networks. Even country villas, with their tiled roofs, bathhouses, underfloor heating and mosaics, depended heavily on wider Roman infrastructure for their upkeep. They needed regulated markets to distribute their farmed produce and to prosper, and the roof tilers and mosaic makers had to be paid.

When Roman administration started to break down, the Roman economy and all state-sponsored security went with it. Military establishments, urban life, villa life, *vici* life, roadside villages, industrial and farming villages, and all the other settlements that depended on the infrastructure of the Roman state, went the same way.

The first Anglo-Saxon settlers pragmatically reintroduced the model of largely self-sufficient farmsteads, hamlets and villages that had allowed British prehistoric populations to thrive for so long. They traded, they were part of a wider network of 'folk' and series of kin groups with affiliations to each other, but there was no grand plan, no central government. Early Anglo-Saxon settlements typically were built where sufficient land was available that could sustain them, rather than according to official directions and imperial requirements. They were not built as grand gestures of occupation, complete with regimented structure and monuments, but developed anywhere that was suitable, including among the ruins of Roman towns, villas, villages and old prehistoric sites.

Anglo-Saxon buildings lacked the scale and pretensions of the grandest Roman buildings. They were usually made from wood, reed and mud rather than stone and tile, and ultimately decayed away. All this has made their settlements quite difficult to find. Archaeologists came to know more about the Anglo-Saxon way of death than they did about their way of life; up until the last few decades of archaeological research, it was far more common to find the remains of dead Anglo-Saxons than to find the remains of Anglo-Saxon settlements.

Early Anglo-Saxon burials are very distinctive. These were pagan people who did not like to go to the afterlife with nothing other than their conscience to comfort them.

Whether cremated and buried in clay pots or laid to rest as inhumations in graves, invariably they were accompanied by possessions that indicated their position in their society, and reflected what they and their kinsfolk thought they would need for the next life.

Nearly everybody in pre-Christian Anglo-Saxon was sent off with something, if only a small iron knife. Primarily these would have been used for eating in this world and the next, rather than defence. Adult males were buried with their spear and round wooden shield with its central iron boss, as befits people who would be expected to form local militias in times of trouble. Women were buried with brooches and 'girdle hangers' of bronze, iron 'latch-lifters' (simple keys), necklaces strung with amber and multicoloured clay and glass beads, and sometimes various gold and silver ornaments. When early Anglo-Saxon graves are disturbed and these types of grave goods come to light, they attract attention. I have been called upon to examine burials of this period in fields, allotments, construction sites, under patios and in a pub car park.

FINDING THE VILLAGES

Early Anglo-Saxon cemeteries are usually situated a little distant from the settlements they served, so finding a cemetery, even a large one, does not lead directly to finding the remains of an Anglo-Saxon village. Settlements of this period are seldom found accidentally by workmen or the public, because they leave very little trace on the surface.

They are not marked by the same sort of dense scatters of building material and pottery that characterise buried

Roman sites. Most early Anglo-Saxon buildings did not have substantial foundations that remain visible even when the building itself has disappeared. They were thatched and built from a timber framework of posts driven into the earth, or planks and beams rising from slots cut into the ground. When the posts and beams have decayed, they leave post holes or long slots filled with soil of different character to the surrounding bedrock and subsoil. These, however, are buried beneath the soil. They are often too slight to register as marks in crops on aerial photographs and they are also difficult to identify in geophysical surveys, the various magical 'geofizz' means by which archaeologists can usually detect features buried under the soil.

Another type of Anglo-Saxon building is based around an excavated oval or rectangular hollow, which in many cases seemed to form an underfloor space like a cellar beneath a suspended wooden floor. These were first called *grubenhauser* (German for 'pit house') and colloquially 'grub huts' by archaeologists, but are often referred to as sunken featured buildings (or 'SFBs') now. This type of feature can produce cropmarks that can be seen from the air and they give more of a response in geophysical surveys, but they look rather like the sort of quarry scoops, watering holes, tree throws and other sorts of hollows that are found on many other archaeological sites.

The early Anglo-Saxons, unlike farming prehistoric people and Romans, did not seem especially keen on digging lots of property boundary ditches all over the place. The soil conditions they favoured and their preferred methods for the management of animals and crops probably required only slight boundaries like fences and hedges, and no great drainage assistance. So unlike many Roman and prehistoric settlements, early Anglo-Saxon settlements are not signalled by surrounding arrays of distinctive, ditch-enclosed field systems and track ways.

It is a sad fact that many enthusiastic antiquarians and early archaeologists simply shovelled crucial evidence for Anglo-Saxon habitation away without realising it, when they set out to expose the masonry foundations and tiled floors of Roman buildings. This early archaeological 'wall chasing' method of excavation has meant that it is now impossible to say whether many Roman settlements excavated in the past 200 years also had significant Anglo-Saxon period features.

Archaeologists are a lot more careful these days. Plenty of Roman sites excavated using modern archaeological techniques now reveal evidence for some early Anglo-Saxon occupation. However, not many late Roman period settlement sites can emphatically demonstrate true continuity of occupation into the Anglo-Saxon period. It is always going to be very challenging to demonstrate the gradual adoption of an Anglo-Saxon lifestyle by the occupants of a settlement or their offspring. The nature of the transition from a Romano-British society to one that was Anglo-Saxon and wholly different in character is one of the big research questions in British archaeology.

Genetics, DNA analysis of human remains in large cemeteries, offers the best chance of showing the extent to which the two populations mixed, or whether the old Brits were driven away by the new English. For now, the archaeological evidence seems pretty clear that at the end of the Roman period and into Anglo-Saxon times, there was a widespread population shift and major reorganisation of settlement patterns.

This meant that *some* places that developed from Iron Age origins and persisted through Roman times, or originated in Roman times, may have also been occupied or reoccupied in early Anglo-Saxon times. But many others were not. Roman farmsteads, villas, towns and villages did not go on seamlessly to become Anglo-Saxon farmsteads and villages; nor did early Anglo-Saxon villages necessarily go on to become present-day villages.

The vast majority of archaeological excavations carried out these days are required to inform the development planning system. They are undertaken at developers' expense to record sites immediately before they are destroyed by new housing estates, quarries, or roads and pipelines. Over several decades, this development-led archaeological sampling of the English landscape has helped to provide a more balanced picture of historical patterns of settlement, and led to the discovery of hundreds of early Anglo-Saxon settlements.

This kind of work, together with targeted archaeological survey, is at last shining significant new light on this elusive period, formerly known as 'The Dark Ages'. The current conclusion, however, is that the distribution of early Anglo-Saxon settlements is much more complicated and uneven than previously assumed. In the Vale of Pickering in Yorkshire, for example, and across Norfolk, decades of intensive survey work has revealed dense patterns of Anglo-Saxon habitation. In other promising locations, such as the huge, open area archaeological excavations that took place in advance of the expansion of Stansted Airport in Essex, surprisingly little evidence of early Anglo-Saxon settlement was found. These excavations revealed dense settlement of almost every other period.

When they are discovered, early Anglo-Saxon settlements invariably comprise a cluster of almost perfectly rectangular timber buildings, which vary in size between around five metres and twelve metres in length. Artefacts are often very sparsely distributed on these sites. The hollows of sunken feature buildings are the best repositories of lost and discarded household items, such as lots of clay loom weights (which look like overbaked doughnuts), smashed pottery and bone pins. You might think early Anglo-Saxon settlements sound dull to excavate, but the challenge of finding them, their relative rarity and the formative period they represent alone make them absolutely fascinating.

Perhaps the most famous early Anglo-Saxon village was found at West Stow, not far from Bury St Edmunds in Suffolk, where excavations were completed in 1972. Helpfully, for people who don't excavate or read archaeological reports, but who are interested in seeing for themselves what Anglo-Saxon villages looked like, the various building types that had been excavated were then reconstructed experimentally using authentic materials and techniques. Now you can wander in and around several buildings that have been recreated, complete with authentic furnishings, using all the archaeological evidence, on their original sites.

The experimentation at West Stow continues by reassessing the performance and longevity of the buildings and their materials, and by holding regular re-enactments of daily Anglo-Saxon life. Even the destruction of Anglo-Saxon homes has been investigated here. One of the reconstructed buildings was destroyed accidentally by a fire in 2005. Its burnt remains were excavated and recorded with standard archaeological and forensic techniques to help inform archaeological interpretations of similar buildings and of similar catastrophic episodes elsewhere.

At least eighty individual buildings were found at West Stow, which makes it sound like a large village. However, this number represents periods of renewal and rebuilding during the settlement's 200-year heyday from around AD 450 to 650, and not the number of buildings that were in use at the same time over that period. Not all the buildings were necessarily dwellings. The original excavation reports and current marketing of the site emphasise that this is indeed an Anglo-Saxon *village*. Some archaeologists, however, see West Stow as never amounting to more than a tight-knit cluster of around four family farmsteads at any one time. A hamlet at best.

Nevertheless, this was not isolated settlement. Evidence points to more Anglo-Saxon homes in the vicinity of the main cluster of buildings and more settlements of various sizes for several miles in both directions from West Stow along the valley of the River Lark. West Stow, whether itself a hamlet or a village, was part of a much larger community, albeit one that was dispersed across the local landscape.

Many subsequent excavations of Anglo-Saxon settlements across England continue to show that West Stow is quite typical of the period in this and many other respects. The settlements vary in size from one or two buildings that formed a farmstead for one family to large clusters of a few dozen buildings. There is usually very little evidence for streets and regular planning, but where there is ample evidence for multiple households and communal living, we can be confident in identifying them as villages.

EARLY VILLAGES INTO LATER VILLAGES

The site of the early Anglo-Saxon village of West Stow was abandoned, and the closest medieval and present-day villages developed over half a mile away. Settlements of this period are often found well away from later villages. Even the most important early Anglo-Saxon villages did not necessarily persist and develop directly into later villages.

The Venerable Bede writing his *A History of the English Church and People* in the eighth century AD mentions the mid seventh century AD baptism of one East Saxon (Essex) royal in the East Anglian *vicus regius* (royal settlement or village) at Rendlesham in Suffolk. Once thought to be under the present-day village of that name, it took until 2008 to find its exact site in the parish. So far, only limited excavation has taken place, but enough evidence already exists to confirm that this was no ordinary Anglo-Saxon village. Metal detecting surveys have revealed a lot of unusual and high status objects, including Continental gold and silver coins. Extending over fifty hectares it is the largest and richest site of this period known in England, and undoubtedly connected to the Sutton Hoo royal burial site, just a few miles down the River Deben.

On the other side of the country another exceptional early Anglo-Saxon period village has recently been re-examined by a new campaign of archaeological excavations. Situated on a rocky headland at Tintagel in Cornwall, this place is unique in this period in having substantial rectangular stone buildings, rather than the usual wooden houses. It is also exceptional for producing rare physical evidence of written language during this period. Celtic, Latin and Greek words scratched on stone slates have been found there. Fragments of fine pottery and glass tableware indicate trading links with as far flung places as Spain and Turkey. Its people interacted with the Roman Mediterranean world, not the Germanic and Scandinavian world to the north-east. In the medieval period this site was associated with the Arthurian legend. It was said to be the place where King Arthur was conceived, and the folklore may contain a grain of truth about its status. It is possible that Tintagel was a regional royal centre, as well as an extraordinary well-connected international trading village.

The site at Tintagel was re-imagined by Richard, Earl of Cornwall who, despite the limited strategic and military value of the place, built a show castle here in the 1230s. It was his homage to Arthurian legend and helped to create an association between his dynasty and the ancient British king. But like so many other early Anglo-Saxon period settlements, this site was abandoned rather than continuing to develop as a village or town. The present village of Tintagel developed on an inland site a quarter of a mile away.

Archaeological work across the country has shown that were a huge variety of settlement types in England, stretching back thousands of years into prehistory. If we were able to time travel and visit briefly ancient settlements at various periods, we would describe many of these places as villages. To most ancient people, however, making the distinction between a village and another type of settlement would not have been relevant.

Their perceptions of the settlements they lived in were rooted in the organisation of their own societies and their own interests, just as ours are. Telling the occupants of a Roman wayside settlement either that they lived in a large village, or a small town, would mean very little to them. Having an officially recognised *mansio* or being designated a *vicus* or *civitas* would mean a lot more.

There is no neat linear evolutionary path from transient human habitation to today's English villages. Villages were never an inevitable development from the establishment of farmsteads and hamlets, or simply stepping stones to the development of towns. Ancient villages were one form of settlement that co-existed with several other forms of settlement. At times, and in many places, it is hardly possible to make a distinction between hamlets, villages and small towns.

Nor is it possible to trace a direct line from a particular prehistoric settlement, through settlements in the Roman and early Anglo-Saxon period, to a particular English village today. Village history books and websites that claim the origins of their village date back to prehistoric or Roman times are invariably making way too much of the evidence for human activity in the locality over those periods. There is hardly a parish in England that does not retain the remains of prehistoric and/or Roman life, but *continuity* of settlement across these periods to the present day is frustratingly difficult to prove archaeologically.

Archaeological evidence of one period of settlement superimposed on evidence for a subsequent period of settlement does not absolutely prove continuity of that settlement, only that people chose the same place to live at various times. The archaeological evidence, now sometimes supported by precision radiocarbon dates, tells us time and time again that there were significant gaps between periods of occupation in any one place from prehistoric periods, through Roman times, and into the Anglo-Saxon period. Snappy local history titles and proud local claims that a present-day English village has prehistoric or Roman origins have to be treated with caution.

We may not be entirely certain how very early settlements directly relate to the formation of a specific later village, but the information captured by archaeological investigations allows us to characterise the trajectory of settlement development and change in one locality and across England over a long period of time. On a macro level, this allows archaeologists and historians to draw trends through time and across regions, but the question of the very earliest origins of any individual village is usually one that requires a lot more research and may always be a matter for debate.

However, we can be much more confident about the direct origins of very many English villages during Anglo-Saxon times and afterwards, not least because the names people gave their places at the time have stuck, and are still in use today.

And that is only one important clue.

CHAPTER 2

THE BIRTH OF VILLAGE ENGLAND

Archaeologists used to talk about something called the 'Mid-Saxon shuffle', which was not a Germanic dance routine or the start of a card trick, but a period from about AD 650 to 850 when scattered farmsteads and hamlets across Anglo-Saxon England were all supposed to have got themselves organised and coalesced into 'proper' villages. Unfortunately, despite the catchy name, a huge amount of archaeological research and excavation over the last few decades has shown that this is not what happened.

The middle Anglo-Saxon period (650–850) and late Anglo-Saxon period (850–1066) were formative and exciting in all sorts of ways. Small kingdoms were absorbed into larger ones and finally forged into one English nation. This took several hundred years and involved Machiavellian machinations and bloodshed that makes *Game of Thrones* seem tame and believable by comparison. Christianity, which had been introduced to Britain in late Roman times, but largely eradicated at the end of the Roman period, took hold once more. Monasteries for religious communities and churches to serve secular communities were built across the land.

Monasteries came to be important instigators of urban and rural growth. They promoted the development of specialist farms (granges) and settlements to help sustain their earthly needs. Some of these places were newly planned for the purpose; other settlements benefited and expanded from the market for produce that the monasteries provided. Settlement patterns began to change again: places were getting bigger, more organised and structured, mirroring the restructuring of kingdoms and the more formal governance of the country, and a healthy economy.

TRADE AND WAR

From the mid-seventh century onwards, a few ports and trading centres were established at various places on the English coast and major navigable rivers. They had place names ending in 'wic', which is related to the old Roman word *vicus*. These places faced north-west Europe, not the Mediterranean centre of the old Roman world.

Ipswich (called *Gipeswic*, the 'g' was silent) in Suffolk was one of the earliest. Though probably only a village-sized enclave to begin with, it grew to become a town. *Hamwic* (Southampton), may have had a population of several thousand in the eighth and ninth centuries and had a grid plan layout of streets. Similar centres were developed at *Eoforwic* (York), Norwich, and in the Aldwych ('old wic') area of London (*Lundenwic*).

None of these trading settlements used the infrastructures of the old Roman towns in these places as a starting point, but instead favoured spots nearby where trading boats could be hauled on to a beach or easily berthed. Both *Hamwic* and *Lundenwic* later shifted to make use of the remnants of walled Roman towns, as security became paramount once again.

From the end of the ninth century, faced with Danish Viking attacks and invasion, the Anglo-Saxons created fortified settlements known as *burhs* (or *burghs* or *burgs*). Though to us, like the *wics*, many of these places would appear to be large villages, at the time they were considered to be special centres of population and administration. They were something new and set apart from normal rural settlements. The word *burh* is related to words that came to be firmly associated with towns and cities, such as borough, burgess, burgage, burger (which of course gives us hamburger, the fast food originally associated with the German city).

Some of the *burhs* used the walls of old Roman forts and towns, or even prehistoric hill forts, but many were newly built. These were laid out with a regular grid of streets and were enclosed by a purpose-built defensive ditch, bank and palisade. The people who lived within a *burh* and under its jurisdiction in the surrounding countryside were required to defend it in times of trouble. The size of each *burh*'s defensive circuit related to the size of this population. It was stipulated that ideally four men should be allocated to defend a pole's length of wall (15 to 16.5 feet).

Burhs were a really clever way of bringing together a generally quite dispersed population, with its part-time fighting force in undefended farmsteads and villages, into concentrated fortified centres, each of which was a serious obstacle to invaders wishing to capture territory.

Burhs were used to recolonise and consolidate territory taken back from the Danish, and they are considered by some to be among the earliest forms of town planning in post-Roman Europe. However, their populations were village-sized by today's standards, and like villages, they were firmly embedded in their surrounding rural landscapes and its economy.

Examples of distinctive purpose-built *burhs* are still fossilised in the structure of places like Wallingford in Oxfordshire and Wareham in Dorset, where subsequent development has not eradicated the core, grid-iron pattern of streets laid out over 1000 years ago. Many other *burhs* also developed into small towns, just like these. Some became county towns, such as Lewes (East Sussex), Exeter (Devon), Oxford, Worcester and Warwick. Winchester and one other place that sounds familiar, *Lundenburh* (which was distinct from *Lundenwic*, but not far from it) eventually became capital cities.

All right, it is not quite accurate to say that Winchester was the equivalent of London today, but it was certainly a Wessex royal centre, and as the kingdom of Wessex came to dominate England before the Norman Conquest, it is sometimes referred to as England's first capital city.

Some of the *burhs* remained village-sized and some were deserted entirely. *Burhs* that occupied excellent defensive positions for times of trouble were sometimes too inconveniently placed in times of peace. *Burhs* situated within floodplains or exposed on hilltops could be too far away from good water sources and productive fields to thrive and develop as long-lived settlements.

At Burpham in West Sussex, an old Iron Age hill fort overlooking the River Arun was refortified as a *burh*, but the villages of Burpham and Wepham developed outside its ramparts. The Iron Age hill fort at Chisbury in Wiltshire also became a *burh*, but only Chisbury Manor Farm and a thirteenth-century chapel can be found on the site now. The small village lies outside the impressive defences. The current hamlets of Lower, Upper and Little Eashing in Surrey also skirt around the site of the former *burh* there.

The village of Lyng in Somerset, however, still lies within the former Anglo-Saxon *burh*. Its position on an island in a marsh limited possibilities for village expansion and relocation elsewhere. Lyng was attached by a causeway to King Alfred the Great's nearby island fortress and monastery, Athelney, which is now itself deserted except for a farm.

The Vikings, or rather the Scandinavians who settled in England from the late ninth century onwards, promoted further urban growth, developing major trading and manufacturing centres in a territory that extended across the east of England, the East Midlands and north of England. York, now known as Scandinavian *Yorvik* rather than Anglian *Eoforwic* (or Roman *Eboracum*), became a major Viking centre. The five great boroughs of the Danelaw – Leicester, Derby, Nottingham, Lincoln and Stamford – were key to the Scandinavian power base in central England.

It was once thought that Scandinavian settlers were also wholly responsible for creating the structured, nucleated form of many English villages that is recognisable today. They undoubtedly played their part by founding and occupying many farms, hamlets and villages, but they alone did not develop the structure of English villages. It is probable, however, that colonisation, recapture and consolidation of territory by both English and Danish regimes prompted some serious reorganisation of rural settlements, beyond simply creating new *burhs*. Armies had to be fed and the countryside had to work efficiently. Villages were key to supplying and coordinating rural labour and managing surrounding farmland, so it is not hard to imagine that they were subjected to some official tinkering and restructuring.

By the end of the Anglo-Saxon and Anglo-Scandinavian period, before the Norman Conquest in 1066, England was organised into shire counties, which were themselves subdivided into *hundreds*. At first a hundred was notionally an area of a hundred *hides* (units of land of around 120 acres, sufficient to support a hundred families), but hundreds simply became conveniently sized administrative districts. They were known as *wapentakes* in Danish areas. Each individual settlement belonged to a hundred and the landscape was further organised and administered in private estates and ecclesiastical parishes. By this time many new villages had been founded and many formerly dispersed farmsteads and hamlets had probably already coalesced ('shuffled') or grown into villages.

Paradoxically, part of the archaeological evidence for the direct growth of many present-day English villages from late Saxon origins comes from the fact that it is rare to find abandoned villages of this period. Unlike earlier villages, late Anglo-Saxon villages are seldom found scattered across the landscape in complete isolation. Most of them seem to lie under villages that continued to develop at least into the late medieval period, or went on to become present-day villages, where archaeologists find it very hard to see them.

An innovative programme of research to investigate 'Currently Occupied Rural Settlements' was set up by Professor Carenza Lewis, who was a member of TV's *Time Team* for many years. Volunteers and school groups dug small test pits wherever they could in selected villages with the dual aims of investigating their origins and engaging people with archaeology. Dozens of villages, mainly across southern England, have been investigated and artefacts have demonstrated hitherto unrecorded Anglo-Saxon activity on several present village sites.

It is difficult to be sure of the character and extent of this activity without large-scale excavations, which can seldom take place in the heart of today's villages. However, archaeological excavations in advance of housing developments do sometimes provide useful larger glimpses of village pasts and it is common for these to find evidence for late Anglo-Saxon habitation.

The archaeological evidence and mentions in early charters tell us that some of the things that characterised the structure of villages throughout the medieval period and into the present day, such as a neatly arranged cluster of houses, the residence of a lord and a church, had come into being in late Anglo-Saxon times. In fact, many of today's English villages had taken their basic form at that time. Nevertheless, it was another foreign invader that further promoted the widespread development of villages and was responsible for shaping many English villages as they appear today.

THE NORMANS HAVE FORM

Nucleated villages comprising a main street lined with rows of houses within their respective plots, perhaps with back streets and a side street or two, a church and a manor house, represent the look of a classic English village for many people. Highly structured villages like this made an appearance in the last part of the Anglo-Saxon period, but they became much more widespread after the Norman Conquest. Many quintessential English villages, once thought of as solidly Anglo-Saxon institutions, are products of the era of the French Normans and Angevins in the last years of the eleventh century and the following two centuries.

The Norman Conquest was not followed by a mass migration of Norman people. Just like the Roman conquest, it was driven by military domination, but not the wholesale removal of the indigenous population. It primarily involved a replacement of the old Anglo-Saxon and Anglo-Scandinavian aristocracy by a Norman aristocracy; and like the Roman conquest, the Norman Conquest didn't happen overnight. It took several precarious years for the Normans to take a firm hold of England. William the Conqueror's ambitions were frustrated by serious Anglo-Saxon rebellions and Danish incursions.

In the early phase of the invasion in the southern counties, and a few years later in the north of England, William employed a terrible scorched-earth policy to destroy all opposition. Such was the devastation that many areas of countryside and its villages took years to recover. However, the Normans, like the Romans, knew that to make the most of their conquest they had to keep the countryside functioning. William had taken over a well-ordered and productive England, which he firmly believed he had a valid right to rule.

He had neither the inclination nor means to loot it and return to Normandy, or destroy everything so he could rebuild it all from scratch, so he left the least troublesome places more or less alone for the time being. He even allowed some Anglo-Saxon and Anglo-Scandinavian lords and abbots to remain in post for a while; though most of them, if not already dead or outlawed, had their estates confiscated and given to William's Norman barons.

The Normans introduced a highly effective defensive structure to England: the castle. The first Norman castles were simply great conical mounds of earth (a motte) with a wooden tower (a keep) on top, and an enclosed annexe (a bailey) formed by a great ditch and bank topped with a wooden palisade fence. Motte and bailey castles could be thrown up relatively quickly using unskilled labour, which was probably supplied by the miserable people who had just been defeated.

The construction of a motte and bailey castle at Hastings is shown in one of the panels of the Bayeux Tapestry. William built this castle soon after landing in England, before the famous battle nearby. The remains of the castle are still there, along with the remains of around 600 others across the country that were built during the Norman period.

The Normans could not have conquered England without motte and bailey castles. Unlike large Iron Age hill forts, Anglo-Saxon *burhs* and walled Roman towns, motte and bailey castles were not intended to hold a large population and they did not need a large garrison of regular soldiers or militia to defend them. If insurgents got into the bailey, the Norman household and a few soldiers could simply retreat to the keep on the motte. Anybody who has tried to scramble up a castle motte to take a sledge ride or while playing soldiers, can picture the carnage that would be inflicted on real attackers burdened by heavy military equipment. Arrows and noxious substances of all kinds would have rained down on them from the lofty keep as they dragged themselves, exhausted, up the dispiritingly steep slope.

Motte and bailey castles were built in strategic locations such as important river crossings, and also to subjugate settlements that might rise up in rebellion. The Normans flattened Anglo-Saxon homes in many places to get the best construction sites for their new castles, but as centres of power, administration and wealth, castles ultimately also attracted people. They went hand in hand with Norman settlement reorganisation and planning. Norman and later castles are fundamental to the growth, establishment and redevelopment of many English villages, more of which later.

Twenty years after his invasion, William wanted to know exactly what his new kingdom comprised, who held what assets, and what they were worth. Armed with a comprehensive survey, he would have full oversight of his kingdom. This kind of information meant power and money.

William would have a basis for taxing his subjects, and if a baron rebelled, he would know exactly what to take from him, and to whom to grant it next. The survey that William demanded was so comprehensive that it was later likened to the reckoning that would be made on the Christian day of Last Judgement, when the world ends and humanity is divided into good and bad: Doomsday.

The Domesday survey, finalised in 1086, was presented in two main parts. The first volume covers much of England ('Great Domesday'). Essex, Suffolk and Norfolk got their own volume ('Little Domesday'), which generally has more detailed entries. Some places were not included in the survey, notably London and Winchester, County Durham, Northumberland and large parts of the north-west of England (Cumbria, the old county of Westmorland and parts of Lancashire).

The Domesday Book mentions over 13,000 individual English settlements and only 112 of these are identified as boroughs or towns. The vast majority of settlements are described as *vills*, a word related to the Roman 'villa' and village. It is tempting to equate *vills* directly with villages, and some translations of Domesday do exactly that, but strictly speaking *vills* were administrative units of settled land that made up hundreds. A vill could be a village and its surrounding land (later to become a parish in many regions), but it could also be a collection of households and farms dispersed right across the same area of land.

Nevertheless, Domesday makes the big picture absolutely clear. England in the late eleventh century was still overwhelmingly rural in character. Of its population of between 1 and 2 million (estimates vary), the vast majority of its people, more than ninety per cent, lived in the countryside, and the countryside was characterised by farmsteads, hamlets and villages. Most of the towns were the size of villages today, and would not appear particularly urban to us. Even the larger towns, such as York, Lincoln and Norwich, which had populations of 4000–5000, would have appeared more like small, rural market towns today. Well into the medieval period, most English towns were well integrated with their agricultural hinterlands, and much more like later farming and market villages than modern towns.

The Domesday Book is organised into sections covering each county. The county sections are not primarily organised under a list of individual places, *vills* or villages, but by estate holders or lords. The lords are listed according to a hierarchy of importance, which means that the county surveys in the Domesday Book start with the manors held directly by the king himself. William considered that ultimately he owned all the land in his kingdom, and others held it only with his agreement, effectively as his tenants. Entries for the manors of the 'tenants in chief' (the major barons, bishops and abbots) follow those of the king.

The estates belonging to these nobles and clergymen are listed under their administrative hundred and by individual *vill*. These estates came to be known as manors, from the Norman French for dwelling, *maner*, and Latin for 'remain', *manere*. All *vills* belonged in whole or part to one or more manors. So the same *vill* can crop up several times in different Domesday Book entries under different lordships, each individual entry listing only the land, people and other assets that were held by that lord. To add further complications, the lord's manor or holdings (or parts of them) could be sublet to others.

Each Domesday entry records the amount of land in *hides* (a 120 acre unit of measurement), *virgates* (quarter of a hide, 30 acres) and acres held in the *vill* by that particular lord. A *hide* was known as a *carucate* in Danish areas. Each entry records the number of ploughs owned directly by the lord, and by his people. The population of the lord's holding in a *vill* is recorded by status, from slaves to knights. Only certain individuals were specifically mentioned singly and for most ranks of peasant, which was almost everybody, only the heads of households were counted. So the total population of a village could be a multiple of probably between three and five times the total number of people mentioned in its Domesday entry or entries.

Domesday entries all end with the total value of the lord's estate in pounds and shillings. They also provide its value up to 1066, and who previously held the land. Each Domesday entry therefore paints a picture both of a functioning estate in 1086, and a place that existed before the Norman Conquest. Domesday also provides a sobering list of dispossessed Anglo-Saxon and Anglo-Scandinavian former landlords and what they had lost to the conquerors.

Important assets such as woodland, meadow, pasture, mills, fish ponds and fisheries are mentioned in Domesday entries. Sheep, pigs and cattle are also noted, wood for building, even things such as the number of eels that are supplied towards rent payments. Specific services owed by people as part of their tenancy are referenced, such as *cartage* (duty to supply a draught animal and/or cart to haul things for the lord) and *escort* (to act as a bodyguard to the lord). Domesday also mentions some industries, such as salt production, lead working, quarrying, mining and pottery production; markets and mints are included, and perhaps more surprisingly, over forty vineyards are recorded.

Domesday Book also provides a great deal of information about the structure of society and gives us a great sense of the character of village populations. Anglo-Saxon society was stratified, with kings and thegns at the top, but the Normans really knew how to put people in their place and label them accordingly. Domesday entries record social stratifications whose nuances were highly significant at the time, but that seem somewhat bewildering now.

Slaves were on the lowest rung of the social scale. They were owned by the lord, worked for the lord, and had no land of their own to farm. The other villagers were virtually all peasants, all tenants of the lord, but with varying degrees of obligation to the lord and varying degrees of autonomy.

Cottars (cottagers), *bordars* and *villeins* were unfree peasants. That is to say they were tied to the lord and manor, and had to work for the lord. But villeins also had their own land to farm, perhaps up to 30 acres or so, and had to spend less time working for the lord. Cottars generally had less land than bordars, perhaps only a garden plot; but bordars had less land to farm than villeins, perhaps only a few acres. Most of the peasant population were villeins.

Unfree peasants could not leave the lord's estate, or marry, without the lord's permission.

Freemen were not entirely free, in that although they had their own substantial amounts of land to farm in the common fields, they might still owe some services to the lord and were subject to various forms of jurisdiction in his courts. They could move around from place to place. *Men at arms*, soldiers or knights, typically held more than a hide of land in return for their military services.

There were several alternative terms for the ranks of peasantry that were used in various regions and it is often now difficult to define and correlate them rigidly with each other. Depending on which translation of the Domesday Book you read, or where in the country the place is situated, you might find peasants also described as *serfs* (slaves), *smallholders* (bordars), *ploughmen* or *oxmen*, *riding men* (escorts or messengers), *sokemen* (freemen), or the more obscure *boors* (unfree peasants, but above slaves).

Nearly all the rural peasants were heavily involved in agriculture in various ways, but they could also undertake other trades that were necessary for the smooth running of a place. Domesday also lists people specifically identified with particular occupations. This includes people you might expect to find in many medieval communities, such as bakers, brewers, carpenters, cobblers, dairy maids, fishermen, fowlers, millers and washerwomen.

Beekeepers are mentioned surprisingly often too. Honey was a very important sweetener before refined sugar and was also the basis for mead, a very popular alcoholic drink.

Niche professionals, such as embroidery workers, gold fringe makers, harpers and even jesters are referenced, but these, along with the bulk of information about industries, trades and other distinct professions, are mostly associated with larger towns.

Official post holders were identified in Domesday entries, though many of these were associated with the royal household and the military, so would not usually crop up in village entries, except when these people were important landholders. Various officials were also drawn from the ranks of villagers. *Reeves,* for example, were important to the running of the countryside. They were the people responsible for the administrative affairs of a landowner or institution, manor, place, hundred or shire (*shire reeve* = *sheriff*). They were a bit like today's councillors and council officials, exercising delegated authority on behalf of others.

The Domesday Book sounds very comprehensive, but it is important to remember that it was not a commentary on everything to be found in a place, or even a quick characterisation of a place. It was primarily a short summary of the main assets of the lords' estates in a place, and a means to ascribe a total value that could serve as a basis for tax. If something wasn't worth anything for tax purposes, the chances are it was not recorded in the Domesday Book. Therefore, for all but this basic core information, the Domesday Book is quite variable and unreliable.

The commissioners who were sent out to survey different counties took slightly different views on what additional information to include. Some were evidently jobsworths, who stuck rigidly to the core task in hand to get round as quickly as possible, but others clearly relished adding interesting notes, clarifications about disputes and other titbits. Some idea of the complexities and disputes about landholdings can be found in entries such as that for Whaddon (Cambridgeshire), which was held by Richard Son of Count Gilbert.

The commissioner added the following note to the entry:

Saevia held this land under Edeva the Fair; she could grant to whom she would. This did not belong to Richard's predecessor, nor was he ever put in possession of it, but Ralph Wader held it on the day he rebelled against the King.

In Abington (also in Cambridgeshire):

Aubrey de Vere annexed this land from the King's jurisdiction, but Picot the Sheriff adjudged it against him and still keeps 1 plough and 300 sheep which Aubrey has from that land, as the men of the Hundred testify.

Under the land of Eustace the Sheriff in Gidding (Huntingdonshire) we are told that:

Alfwold and his brothers claim that Eustace took this land from them unjustly. William the Artificer [military engineer] claims ½ virgate and 18 acres of this land. This is the witness of the whole Hundred.

These examples all come from Phillimore editions of the Domesday Book. The Phillimore series of Domesday county volumes, begun in 1975, was a landmark in making available all the Domesday survey entries available in a consistent and easily accessible form. Now various other facsimiles, transcripts and translations are available online and some offer the ability to search, analyse and map Domesday information in various interesting ways.

Whether looking at the original text or translations of Domesday, we have to think about the limitations of the Domesday survey objectives and about its inconsistencies. We can have a guess at some of the omissions. For example, only forty-eight castles are recorded in the Domesday Book, which doesn't seem to accord with their importance to Norman military and administrative strategy, or the surviving archaeological evidence. Around 2000 churches are mentioned in the Domesday Book, but some of those that were definitely in existence before 1086 (including some that are still there today) are not mentioned at all.

When we come to explore the history of villages, or a specific village, the basic message is that just because the Domesday entry does not mention something, it doesn't mean it was not there in 1086. However, despite some frustrating shortcomings and lack of clarity in some respects (which at least keep academics debating), the Domesday Book represents an astonishing medieval achievement. The National Archives describe it as 'by the far the most complete record of pre-industrial society to survive anywhere in the world'.

It opens wonderful windows on an England of nearly 1000 years ago. It tells us a huge amount about the structure of society and the governance of the countryside before the Norman Conquest, and it describes a world that remained broadly similar for a good while afterwards, into the medieval period. But the Domesday Book does not seek to describe how people actually lived from day to day, and it doesn't describe the physical structure of their homes and villages.

DOMESDAY: FARMS, HAMLETS OR VILLAGES?

England shortly before and after the Norman Conquest was a land heaving with rural settlements, but what exactly were these places like? The places recorded in the Domesday Book range in size from very small settlements comprising a family or two, to settlements with populations of several hundred. Most places have a population in-between these extremes. The implications seem obvious: by 1086, the English countryside is full of villages large and small. Furthermore, most of the places named in the Domesday Book are still identifiable in one form or another today. This allows the origins of most of today's English villages to be traced back 1000 years with absolute certainty.

But there is a catch. Neat Domesday entries do not necessarily imply neat, nucleated villages. The 'villagers' mentioned might be people dispersed across the manorial estate, or living in several detached small hamlets, rather than living in a single large village. Nevertheless, there is other evidence that in the Norman period many villages had already taken forms that became very familiar throughout the medieval period, and are still recognisable today; and the pace of change was accelerating.

The Normans had to repopulate the areas they had laid to waste and stolen from Anglo-Saxon lords, and this gave them a chance to plant some new settlements, or redevelop old ones. In the north of England, villages such as Wheldrake and Appleton-le-Moors (both in North Yorkshire) were laid out on regular plans as rigid as anything that Roman military engineers had produced. Their long, narrow, rectangular property plots of regular size were laid out from a main street, with houses at the street front and lanes running along the back of the properties.

At other places, this kind of development went hand in hand with the construction of a castle. Planned castle villages can be found along the troublesome Welsh border at places such as Kilpeck in Herefordshire. At Warkworth in Northumberland, in the region disputed by Scotland and England, the castle founded in the Norman period looms over the planned settlement. Warkworth is situated on an important road and river crossing, and it has a long main street with long, narrow property boundaries running from it on both sides. The village is nearly totally enveloped by a loop in the River Coquet. The castle closes the open end of the loop and makes the place look either firmly under the Norman thumb, or very well protected indeed, depending on your point of view.

As time went on, Norman lords sought to develop, rather than suppress, the places they had stolen from the defeated English. William de Warenne fought at Hastings with William the Conqueror and then helped fight off rebellion in the east of England. He was rewarded for these efforts and for his companionship with the king by being given vast estates in thirteen English counties. De Warenne built his main fortified residence at Castle Acre in Norfolk and he, or a successor, laid out a planned settlement enclosed by defences alongside.

The village of New Buckenham in the same county is also distinguished by its regular, grid-based, compact plan. New Buckenham was laid out by William d'Aubigny (also spelt d'Albini) in the middle of the twelfth century on a greenfield site; he also built a castle there. Both castle and village are some way from the original old Anglo-Saxon village of Buckenham, which became known as Old Buckenham. The d'Aubignys originally were from the Normandy village of Saint-Martin-d'Aubigny and, like the de Warennes, they rose to great prominence after the Conquest. The d'Aubignys also built the magnificent Castle Rising in Norfolk, where again an adjacent grid-plan settlement was laid out.

Though all these places are now villages, their Norman lords apparently had urban aspirations for them, and arranging all their tenants' houses in neat rows under their watchful eye was one step towards this aim. Obtaining a charter to hold a regular market and/or an annual fair was another important step on the path to prosperity and growth. The lord could extract tolls and charges from traders and the people could make a bob or two as well.

At New Buckenham, the remnants of the large rect-angular market area is now a village green, though it still retains its sixteenth-century Market House as a reminder of its continuing market-centre function throughout the medieval period. The Market House variously housed shops and acted as a toll house or court house.

At Warkworth, the old market area was formed by a widening of the main street into a triangle shape in front of the Norman church. This area is now partly infilled by later buildings and is mostly used as a car park today, but it is still recognisable. It has a later market cross as a reminder of its former use. Warkworth, though never bigger than the village it is today, had an urban-style administration of citizen *burgesses*, who held the long, narrow *burgage* plots of land running in two rows on both sides of the main street.

This sort of new town ambition was possible because once England had recovered from the shock of invasion, and its subjugation by a foreign elite had begun to turn into more of a co-operative enterprise, the economy started to recover and the population rose. This growth is not only seen in newly planted Norman villages, but also in the expansion of existing small Anglo-Saxon settlements into larger villages. Nucleated villages: compact in form, centred on a focus such as a castle, monastery, market place or main street. Sometimes they were planned this way from the outset, but many simply developed from more scattered communities.

VILLAGES IN THEIR FIELDS

Pressure to produce more food for an increasing population had a profound effect on the form of villages. One important reason for the increasing prominence of large, nucleated villages in late Anglo-Saxon, Norman and medieval times goes hand in hand with the relatively intensive, mixed farming regimes practised in the places where they tend to be found. This type of farming nucleated village is particularly associated with the middle part of England, the Midlands in its broadest sense, rather than its fringes.

Midlands-type nucleated villages were typically at the epicentre of a territory (later known as a parish) that contained a variety of useful resources such as woodland, pasture, meadow and marsh by rivers and streams, but which crucially also comprised a lot of arable land. Each village was surrounded by its own 'open' field system (that is to say not partitioned by hedges and walls), which was farmed in common by the villagers. They variously worked directly on the local lord's land (his *demesne*, pronounced de-main) and farmed their own strips of land as tenants, side by side with their neighbours.

The variable qualities of soil surrounding a village, and the possibilities of crop failure in one location or another, were mitigated by each villager having their strips of land distributed across the fields, rather than all clustered together in one location. Typically there were two or three large open fields surrounding a village, though sometimes more. Cereal crops (barley, oats, rye, wheat) would be planted in one field in one year and crops such as beans and peas in the other; one field would remain fallow (not planted with anything) for a year. The cropping of the fields would swap around the following year.

This regular coordinated 'rotation' of cropping and fallow periods gave the soil in the fields a chance to recover before the next crop, and helped to break cycles of persistent crop pests and diseases. Everybody growing the same things at the same time in the same place enabled co-operative effort to be maximised. At certain times of year, such as harvest, all village labour had to be carefully coordinated and brought to bear on a task, rather than dissipated by everybody having to tend different crops with different needs. When fields were fallow, and after harvest and before ploughing, they were treated as vast commons for grazing by the villagers' livestock.

The open fields were divided into parcels or *furlongs* (from 'long furrows'), which should not be confused with the horse racing distance measurement. Just like fields, furlongs were named to distinguish them from each other. The individual strips of land (*selions* or *lands*) were raised in the centre and fell away on both sides into a hollow before rising up again to the apex of the next strip. The curious corrugated effect this produces on a field's surface can be seen fossilised in land that has not been levelled by modern ploughing. It is still particularly noticeable across the Midlands counties, but also survives elsewhere. It is known as 'ridge and furrow', or 'rig' in the north of England.

Creating and maintaining this undulating land was a deliberate and purposeful choice by medieval farmers. Continuous ploughing in one direction meant that the plough share always turned the soil inwards to the ridge and away from the furrow, which helps to maintain their profiles. There is another visible clue that ploughing consistently followed one direction season after season. Plough teams had to be turned at the end of the strip of land, and because they were unwieldy, they had to start a wide turn well before they reached it. This gave the strips a slight curve at both ends, so that each strip tended to form an elongated reversed 'S' shape that perfectly matched the shape of its neighbour.

But why create an undulating field surface? There are a few theories about the benefits of doing this, including the mathematically accurate but pedantic reason that a corrugated field has a greater surface area than a flat field of the same dimensions.

However, I prefer to think that it is primarily to do with hedging bets with nature and lessening the chances of crop failure. Draining off excessive rainfall was a problem for medieval people, and they had little prospect of artificially irrigating crops that were too dry. Many types of soil become easily waterlogged, but can also dry out and bake hard. In very wet times and in damp places, the furrows would act as drainage channels or sumps, and crops on the ridges would be clear of excessively damp conditions. In very dry years, the furrows would at least retain some moisture.

Perhaps it is something to do with the effects of the climate changing and heavier rainfall, but I seem to see old fields of ridge and furrow with water standing in the furrows much more frequently now than in the past. I look at it and think about the complete disaster that the sight of drowned and rotted crops represented for medieval villagers. They didn't have many options for mitigation and could not afford to leave matters to nature and chance.

I also wonder what medieval villagers would make of the fact that many of the fields that they worked very hard to cultivate, fields that were ploughed for centuries and whose productivity was a matter of life or death, are no longer used for growing crops at all today? A surprising amount of ridge and furrow land still survives in very pronounced earthwork form in grassland, never having been levelled by subsequent ploughing. You can find ridge and furrow that ascends very steep hillsides that would test modern tractors, never mind plodding ox teams, and you can find it in areas that seem far too deep in flood zones to be worth the effort and risk of sowing crops.

You can also find ridge and furrow in areas that have since found non-agricultural uses. I have played on plenty of cricket fields that were once part of the village's old open field system. Care might have been taken to level the central 'square' so that half-decent pitches can be laid out, but the outfields still retain the tell-tale undulations of ridge and furrow. It is a bit unnerving to be running to take a catch on the crest of a ridge, only to find yourself collapsing into a furrow. It is hilarious to see opposition fielders confidently swooping to stop a ball that is skipping to the boundary, only to find it shoot between their legs, or leap over their shoulders: 'Village!'

Modern farming has levelled the vast majority of ridge and furrow that survived up to the twentieth century, but the evidence from old aerial photographs, maps, documents, and early landscape paintings and drawings shows how widespread it once was. This, along with the sheer extent of surviving ridge and furrow in marginal land that isn't ploughed now, indicates medieval village communities that were trying to squeeze every last bit of arable productivity out of their available land. England's population expanded massively in the first half of the medieval period, there were hungry mouths to feed, and plenty of hazards that could not be countered by pesticides and artificial fertilisers. Crop failure meant starvation for villagers.

The medieval open field system of farming in strips was not very efficient. Crop yields even in the very best years were much lower than the very worst yields today. But it was a system that almost certainly was introduced before the Norman Conquest and it was widespread across England for centuries afterwards. Incredibly, two villages in England still farm by this method today.

Braunton is a large village just inland of Devon's north coast. Its 'Great Field' is now farmed by a handful of farmers, rather than hundreds of villagers, and most of its strips have been amalgamated into fewer, larger strips over time. But the strips are still marked by ancient unploughed turf bulks (known as *landshares*) and large stones (*bondstones*) and farming still has to be coordinated to maintain the system.

At Laxton in Nottinghamshire, three open fields (Mill Field, South Field and West Field) are still functioning in medieval fashion alongside the modern fields in the parish. As at Braunton, the individual strip size has increased since medieval times to suit modern farm equipment. Here the strips and grass areas (*sykes*) are marked with stakes rather than stones and bulks. In order to ensure that the obligations of common farming are maintained and the system functions smoothly, the old Court Leet, a medieval committee of villagers operating under the lord's authority, still sits. It appoints a 'jury' to go and check on the state of affairs in the fields each autumn, making sure everybody has followed the rules.

Co-operative farming in medieval times required more than neighbourly goodwill among villagers. There were complex suites of by-laws governing everything that went on in the fields; transgressions were dealt with in manorial courts and were punished with a fine. In earlier times, similar stipulations must have governed village farming, but they were either never written down or have not survived.

In the medieval period, records of these by-laws and fines survive in *court rolls* or *manorial rolls*. They were so-called because they were written on parchment and stored in rolled-up form. They give a good sense of the regulation necessary to make this type of agriculture work, and medieval village life generally. Villagers needed a good memory and eye for detail if they wanted to avoid penalties.

For example, in the village of Newton Longville (Buckinghamshire) in 1290, it was stipulated, among many other things, that: 'anyone who wants to gather peas, beans or such like shall gather them between sunlight and prime in le Hech [a field name] and this [must be done] after the Feast of the Blessed Virgin Mary.' *Le Hech* was a field name and *prime*

Iron Age roundhouses, based on examples excavated at places such as Glastonbury Lake Village and Danebury hill fort, have been reconstructed at Butser Ancient Farm in Hampshire. They are arranged in an enclosed village-like setting.

© Tony Watson / Alamy Stock Photo

Excavating the remains of a Bronze Age roundhouse at Must Farm near Peterborough. The radiating timbers of the collapsed conical roof structure are clearly visible, along with the stumps of posts that raised the building above the mud. The remains of the wooden palisade circuit that enclosed the settlement can be seen far right.

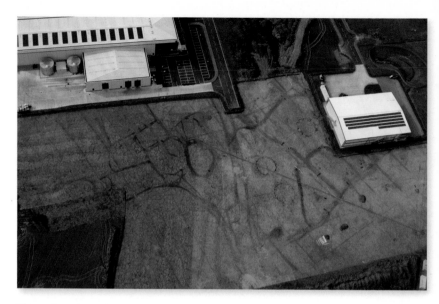

This archaeological excavation in advance of new development has revealed Iron Age and Romano-British habitation, greatly adding to knowledge about ancient settlement patterns in the locality. The dark fills of ditches define lanes, property boundaries and roundhouse sites.

The site of the walled Roman town of *Durobrivae* (centre) between the A1 Great North Road and the River Nene. The town developed as a roadside settlement near a fort. The course of Ermine Street, a major Roman road, can be traced as a parch mark running through the centre of the town. Some side streets can be seen branching off. The site was later abandoned, though Anglo-Saxon and medieval villages developed nearby.

The reconstruction of an Anglo-Saxon village at West Stow in Suffolk, based on evidence excavated at the site. The loose layout and buildings of West Stow are typical of early Anglo-Saxon settlements. The building in the foreground is a 'sunken feature building', based over a large hollow excavated in the ground.

A medieval village with a small manor or manorial farm in the foreground, village houses behind, and a manor house near the church in the background. The circular building is a dovecote, which provided pigeon and dove eggs and meat in medieval times. The picture is based on evidence from the medieval village of Botolph Bridge near Peterborough. This village is listed in the Domesday Book but had dwindled away by later medieval times. Modern homes have now been built on the site.

Woodhurst was one of three adjacent medieval hamlets all with 'hurst' names (Old English for 'wooded hill'). The woodland disappeared as the medieval village developed here, surrounded by its open fields. As the village grew, houses were built along the main street, parallel back lane and on the land between. The former open fields of 'ridge and furrow' finally were enclosed and overlain by hedged fields. Some survives in pasture, but further from the village it has been levelled by modern ploughing.

Kimbolton village typifies the layout of many Norman and medieval planned 'new towns'. Kimbolton belonged to King Harold before 1066 and was already a substantial place of 120 or so households in 1086. In 1200 its lord, Geoffrey FitzPier, obtained a charter for a Friday market and annual fair. He replanned the village as rows of regular properties along a wide market street in front of his new castle. The present Kimbolton Castle (bottom left) was built in the late seventeenth century and eighteenth century on the site of its medieval predecessor.

Caxton in Cambridgeshire developed along the line of Ermine Street, a major Roman road, but this is not a Roman village. The medieval village first developed around the church, well to the west of the road (far right). From the thirteenth century, the road regained its importance to travellers. A market site and new village was then laid out alongside. Caxton is now bypassed by a modern road (left).

Outwell is a sprawling village that developed where rivers meet. The junction of the Old River Nene and the Well Creek is in the centre of the village. Their banks, the course of a former river leading north (Wellstream), and a lane leading out to the fields are all lined with houses. Remnants of curving medieval cultivation strips can be seen in the foreground. They are a local variation of ridge and furrow called 'darlands'.

Gedney Hill in Lincolnshire. The medieval Church of the Holy Trinity (centre) indicates the village had developed by the fourteenth century. Several villages in the Fenland region are strung out along long straight drove roads that were laid out across drained marshland. The 'Hill' element of the name surprises many people as the village is only a few feet above sea level.

was a period of day between dawn and the first division of the medieval morning, which varied with the seasons.

In 1332, the villagers of Great Horwood in the same county were instructed:

> No one shall be allowed to glean who can earn his food and a penny a day if there is anyone who wishes to hire him.
> No stranger shall be allowed to glean among them.
> Everyone shall cause all lanes and suspect gaps next to the fields to be stopped up.
> No one shall gather stubble in the field from the Feast of St Michael to the Feast of St Martin except in his own land.
> No one shall cart at night time.

Gleaning is picking fallen grain off the ground after harvest. Villagers were permitted to do this to accumulate meagre supplies for their own use.

The records show that in Newton Longville in 1290: 'Roger Adekyns puts himself in mercy for trespass in the lord's grain with three sheep and four lambs.' He was one of many Newton Longville villagers, male and female, that year who either deliberately or accidentally let their pigs, sheep, cows, horses or geese roam into the lord's crops, pasture or meadow. The penalties were one to four pence each.

Alongside these misdemeanours are 'fines' or charges for various permissions required from the lord such as: 'It is granted by the lord to Agnes Bouere that she may marry wherever she wishes in the lords fee' (fine, 12 cocks; Newton Longville, 1283).[1]

ENGLISH VILLAGES TAKE SHAPE

The level of co-operation, regulation and scrutiny required to operate open, common fields were far more suited to communities that were concentrated in one principal, central location: hence the nucleated village. In this structure, practically everybody in the village was equally close to, or far away from the strips of land they had to farm dispersed across the open fields. People in a compact village could quickly get together to communicate, agree action and martial their resources without having to send messages off to far-flung dwellings and wait for others to arrive. It was an arrangement that allowed all villagers to play their parts in managing the surrounding agricultural estate that kept them all alive.

If all went well, it also generated a healthy surplus for the lords and tax revenue for the king and church. Parish churches were built conveniently within these centres of population. The principal manor houses of a resident lord would not be situated right among the peasants' homes, but it would not be too far away either. Nucleated living also meant that villagers could share centralised village amenities more easily, and more readily enjoy a sense of community. They could worship, celebrate and party together. The medieval

---

[1] All examples drawn from *Open-Field Farming in Medieval England* by Warren O. Ault.

village calendar was not all work: fairs and religious festivals gave a chance for some time off and for some fun.

This basic nucleated village form, which started to appear in late Anglo-Saxon England but became widespread following the Norman Conquest, can still be seen in a huge number of English villages today. However, this type of compact village was not ubiquitous in medieval times, nor is it now. It doesn't represent the diversity of rural settlement and villages right across England.

There were linear villages that developed along important highways, just as Roman roadside settlements had, or alongside rivers. Medieval villages also evolved with more than one centre; we now describe these as polyfocal villages. The term 'polyfocal villages' is a bit like those medical terms that doctors reel off as a diagnosis, which when you drill down to the actual meaning of the words are merely vague or oblique *descriptions* of the condition in Latin or Greek.

'Doctor, I am losing my hair. What could it be?'

'I'm sorry to say it's alopecia.'

'Isn't that something to do with mange in foxes?'

What you really want is an accurate *explanation* of what causes the condition, which then helps you to understand and treat it.

So here goes. There are lots of reasons why villages might develop in a compound, polyfocal way over hundreds of years, but one of the simpler ones is that several nearby formerly detached hamlets and farmsteads grow outwards towards each other, until eventually they are recognised as belonging to one large village made of several parts. Families split land amongst heirs, or sell it, and each new offshoot family might build a new house on their newly acquired land near to the others.

The presence of multiple lords, with their own manors and manor houses, is another factor in the development of polyfocal villages. Each manor might form a distinct focal point around which the respective lords' people cluster. Another reason is that a village might gain an additional planned annexe. If d'Aubigny had built his new castle and planned settlement closer to the original village of Buckenham, we might now have one large, polyfocal Buckenham, rather than Old Buckenham and New Buckenham. Similarly, a newly planned village might later gain another planned annexe at a later date, or simply grow towards another focus. A new market area or green could also create a new focus for a group of houses.

Whether polyfocal, linear or nuclear, the arrangement of individual properties within a medieval village tended to be similar. I have already mentioned that many villages were arranged with property plots set out from main streets. Peasant homesteads in their own grounds, *tofts*, often stood close to the street front with their individual *crofts* (allotment-like plots of land) behind. These were distinct from the strips farmed in the open fields. Fences, hedges, walls and ditches would be variously used to enclose these pieces of land, either to keep a few animals in, or to keep village livestock from ruining the gardens and crops.

Despite hundreds of years of subsequent village development that has created new houses, new streets, and resulted in the joining together or splitting up of properties, these early toft and croft boundaries are still perfectly distinct in very many English villages.

Manor houses with their barns and other farm buildings stood in larger enclosures, which often had much beefier boundaries that were defined by ditches and banks. Closes, or small fields enclosed by hedges, fences or walls, might be found next to the manorial complex and alongside the village. Most villages have an easily identifiable main street, or High Street, and other lanes and roads that lead from it to other nearby places. Lanes also formed along the backs of tofts and crofts (back lanes) and these sometimes formed a full circuit around the village.

A variety of village forms developed in medieval times, and in some parts of the country large villages were not the most common form of settlement. In large parts of the north, south-west, east and south-east of England, an ancient pattern of dispersed farmsteads and hamlets persisted throughout medieval times. Even today, smaller dispersed settlements characterise large parts of several counties, such as Cumbria, Cornwall and even parts of Norfolk, Suffolk, Essex and Kent. In these parts of the country, poorer soils, difficult terrain or lots of woodland, heath, moor or marsh, meant that arable land was more piecemeal and scattered, and therefore farms and homes tended to be scattered across the landscape.

CHAPTER 3

MEDIEVAL FEATURES

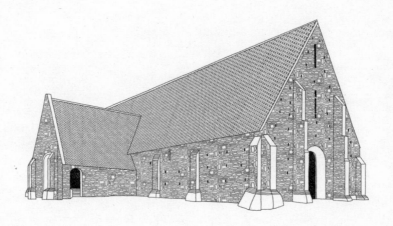

The basic structure of many English villages today had been established in the medieval period. So too had many of their defining features and buildings. It is worth keeping an eye out for these classic village elements if you're looking to understand the origins and development of a village you are exploring. Some features have been masked or modified by later development and there are, of course, also many other medieval features that have been lost from the village scene, but await rediscovery.

VILLAGE GREENS

Village greens, a characteristic and delightful feature of many English villages today, proliferated in medieval times, though some may have predated the Norman Conquest. Greens were simply open areas of grassy common land onto which villagers could bring grazing livestock. Bringing livestock in from the fields to graze right under the watchful eyes of the village was sometimes necessary for protection, as well as for routine husbandry tasks. Greens were also places where villagers congregated for fairs and markets, celebrations and sports.

Some greens were integral to the design of a planned village. Milburn in Cumbria, one of the new type of planned villages built after the Norman Conquest, was laid out around an almost perfectly rectangular green. Rows of houses and farms front on to it on all sides. Coneysthorpe in North Yorkshire is similarly based around a rectangular green.

Greens could be established in a casual or opportunistic way by taking in pieces of land from adjacent fields. They could develop around road junctions and where droves and tracks funnelled into a village from its surrounding fields. Greens can be elongated strips of land, or compact, more or less circular, square or triangular areas. They can also be very large and completely irregular in shape, simply responding to the lie of the available land and its natural and built obstacles. They might simply develop in awkward, marginal areas that were less convenient for cultivation, such as alongside streams.

Greens could dictate how a village developed over time. Even if not planned from the outset, it was common for houses to be built fringing a green and facing on to it. Where greens formed in areas of dispersed settlement, well away from village centres, they might later attract a cluster of houses that gave rise to an entirely new hamlet or village. This might simply use the name of the nearest existing place with the word 'Green' appended. Rural Essex, north of Epping Forest, is peppered with villages and hamlets whose names are post-fixed by 'Green'.

On the north-east fringes of Stoke-on-Trent in Staffordshire, there are clues about the character of the area before it was enveloped by potteries, coal mines and housing. The historic village and hamlet names Baddeley Green, Norton Green, Ball Green, Bemersley Green, Sneyd Green and Ford Green, can all be found within a few square miles.

Many village greens have changed considerably over time, either being entirely built over or nibbled away by later housing development or fragmented by roads. In fact, sneaky encroachment onto greens by the construction of roads, houses and their gardens began quite early in many cases, and roads and streets that criss-cross greens are often a formalisation of old paths of convenience and tracks from one village location to another.

No village green is complete without a pond or two. Village ponds were not solely places for dunking suspected witches, but were important watering holes for livestock. *Pounds* sometimes still survive on village greens, and these small wooden, stone or brick-walled enclosures were built to imprison animals that had strayed where they shouldn't have, pending the payment of fines and collection by their owners.

Goathland, a village in the North York Moors best known to fans of nostalgic 1960s period drama series *Heartbeat* as 'Aidensfield', is strung out around a series of massive greens. Surrounded by wild moorland, the greens were a very important sanctuary and source of good grazing. In fact, the tenants of the Duchy of Lancaster still have rights to graze sheep on Goathland's greens, an arrangement that dates back hundreds of years.

In contrast to the spread-out, rough pasture greens of Goathland, the village green at Leigh, near Tonbridge in Kent, is now a large, neatly mown area in the centre of the village, encircled by streets, where cricket and football pitches are laid out. The parish of Wellow, in Nottinghamshire, still retains an unusual amount of common land, but the small triangular green in the centre of the village is barely wide enough to accommodate dancing around its impressive maypole.

Village greens continue to be valuable amenities for the villages that are fortunate to retain them. They are appreciated equally either as informal meadows, perhaps with a scattering of shady mature trees, or closely mown grass that provides setting for the village football pitch, cricket pitch, bowls greens or children's play equipment; or a mixture of all of these things. Today's village fêtes, shows and fairs reflect the sort of functions held on this same land for hundreds of years. They are so well recognised as useful and attractive features of any settlement that modern versions of greens are built into new housing developments.

HOMES

Just as today, the quality and size of medieval houses largely reflected the means and status of their occupants. Most peasant houses throughout the medieval period would have been very basic, and pretty disgusting by today's standards. None of these early, simple peasant houses survive to the present day: our knowledge about them comes almost exclusively from archaeological excavations.

The seminal research excavations at the site of the village of Wharram Percy, in the Yorkshire Wolds, shed a lot of light on the development of medieval village homes and other village buildings, and on the structure and development of medieval villages generally. Investigations began there in 1948 and the programme of archaeological excavations spanned four decades.

Another important early excavation programme was carried out at Goltho in Lincolnshire during the 1970s, and another in the 1980s on the hamlet of West Cotton near the town of Raunds, in Northamptonshire. It is no coincidence that these places, and other places where the most substantial archaeological research and rescue campaigns have taken place, are all deserted villages.

In villages that ceased to be occupied before the modern era, no modern houses have disturbed and destroyed the flimsier foundations of earlier houses. In deserted villages, there are fewer physical barriers to excavating the large areas necessary to get a comprehensive picture of the extent of buried archaeological remains, and much more chance of understanding the full sequence of village development.

Archaeological excavations across the country have consistently shown that the earliest medieval peasant houses were similar to the Anglo-Saxon houses described in previous chapters. They were rectangular and comprised one or two rooms, or at least separate spaces in one room marked by some form of partition; animals would be housed at one end, the human household at the other. In all but the most stone-rich areas, most houses were largely timber-built. Their frames were either secured directly in the ground (as they had been in earlier periods), built off levelled clay platforms, or from stone foundations or low walls of stone rubble. Reed, straw, heather or even turf thatch provided a roof covering; whilst wattle and daub, or cob, were all cheap, earthy walling materials ready to hand.

Better-off peasants inhabited longhouses. These long, thin, single-storey houses had a byre for livestock at one end, which was partitioned off from the living quarters of the household, and there were opposed entrances in the long parallel walls that provided a route through the width of the building (a cross passage). The family lived in a room open to the rafters, heated by a central fireplace, and living conditions and the household scene generally were not much different to family life in a prehistoric roundhouse.

The longhouse, in modified forms, persisted throughout the medieval period and into the modern era in remote locations. Excavations of peasant homes at Wharram Percy and elsewhere have produced hinges for doors and shutters and keys, which show that at least a basic degree of security and draught-excluding comfort was available even to the lowliest households.

MANOR HOUSES

Early manor houses and smaller manor houses were often more substantial versions of the longhouse or hall house, but usually with more outbuildings and larger outbuildings than peasants would have required. Over time, additional wings and courtyard-shaped arrangements might develop. When a lord felt safe enough not to need a full-blown castle, or was not influential or rich enough to have one, he could nevertheless build in some additional security to his residence.

First he could build his house from stone and make the entrance on the first floor accessible only by a narrow stair. This would make the living quarters much easier to defend against intruders.

Openings could be set high up and would be small; as many windows were shuttered, not glazed, this minimised draughts as well as attackers. Arrow loops, narrow slit openings from which longbows and crossbows could be fired, were built into the walls. The ground floor would be a storeroom or basement in which livestock and produce could be locked away. Again, only narrow openings (ventilators) too small to climb through were needed. Examples of these types of manor house were excavated at West Cotton and at Wharram Percy, and have been revealed in several other excavations. Remarkably, a handful are still standing.

The late Norman manor house in the village of Boothby Pagnell in Lincolnshire was eventually replaced by a much later manor house, but this venerable building was still in use as a dwelling in the early twentieth century. It is still roofed and stands in the private grounds of the house that succeeded it. At Hemingford Grey in Cambridgeshire, the Norman manor house, built around 1150, is still a home. Both houses were built of stone and arranged with living quarters on the first floor, which were accessed by external steps, with undercroft storerooms beneath. Both houses retain Norman architectural features, such as forms of semi-circular headed windows and doors that are now more commonly seen in churches, monasteries and castles. They are among the few places across the country where Norman domestic architecture can still be seen in either village or town settings, but they are representative of the manor houses that would have been quite numerous in villages across England in Norman times and into the medieval period.

A lord worried about security, or simply wishing to signal his status, might also choose to surround his residence with a moat. Remains of moats survive both at Boothby Pagnell and at Hemingford Grey. Around 6000 medieval moated sites can be seen across England and the majority of these seem to have been built in the period from around 1250 to 1350. The moats usually enclose a square or rectangular island on which the principal manorial buildings clustered. Causeways or bridges crossed the moat and some had a gatehouse to protect the main entrance.

A licence was required to fortify a residence with walls and battlements (a licence to *crenellate*) and this could only be granted by the Crown, or by an authority delegated by the Crown. As time went on, many manor houses became difficult to distinguish from small castles and some became known as such, but much of their elaboration was about showing off, rather than solid military purpose.

One of the best preserved and most picturesque examples is Stokesay Castle in Shropshire. There was an early castle on the site there, but the result of Laurence de Ludlow's rebuilding campaign late in the thirteenth century is a fortified manor house. A splendid timber-framed gatehouse leads to a courtyard. On the west side of the courtyard, an impressive stone-built great hall and living accommodation (the *solar* block) is flanked by two towers. The towers, walls, moat and gatehouse offered some protection for the household and staff, but the buildings have very large windows facing the outside world and are lavishly ornamented internally and externally.

Laurence de Ludlow was one of England's leading wool merchants and a very wealthy man. Stokesay Castle is an architectural status symbol, rather than a fort or true castle. Its only real test as a stronghold came in 1645 during the English Civil War. However, the temporary Royalist garrison there quickly saw the futility of trying to defend it and gave the place up without a struggle when a Parliamentarian force appeared.

MILLS

Other building types that once characterised many English medieval villages can still be found in many of them today, though the surviving buildings themselves are later in date. Around 6000 mills were recorded by the Domesday survey, which is nearly one for every two places listed. Most of the mills mentioned in the Domesday Book were watermills and grinding wheels powered by animals.

Windmills became increasingly common later in the medieval period. The earliest were post mills, whose machinery and housing all rotated on a large central post. This had to be turned by hand to face the wind. Mills were absolutely vital to the operation of a village and making villagers pay to have their grain milled in the lord's mill was a big money-spinner. Windmills can be accurately and metaphorically described as the primary engines of the English medieval economy. The workings of a mill, with its interlocking mechanism of cogs, shafts and stones, would have been deeply impressive to people not at all used to machines.

Post mills were built on small mounds like mini castle mottes. These mounds often survive close to villages, even though the mills themselves have long gone, or have been replaced by the smock mills and tower mills that came later. Both of these types of mill were a considerable technological leap forward, having fixed towers, rotating caps, and then an inbuilt ability to self-correct the orientation of the sails. No medieval post mills survive, but seventeenth-century examples can still be seen. The post mill that served the village of Outwood in Surrey was built in 1665, and is thought to be Britain's oldest working example.

BARNS

From the earliest times, barns and sheds were built to shelter animals and crops by better-off villagers and lords alike. Some medieval barns, especially those associated with large monasteries and estate centres, such as the twin thirteenth-century barns at Cressing Temple, are positively cathedralesque. The great early fifteenth-century barn at Harmondsworth, a village just north of Heathrow Airport, was part of the manorial complex belonging to Winchester College. It is nearly 60 metres (around 200 feet) in length and formed from a thirteen-bay frame of giant oak trusses. English Heritage rescued it from dilapidation.

The impressive fourteenth-century barn at Lacock in Wiltshire, now in the care of the National Trust, once belonged to Lacock Abbey, and had a spell of use as a village market hall in the eighteenth century. It is built of lime-stone, with oak crucks supporting the roof. Most medieval villagers would not have seen barns of quite this magnitude in their own village, but large barns would have been notable buildings in most villages, when nearly everybody lived in simple, single-storey homes. In addition to the obvious agricultural functions, many occasionally hosted village meetings, dances and touring theatre productions. Magnificent medieval barns, large and small, still survive in many villages.

EARLY CHURCHES

Parish churches were usually by far the most substantial, lofty and impressive buildings in a medieval village, and remain so today. Churches have also been the most enduring of all village buildings. Throughout more than 1000 years, parish churches have acted like giant masonry barometers of the fortunes of their villages. They are woven into the changing fabric of a place. The construction, enlargement, decline, abandonment and rebuilding of churches not only indicates the spiritual health of villages, but also a lot about their politics and economic wellbeing, and about their lords.

There were probably a few buildings in England broadly equivalent to Christian churches in late Roman times, but not until after the widespread reintroduction of Christianity to England, from the seventh century onwards, would churches as we recognise them start to become a defining feature of the English landscape.

The parish church usually has the most lavish architecture of any village building, and it has usually cost much more to build and maintain over the years than even the grand houses of local lords and squires. Well before the Norman Conquest, village communities paid a *tithe* (notionally one tenth of all that they produced or earned) to the upkeep of the church and its officials. If they were lucky, the local lord would dip into his pocket for major building campaigns and endowments of land to provide additional income for the church. Sometimes benefactors would pay to have prayers said in their name for evermore, and some would mark their contributions firmly in stone: coats of arms and initials label their good work on the building.

In medieval times, giving money to the church was seen as a sort of spiritual insurance policy. It was considered to be a good investment for those with excess wealth, as it secured 'priority passenger' status through purgatory and hopefully a favourable reception at the pearly gates of heaven. It is not just the exterior of a church building, its size and architectural quality, that gives a sense of the capacity of the village community and its big hitters. Most church interiors are adorned with all sorts of fixtures and fittings, memorials and ornaments that give clues about the history of a village and its people.

The first churches served monastic communities, and were the spiritual bases from which missions to convert the pagan people of the various Anglo-Saxon kingdoms were launched. The founding of these churches required royal approval and grants of land and money. Later, local lords built private chapels for their own households and churches to serve the communities working on their estates. These estates and vills formed the basis for parishes, which were all served by a parish church. Many present-day parish churches originated as manorial churches.

A handful of village churches that date from Anglo-Saxon times survive in a substantially complete form and are still in use today. The original village church at Escomb, in County Durham, is one of the earliest. It dates to the late seventh century or eighth century and its design is typically Anglo-Saxon. It is a small, narrow but lofty building, with small windows. The variably sized blocks of stone used for its walls were probably recycled masonry taken from the ruins of a nearby Roman fort at Binchester; a stone bearing the mark of the Sixth Legion has been used (the wrong way up) in the north wall.

The church of All Saints in the village of Brixworth, in Northamptonshire, is probably even earlier, dating to before 675. This church was modelled on the format of Roman basilicas, and it also reuses Roman stone and tiles. Truth be told, Anglo-Saxon builders were more comfortable with timber work. Most Anglo-Saxon churches were built of wood. They have not survived, and only their shadowy foundations remain to be revealed in archaeological excavations.

Almost miraculously, however, one wooden church of the period still serves its parish. This church, at Greensted in Essex, may well be the oldest timber building in Europe still standing, and is probably the oldest wooden church anywhere in the world. Once thought to date to the ninth century, tree-ring dating (dendrochronology) has now placed it in the eleventh century. Its walls, formed by huge, split-oak staves, are reminiscent of old Scandinavian buildings and Anglo-Saxon halls.

Even the style of late Anglo-Saxon stone churches contains echoes of an earlier timber building tradition. Some say that the curious, narrow stone strip (pilaster) detailing that can be seen in the towers of churches such as Barnack in Cambridgeshire, Earls Barton in Northamptonshire, and others, is intended to mimic timber work. Substantially complete Anglo-Saxon churches are very thin on the ground now, but several hundred village churches still retain some Anglo-Saxon features, even if the churches have been modified many times over the centuries since.

Apart from pilaster strips on external masonry, the features to look out for are triangular headed windows, baluster shafts (squat, bulbous columns), small semi-circular headed windows, and a distinctive 'long and short' arrangement of quoins (corner stones). This looks exactly as its name suggests, with a stone block on its side supporting a long thin upright stone block, which supports another block on its side, and so on up the wall.

The centuries after the Norman Conquest were boom years for church building. The church, like the castle, was one of the key expressions of Norman power. Cannily, the Normans did not immediately go for a wholesale destruction of existing Anglo-Saxon church administration, or demolition of the church buildings themselves, but instead took them on and made them their own. When the Normans did decide to rebuild churches, their architecture was based on the same fundamental engineering principles and architectural forms that governed Anglo-Saxon architecture, but Norman builders were able to take these to another level entirely.

Doors, windows and chancel arches were largely the same semi-circular headed Romanesque format as their Anglo-Saxon predecessors, but Norman masons showed off their mastery of stoneworking with zigzags, hatching, billets, pellets, lozenges, cabling and wavy line effects. These were carved very precisely in deep relief into fine, tightly jointed stonework, and sometimes covered every square inch of prominent arches, columns and pilasters. To be brutally honest, Anglo-Saxon architecture tends to look a bit crude, chunky and plain in comparison, though it is nonetheless thrilling for its antiquity and rarity.

LATER MEDIEVAL CHURCHES

From around 1200 onwards, what is now known as the 'Early English' style of architecture started to replace the old Saxon and Norman Romanesque styles previously used in village churches. Rather than semi-circular and squat, arches became high and pointy. In engineering terms, this was a better way of spreading the weight bearing down on them, so walls did not have to be so thick and greater heights and spans could be achieved. Larger windows were built. Intermediate stone mullions (thin vertical bars) increased the span of a window and light stone tracery, forming geometrical shapes, filled the space in-between.

The 'Decorated' style came in around 1300, which added even more florid cusps, quatrefoils and curves to tracery. New shapes, such as the *ogee* arch were introduced. These were formed by joining two reversed S-shaped curves at an apex and were inspired by Middle Eastern architecture. Finally, the pinnacle of medieval church design was reached with the 'Perpendicular' style. The objective there seemed to be to demonstrate that stone had no weight at all, and that huge airy buildings were able to soar skywards, mainly due to God's grace.

Flying buttresses, pinnacles and turrets seemed to float in mid-air. Stone was worked delicately into intricate lace-like patterns and blooming flower shapes. Windows became vast and let in more light than ever before through ever thinner and more translucent coloured glass. Masons and glaziers were really showing off now. Not to be outdone, carpenters put all the intricate patterns used in stonework, and more, into their timber panels, screens and roofs. Vibrantly coloured wooden flying angels projecting from beams would meet the gaze of villagers who turned their heads up towards the heavens during worship.

I used to be a little bit disappointed with my village church, St Andrew's. I now appreciate that it is a very fine church indeed; a magnificent medieval building and a striking local landmark. It is a very large, late fourteenth-century Perpendicular-style church with a tall, elegant 'pepperpot' tower, said to have been inspired by the famous Octagon Tower of nearby Ely Cathedral. But as a child looking for some distraction during services, I found its interior a bit too plain.

I vaguely knew that after Henry VIII changed the English state religion from Catholicism to something a bit more palatable to the governance of his country (and more tolerant of his serial marriages), churches were altered in various ways. Too much bling and idolatry was considered ungodly to church reformers in the sixteenth and seventeenth centuries. A considerable amount of ornamentation was stripped from village churches at the time and a good deal of colour was washed over. It wasn't the lack of glittering ornaments that I found disappointing in my village church, but the paucity of ancient memorial tablets and other historical paraphernalia hanging from the plain, whitewashed walls.

Where were the ranks of brasses depicting priests and nobles that should be set in the floor? Where were the tombs adorned with cross-legged sleeping knights and their ladies? Where were the frilly-ruffed gents and ladies dressed in black, kneeling in prayer? Where were the anatomically suspect stone skulls and dancing skeletons? Most other churches I saw seemed to have these types of memorials, even if they were mutilated with missing hands and noses. Another casualty of church reformers.

All this kind of thing seemed to be missing in St Andrew's, and with it much of the interest for children who thrived on weaving stories around such morbid curios. But the truth is that St Andrew's never had many of these monuments in the first place. The monuments in the church, or in this case the lack of them, tell us a lot about the movers and shakers in a village over time. Monuments reflect the ebbs and flows of the village dynasties; they represent manorial lords and later gentry recording their military exploits, sacrifices and good works, and sometimes their misfortunes. These memorials reflect how they, and their relatives and friends, wanted them to be seen in perpetuity.

My village, like many others, had an absentee landlord, a lord of the manor who lived elsewhere. The manor was held by the Abbots of Ely since before the Norman Conquest. They had a manorial site there, a grange later called the Burystead, and it was at the centre of one of their most valuable holdings; it remained in church hands until recent times. The very large chapel of this complex, dating to around 1300, still stands within a moated enclosure. It was later converted to a house and extended by a large, eighteenth-century wing.

I used to cycle by quickly on my way back from Cub Scout meetings, as the dusk descended and the mist rolled in, because ghosts of monks were rumoured to appear occasionally. The Abbot of Ely himself didn't actually live there, but there was no room for any other big manorial players in the village until relatively minor gentry appeared in the eighteenth century. The abbots and other major officials were buried in the cathedral at Ely and did not feel the need to adorn this parish church with symbols of their influence.

The parish church in the village of Flitton, in Bedfordshire, is a different matter entirely. It has a curious, plastered cream-coloured extension at its east end that seems totally out of proportion with the rest of the church. A glance inside immediately answers why this extension was built, and leaves you in no doubt about who ruled the roost in this neighbourhood. The extension is the chapel and mausoleum of the De

Grey family, Dukes and Earls of Kent. They lived at nearby Wrest Park and had built the church in the fifteenth century. Henry Grey, the 6th Earl of Kent, paid for the extension to be built around 1605. It now houses one of the finest collections of funerary monuments that can be seen anywhere in England. The effigies and memorial tablets span three centuries and exclusively commemorate the De Grey dynasty.

The church of St Mary and All Saints at Fotheringhay, Northamptonshire, is out of all proportion with the surrounding village. Its magnificent octagonal lantern tower is a beacon visible for miles around. A closer look suggests that the tower and lofty nave is also out of proportion with the rest of the building. That is because the church used to be even bigger, about twice its current length, before it lost its chancel.

Why is there such a huge church in this quiet corner of Northamptonshire? One clue to the former prominence of the place and its church can be found down a track at one end of the single village street. The earthworks of a large motte and bailey castle overlook an ancient crossing of the River Nene. Only a fragment of masonry now remains, but this was a substantial castle in medieval times. It was here that Mary, Queen of Scots, contender for the English throne and therefore perennial problem for Queen Elizabeth I, was held prisoner and finally beheaded in 1587. The castle had been owned by royalty, and royal connections explain the magnificent church.

Fotheringhay church was effectively two churches, one part for a college or community of priests founded by Edward III, and the other part for the people of the parish. It is the former part and the attached cloisters of the college that have gone. Fotheringhay church was intended as the mauso-leum for one of the great dynasties of the medieval period, the House of York. King Richard III's brother, parents and great-uncle are buried here, and Richard himself had been born at Fotheringhay Castle. His death at the Battle of Bosworth in 1485, the last English king to die in battle, is usually taken to mark the end of the medieval period in England.

The great 'wool churches' of Suffolk are also more like small cathedrals than parish churches. Their scale and quality is due to new medieval money, though, rather than old medieval dynasties. The Church of St Peter and St Paul in Lavenham testifies to the rise of the merchant class in the medieval period. When the lord of the manor, John de Vere, Earl of Oxford, had the idea of building a new church to mark the Tudor victory at the Battle of Bosworth, he turned to Lavenham's wealthy woollen goods merchants, clothiers, for the necessary cash.

Thomas Spring II gave a considerable sum of money towards building the huge tower, and his son, Thomas Spring III, finished the job with no expense spared. He also paid for the south chapel and a tomb for him and his wife within a lavish enclosure inside the church. Another clothier, Simon Branch, built a chapel on the north side of the church. The De Veres were an old Norman family. By the time Thomas Spring III had made his will (in which he described himself only as a 'clothmaker'), he was in fact one of the richest men in England. The Spring family married into the De Veres, and Thomas III's son later joined the nobility as Sir John Spring.

Medieval parish church builders often preferred to modify and extend existing buildings, rather than demolish them and start again. Obtaining new stone, hauling it from quarries, cutting it to shape and chiselling fashionable new tracery was incredibly expensive and time-consuming. Therefore, though first appearances might suggest a wholly late-medieval date for many village churches, a closer look can reveal much earlier fabric, features and origins.

A final note of caution: Victorian architects restored and rebuilt a huge number of medieval churches, often using a fantasy mash-up of medieval styles that made them look more medieval than even medieval people would have been entirely comfortable with. There are very few village churches whose fabric missed Victorian attention. Some of their work was way too radical, bordering on vandalism and near total demolition.

However, many medieval churches had entered the nineteenth century in very poor condition. They would not survive at all today, but for Victorian piety and their church restoration mania; and even the most heavily restored churches usually retain some features from their medieval past.

CHAPTER 4

LOSS AND REINVENTION

LOST, DESERTED, SHIFTED AND SHRUNKEN VILLAGES

Villages have been destroyed by sudden, catastrophic events such as accidental fires and warfare, and they can be swept away by the sea. Dozens of medieval villages in the East Riding of Yorkshire, from Flamborough Head to the Humber Estuary, were lost to the erosion of the coastline. Dunwich on the Suffolk coast was an important port and sizeable town in medieval times, but the soft mud cliffs it stood on were eaten away by storms until the place was reduced to a small village. The cliffs continue to erode towards the ruins of Greyfriars Priory, the last of the former town's many medieval churches, chapels and religious precincts that long ago fell into the sea.

The village of Slaughden, further down the Suffolk coast, near Aldeburgh, suffered the same fate. The shingle spit on which Slaughden lay was battered by the North Sea, until by the 1920s nothing at all remained but a Martello tower. This sturdy defence against Napoleon still stands, but is itself now highly vulnerable to invasion by the sea. The medieval town of

Aldeburgh was also half-eaten away by the sea. Happisburgh, the Norfolk village that gives us the earliest evidence of human life in England, is also being washed into the sea at an alarming rate. It sits on the soft cliffs whose erosion has revealed the tools and footprints buried beneath.

Coastal erosion is not all about the power of nature. The choices that society makes about defence, retreat and management of landscape and seascape can have a dramatic effect. The Devon village of Hallsands' demise was precipitated by the offshore dredging of vast quantities of sand and gravel to build docks at Plymouth. The seabed shifted and the beach and wall that protected Hallsands slumped and slipped beneath the waves. The village buildings then had no defence against storms and many buildings succumbed to the sea during 1917. Ruins can still be seen at the foot of the cliff.

These sorts of calamities can only explain the demise of some villages. Historians had long known that many of the inland settlements mentioned in the Domesday Book and later medieval records had been 'lost'. It was not simply that their names had changed over time; no equivalent existing place could be found that correlated with them. Where were these villages and what had happened to them?

After the Second World War, as aerial photography became more available and archaeologists began to recognise, explore and excavate the buried remains of deserted villages such as Wharram Percy, the true scale of village loss became apparent. Over 2000 deserted medieval village ('DMV') sites are now recorded in England, though it is difficult to be precise about the exact number, as the distinction between clusters of farmsteads, hamlets, separate villages and parts of polyfocal villages is sometimes difficult to make. Many archaeologists prefer to use the term 'deserted medieval settlements'. Nevertheless, it is now certain that a huge number of once thriving medieval villages did not survive to become villages today.

PLAGUE VILLAGES

The theories about what happened to these places have shifted over the last seventy years or so. It was once thought that the terrible 'Black Death' between 1348 and 1350 was wholly responsible for the loss of all these medieval 'plague villages'. In turn it then became fashionable to play down the effects of this pandemic and to emphasis social and economic causes instead. Now the severity and far-reaching consequences of medieval plagues are better known, and now that the decline of many more villages has been examined through documentary research and archaeological excavation, it has to be concluded that there is no neat, single universal answer for village desertion. Plague, changing economic and social forces, and changing environment all had a part to play.

Villages boomed in the early part of the medieval period. From 1086 to around 1300, the population of England at least doubled, perhaps trebled to over 6 million people, and in many villages the rate of growth was even greater. Entirely new villages were founded or grew from smaller settlements. But the fourteenth century saw a dramatic reversal of this growth. It would take another 300 years for the country's population to reach pre-fourteenth-century levels again. Many villages never recovered at all.

The first half of the fourteenth century was marked by livestock disease, terrible weather, crop failures and famines. The effects of the 'Little Ice Age', a deterioration to a generally colder, wetter climate that lasted until the nineteenth century, were beginning to make themselves felt. Things got far worse as the century went on. A terrible disease carried by rats and fleas spread from the Near East across Europe, and on to the south coast of England. It swept through towns and countryside with staggering speed.

The causes of the plague were not understood by medieval people and the various symptoms reported at the time are confused. There were strands of plague that attacked the lungs and that caused blood poisoning. There was fever, and coughing up blood, but the appearance of pus- and blood-filled 'tumours' or buboes on the body was a common and frightening feature, and gave the infection its name: bubonic plague.

It is now thought that somewhere between forty and sixty per cent of the entire rural population of England died during the first bubonic plague epidemic of 1348 to 1350. Subsequent waves of plague over the next fifty years or so killed off more of the remaining population. Other plagues struck at various other times over the next few centuries. The last major outbreak of bubonic plague in England took hold in 1665 and 1666. This outbreak is most famously associated with London, by then a vast, crowded metropolis, but it spread to provincial towns and cities.

Most infamously, it arrived in the village of Eyam, in Derbyshire. It is said that a box of material sent from London to the village tailor was the culprit. Under the leadership of its new vicar and former vicar, the villagers were persuaded to 'lock down' rather than leave and risk spreading the plague throughout the neighbourhood. They knew their chances of survival were small. The villagers held church services outdoors, cared for loved ones, and then buried them.

Nobody can agree about exactly how many Eyam villagers died. Accounts range from about a fifth of the population of a few hundred to around half of its population, but the village endured and thrives today. The self-sacrifice that seventeenth-century Eyam made has been widely celebrated in prose, music, and by an annual 'Plague Sunday' commemoration.

Even these sobering insights into the fragility of medieval and early modern village life do not indicate that the loss of the entire community to infectious diseases was the most frequent cause of village desertion. Historian Michael Wood's detailed research on Kibworth Harcourt (based on copious documents kept by its former manorial lord, Merton College, Oxford) revealed a mortality rate of perhaps over seventy per cent in this Leicestershire village, but he notes how exceptionally high this figure seems to be and how much lighter the casualties were in neighbouring places.

Wood speculates about whether Kibworth's proximity to the London to Leicester highway and the villagers' exposure to infected travellers was to blame, but concludes by saying it could have simply been bad luck. Luck, or rather the complex set of factors behind the transmission of disease and degree of resistance to its effects, meant that not everybody in medieval villages affected by plague contracted the plague, and some people caught it and recovered. Nevertheless, during the most severe plague years in the fourteenth century, very few English villages could have escaped without being seriously depleted by death, illness and by villagers' attempts to flee elsewhere. However, there were probably not very many villages whose populations were entirely wiped out by plague.

The huge loss of life had profound consequences for the future of villages. Prior to the plague, in many places, there was hardly enough land for all the villagers who wanted to farm. After the plague, hardly enough able people could be found to farm the village land. The balance of power was shifting slightly away from old landlords in favour of those who could still work the land and had some means to acquire more land.

BROKEN FEUDAL SYSTEM

The old Norman, rigid feudal system was already gradually breaking down before the 1300s. More peasants were paying rent to the lord of the manor, rather than providing the lord with labour in return for the right to farmland. Villagers were gradually becoming less bound to the lord's manor and were moving around more. The economy was also diversifying; industry and trade were growing and so were towns.

After the fourteenth-century plagues, these changes accelerated. Peasants did less work for the lord and demanded higher wages; and if they didn't like the terms in one place, they moved to another. Some peasants were able to rent much more land at less cost to become farmers of substantial holdings. The ordinary villagers of England were getting more assertive and more able to act on their various disgruntlements. The flexing of newly found muscle erupted into armed rebellion at the end of the fourteenth century. One trigger was a new tax.

As the Hundred Years War with France dragged on, the huge expense of keeping large armies on the Continent and to fight off French raids on England emptied state coffers. In 1377, Edward III's government decided to tax every person in England over the age of fourteen, rich and poor, at a flat rate of four pence, as a one-off contribution to the progress of the war. The one concession was a married couple's allowance. In 1380, another 'Poll Tax' was collected, but the announcement of a third round in 1381 was too much to stomach. It was certainly far too much for the villagers of Corringham, Stanford-le-Hope and Fobbing in Essex. They didn't pay up and village representatives were summoned to Brentwood by officials to explain themselves.

A man from Fobbing, Thomas Baker, stated that the villagers had already paid enough and were not going to pay any more. When the government officials tried to arrest him, other village representatives stepped in, a fight broke out, and lives were lost. Similar trouble was occurring across the Thames in Kent. Soon a peasant army from Kent, Essex, Norfolk and Suffolk was marching into London with a list of grievances and demands, and all the weapons they could find.

They managed to take the Tower of London and behead some of the officials, nobles and churchmen whom they had particularly identified as representing everything that was wrong with the management of the nation. The rebels then went into negotiations with the seriously rattled government and arranged a meeting with the fourteen-year-old King Richard II and his retinue at Smithfield. It was here that the rebel leader Wat Tyler apparently offended Richard's companions with his lack of deference, or outright rudeness, to the king, and was stabbed to death by the Mayor of London and others.

The Peasants' Revolt fizzled out with the usual brutal medieval reprisals against the ringleaders, but not before serious mayhem and destruction had occurred elsewhere across the country, where villagers and townsfolk marched on rich monasteries and rioted in towns. The Poll Tax was not levied again. Although the rebels' demand that serfdom should be abolished was never seriously considered, it was clear that the Crown, government and manorial lords could not count on exerting the same control that they once had over England's villagers. However, this changing social and economic environment was a two-edged sword for many villagers and villages.

Fewer villagers working the land at much higher cost meant that the old communal, labour-intensive system of open-field agriculture could not be sustained in the way it once was. It was particularly difficult to carry on in places surrounded by a lot of marginal land, such as the heaviest clay soils, the thin chalky soils, and the land that was most marshy and prone to flooding. In many parts of England, struggling with poor soils, short of labour and unable to bear the cost of in-demand labourers, landlords turned to a less labour-intensive, monoculture approach to agriculture: sheep farming.

There was a big market for wool. Everybody in England wore woollen clothes. There was not much choice of alternative materials for much of society, but English woollen cloth was also in demand abroad. During the fifteenth century and early sixteenth century, as woollen cloth production became England's premier export business, vast areas of former arable land were given over to permanent pasture.

WOOLLY WOLDS

The new emphasis on sheep farming generated some winners. Places such as Lavenham in Suffolk grew as a centre of woollen cloth production from a village into a substantial town. In 1524, Lavenham had the fourteenth-highest tax return of any town in England. This formerly obscure village deep in the Suffolk countryside paid more tax than the cities of Lincoln, Gloucester and York. Lavenham drew on the weaving skills of its surrounding villages, rather than the wool of the surrounding region's own sheep, and much of the wool the villagers spun and wove came from far across England, such as Lincolnshire and the Welsh border.

There were many losers too. Many villages already decimated by plague shrank and dwindled away as the agricultural landscape changed around them, and villagers drifted away to more hopeful places. Some landlords turfed their remaining tenants out of their dilapidated villages, dismantled cottages and barns, and then allowed the villages themselves to become turfed over as pasture.

The sites of deserted medieval villages and shrunken medieval villages (where a village has significantly contracted) can be seen right across England, but these places are mostly concentrated in the areas that were most difficult for arable cultivation and more suited to livestock rearing. Grass-covered humps and bumps indicate the buried remains of buildings and streets of formerly busy villages, given over to leisurely grazing by sheep and cows.

Not far from the famous deserted village at Wharram Percy in the Yorkshire Wolds (now managed by English Heritage), the sites of the deserted villages of Burdale, Raisthorpe, Mowthorpe, Cowlam, Cottam and Eastburn can also be found. They sit alongside the plentiful archaeological evidence of other former settlements whose names are not known, and among villages that survived but shifted and contracted. Gainsthorpe in Lincolnshire, another strikingly complete and well-preserved deserted medieval village site that is open to the public, is only one example of around 130 named 'lost' villages in Lincolnshire. Many of these are on the dry chalky landscape of the Lincolnshire Wolds.

It doesn't take much imagination to come up with reasons for the desertion of the small medieval village at Hound Tor, in Devon; clambering up to the Tor on the east side of Dartmoor leaves a firm impression of the character of life in the village. There is desolate beauty there undoubtedly, but my goodness this is an unforgiving landscape. Craggy, rocky, undulating land, incised by streams in maze-like ravines and dotted with treacherous marshes. At around 1500 feet above sea level, it is battered by the weather, and more often than not is actually among the wet clouds.

The wonder is not why the village was abandoned, but why it was established there in the first place. This cluster of longhouses, smaller houses and barns surrounded by their gardens and strip-cultivated fields, originated in the thirteenth century or earlier. It was abandoned by the early years of the fifteenth century. The ruined, low granite-stone walls of the former village buildings and their gardens and paddocks are easy to pick out among the surrounding moorland.

The remains of deserted villages more like Wharram Percy and Gainsthorpe in character are abundant across the middle part of England, from The Wash in Norfolk to the Welsh Marches. They are especially frequent in the clay lands of the southern Midlands in counties such as Northamptonshire, Leicestershire and Warwickshire. Their abandoned fields of ridge and furrow surround them.

Deserted and shrunken villages in these counties are neighbours to hundreds of medieval villages that went on to thrive and grow, as some parts of the countryside were more resilient to being run down, and more able to bounce back when times improved. Medieval plague and rural depopulation undoubtedly hit places such as Kent in the south-east of England as hard as anywhere else, but the different settlement patterns of parts of the south, less total reliance on large-scale open-field farming and more wealth, meant that places could usually recover and grow again. There are fewer traces of total village abandonment to be found in these regions.

In nearly all parts of England you can find intact churches, or the remains of churches, completely alone amid fields, apparently in the middle of nowhere, or accompanied by a solitary rectory, former manor house, farmhouse or cottage or two. Churches, invariably the most substantial buildings in any village, are often the last standing remnants of a village that has moved elsewhere, or even disappeared entirely. The challenge is to find out what happened to the village.

The position of a medieval church in relation to the rest of the village is often a very good indicator of how a village has changed since then. Churches were usually built quite centrally within the communities that they served, even when these communities were dispersed across the local landscape. Churches did not turn their backs on their villages, but villages sometimes wandered away from their churches.

This is what happened at Boughton in Northampton-shire. The old Church of St John was situated at Boughton Green, part of the polyfocal medieval village. There was a famous annual fair there, where all sorts of goods and live-stock could be bought; it was particularly noted as *the* place to buy brooms and wooden goods. The last day of the fair was marked by wrestling and other sports. Old St John's was the original medieval church of the parish, whilst the other focus of the village, close to the Northampton to Market Harborough road, had its own medieval chapel.

The settlement at Boughton Green dwindled away as the new village centre nearer the main highway grew. As early as the sixteenth century, it was noted that there were now no houses at Boughton Green and the villagers and priests preferred to worship in the chapel rather than walk the inconvenient mile to their parish church. The chapel became the new parish Church of St John the Baptist, and the original Church of St John was left to decay. It is now a romantic ruin and reminder of the how villages can shift and change their focus.

Incidentally, though Boughton Green was no longer a settlement, the green continued to host its fair. It was at this fair that the infamous 'Captain Slash' was finally captured. The highwayman and his huge gang of thugs toured the country pillaging fairs and robbing fairgoers, but at Boughton, the outraged villagers and stall holders armed with guns and swords fought them off. The 'Captain' was hanged at Northampton in 1826. The fair carried on into the first few years of the twentieth century. The former green is now largely farmland, but its site is outlined by converging minor roads.

HEDGING AGAINST THE COMMONERS

Whether villagers wandered off in search of a better life elsewhere, or landlords actively pushed them out, enclosure of former village common fields was usually involved. Landlords took abandoned land into their own farm, or rented it to others who had sufficient means to farm it. Some villagers managed to get themselves in a position to benefit and become independent farmers, but most could not. Newly partitioned village land was then physically enclosed and separated from the remaining common land by hedges, fences and walls. Villagers' common rights to use land for grazing at certain times of the year, or to dig peat for fuel, gather firewood, forage and hunt, and so on, were also lost. Many of the poorer villagers depended on these various concessions and rights to survive.

Patchworks of fields bordered by hedgerows or dry stone walls are a much-loved characteristic of the English countryside today. In the fifteenth century it was a cause of great friction, dispute and even violence. In 1549, spurred by the furious followers of Robert Kett, it came close to provoking a civil war.

Ironically, the Kett family had been a beneficiary of increasing social mobility in the later part of the medieval period; Kett was also one of the biggest farmers in the area around Wymondham in Norfolk and latterly had enclosed his own land. When an angry mob went to tear down fences and hedges in the nearby villages of Morley St Botolph and Hethersett, the lord of the manor there, Sir John Flowerdew, a lawyer, persuaded them to attack Kett's enclosures instead, with the help of a little financial inducement.

The two landowners had fallen out previously over the rights to the dissolved Wymondham Abbey. Many officials, nobles and gentry had done very well out of Henry VIII's Dissolution of the Monasteries, acquiring the vast former manorial estates of closed religious houses. Flowerdew had acquired rights to half of the former Wymondham Abbey site, and the townsfolk had acquired the other half and wanted to use the former abbey church as their parish church. Flowerdew refused to sell his half to them and instead tore down half the church and carted off the stone. Kett had sided with the townsfolk in this dispute.

When the angry townsfolk and villagers now turned up on Kett's doorstep, he listened to their complaints. Incredibly, he helped them tear down his own fences, then got them to march back to finish the job on Flowerdew's land. Robert Kett entered a highly select band of laypeople who have managed to turn the tables on a lawyer. Even more unbelievably, Kett also agreed to become the leader of this growing army of dispossessed villagers and various townsfolk from the region with various grievances against the gentry classes.

The rebel army, thousands strong, positioned itself on Mousehold Heath, the high ground that overlooks the east side of Norwich. They had got hold of some artillery pieces and lobbed cannonballs into the panic-stricken city. The city's defenders returned fire; this was not a provincial spat, as Norwich was England's second largest city at the time. Kett's rebel army attacked and beat off a government force sent to relieve the siege of the city, before eventually succumbing to a much larger army that had been bolstered by European mercenaries. Around 3000 rebels were said to have lost their lives; Robert Kett, his brother and many followers were executed. Kett's rebellion was the major insurrection of several elsewhere in England at the time.

In neighbouring Suffolk, historian Peter Warner has investigated the consequences for the villagers of the lord's enclosure of former common land at Walberswick. His book, *Bloody Marsh: A Seventeenth Century Village in Crisis*, pieces together the complex sequence of events surrounding access to land that in 1644 led to one of the lord's hired hard men being murdered, and the execution of three villagers. The Bloody Marsh incidents and Kett's Rebellion are episodes in a long series of often violent rural disputes and unrest that rumbled on across England. Countless examples of physical confrontations and numerous local legal cases centred on village land and exactly who got to benefit from it.

PARLIAMENTARY ENCLOSURE

As the Industrial Revolution took hold in the eighteenth century and demand to feed a growing urban population in England grew, it became increasingly obvious that farming had to be modernised. The old open-field, strip-farming system, whereby many villagers farmed their own fragments of land with variable degrees of competence, success and much duplication of effort, was looking increasingly anachronistic. It could not compete with what could be achieved by specialist farming landowners and tenants with larger holdings.

During the eighteenth century and nineteenth century, the enclosure of the remaining open fields around villages was facilitated by a series of individual Acts of Parliament that progressed through most parishes in England. It had a profound effect on villages and their surrounding landscapes. Over 5000 individual enclosure bills were passed by Parliament, relating to about a fifth of the English landscape, and affecting nearly 7 million acres of land. Some parishes had already been mostly enclosed and parcelled up into private

Finchingfield village green in Essex has many of the classic characteristics of large village greens. It is in the centre of the village and surrounded by historic houses. It has a large pond, a war memorial, and is cut through and fringed by roads and lanes.

Mills were very important assets for villages. This fine tower mill dates to the early nineteenth century and is unusual in being situated on what was once a shoreline. Cley next the Sea in Norfolk is further from the sea than it once was. The medieval harbour here silted up. Reclamation of coastal marshes from the seventeenth century onwards means that this former port village is now half a mile from the sea.

The Church of St Andrew at Greensted, Essex, is probably the oldest surviving substantial timber-built church in the world. The large oak staves of the nave (centre) date to the eleventh century. The weatherboarded tower, brick chancel, plain tile roofs and dormer windows were built hundreds of years later.

The Church of St Mary and All Saints in the small village of Fotheringhay in Northamptonshire is cathedral-like, but used to be bigger still, extending to around twice its present length. It served as a parish church, a collegiate church, and as a mausoleum for one of the great medieval royal dynasties: the House of York. The earthwork platform behind the church is the site of the cloister and other college buildings.

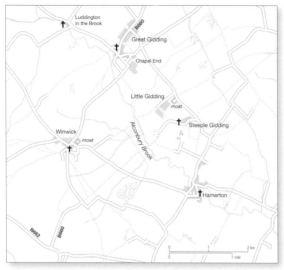

A group of villages near the boundary between Huntingdonshire and Northamptonshire illustrate the changes many villages and parishes have undergone over the last millennium.

© Phoenix Mapping

The population of Winwick today, roughly 200, is around double what it was in 1086, but the village has been larger in the past. In 1851, over 430 people lived here. The site of a medieval moated manor house is marked by a rectangle of trees (right of centre) and earthworks of former adjacent paddocks and house plots can be seen in grass under low raking sunlight. The church was not mentioned by the Domesday Book but has Norman origins.

The Domesday Book records a place called 'Redinges', later 'Geddinge'. The forty or so households recorded at that time (perhaps 120-160 people) may have all clustered along the main street in what is now Great Gidding (pictured). However, several lords had property here and it is likely that some homes were established in detached manorial centres that later became the villages of Little Gidding and Steeple Gidding.

Little Gidding is not specifically named in the Domesday Book, but was identified as a distinct village and parish in the thirteenth century. T.S. Eliot's poem named after this village was partly inspired by the Anglican monastic community founded here in the seventeenth century. There were around seventy villagers in the early nineteenth century, but only around half that live here now. They now share a joint parish council with Great Gidding. The earthwork remains of a square moated manorial house (left of centre) and former village houses (centre) are protected as a scheduled monument.

Steeple Gidding is not specifically mentioned by the Domesday Book either, but was a distinct village and parish by the late thirteenth century. The Church of St Andrew, with its steeple, is largely fourteenth century in form but it has Norman origins (top centre). There are only a handful of households remaining in the hamlet today, which is now part of the merged parish of Hamerton and Steeple Gidding.

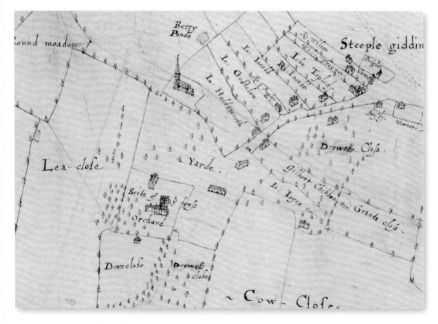

This map of Steeple Gidding was produced in the seventeenth century. The loss of buildings and village shrinkage since then is obvious from the aerial photograph, but the basic historic layout of the village is still apparent. © Huntingdonshire Archives, Ref. Map 120

The deserted medieval village of Childerley on the Cambridgeshire claylands. Childerley Hall, a sixteenth-century mansion, is top right. The last buildings of the dwindling village may have been cleared to create a deer park around the Hall. By the time Charles I spent a night here in 1647 as a prisoner of Oliver Cromwell, there would not have been any villagers to either jeer or cheer him. Shadows cast by a low sun pick out the earthwork remains of house sites in their plots of land, a probable manorial enclosure (top centre) and the 'ridge and furrow' of part of the old open field system.

Part of the village of Avebury in Wiltshire lies within a great Neolithic henge monument (top). Sir John Lubbock, who introduced the Ancient Monuments Protection Act in 1882, bought part of the village to protect the site. The monument and several village buildings now belong to the National Trust. Several hundred thousand tourists visit Avebury each year.

ownership by this point, but many villages still had considerable areas of surrounding open-field, strip-farming and common land, with its customary and common rights.

Under the legislation, commissioners were appointed to decide how to divide up the land in each place and exactly who got hold of it. You can imagine the wrangling, claims and counterclaims. Enclosure Awards were then drawn up that listed the land parcels and their owners, and these were often accompanied by detailed annotated maps. The resulting individual private farms, large and small, tended to be in manageable blocks in one place, rather than fragmented and scattered around a village like the old strips.

The boundaries of the new properties did not necessarily coincide with the ancient grain of the fields, or the old units of land such as whole open fields or furlongs. The new fields that were created by this formal enclosure process tended to be more regular in shape than the old fields; preferably they were laid out as rectangles, with long straight boundaries. The teams of horses and much better farm equipment now working the land were quicker than the old medieval ox teams, but their efficiency could be maximised even more if they did not have to turn so often.

When the inevitable new hedges, fences, ditches and stone walls appeared around the newly enclosed fields, they often ran across ridge and furrow rather than with its line. You can sometimes still see fences and walls that undulate because they were built across underlying ridge and furrow, even though the ridge and furrow in the fields has itself been flattened long ago. Just as the old village fields were straightened out, old meandering ancient tracks, droves and field ways were formalised into wide, straight lanes and roads.

Villagers who were not landowners, tenants or employed as farm labourers had no right to enter the enclosed private land. The 'Peasant Poet', John Clare, who was a passionate wanderer and observer of landscape and wildlife in his own neighbourhood, summed up the feelings of many villagers right across England, when he wrote:

> There was a time my bit of ground
> Made a freeman of the slave.
> The ass no pindar'd dare to pound[2] When I his
> supper gave.
> The gipsies' camp was not afraid;
> I made his dwelling free.
> Till vile enclosure came and made
> A parish slave of me.[3]

The final line refers to completely landless and jobless villagers having to depend on charity administered to the poor of the parish, rather than eking out a meagre living from farming common land. On the other hand, many former village labourers and small-time farmers, who would never have otherwise been able to progress, did very well out of

---

[2] A pindar is a person who impounded stray livestock.
[3] Extract from *The Lament of Swordy Well* by John Clare.

Parliamentary Enclosure. It freed them from remaining ties to a landlord and gave them opportunities for innovation, enterprise and expansion.

The wholesale enclosure of fields around a village affected the structure of the village itself. Now farmers and labourers who formerly lived near the centre of the old field system, in the middle of the village, could find themselves a very long way from the block of land they had to farm, rather than a roughly equal distance from all their scattered strips. The long, daily traipse to distant fields ceased to make any sense and as a consequence many new farmhouses, farmyards and labourers' cottages were built away from villages, among their own farmland.

These new farms, dotting the landscape around villages, are still very distinctive in today's landscape. Many farmers and estate owners took the opportunity to invest in 'model farms', where the farmhouse in stone or brick was accompanied by a state-of-the-art suite of farm buildings, often arranged in a courtyard, within which and from which the latest farming techniques were deployed. Their form is reminiscent of farming Roman villas, medieval manors and monastic granges. Ancient village farmhouses and yards in village centres found other uses.

Enclosure went hand in hand with various other efficiencies and improvements in agricultural technology, including land drainage. Thousands of miles of buried gullies lined with brushwood or stone were excavated across fields to improve drainage; maintaining permanent ridge and furrow was no longer necessary. In the early nineteenth century, it became more common to lay clay drainage pipes beneath fields. These were either in short, horseshoe-shaped sections placed on flat tiles, or short circular tubes.

Smashed clay fragments of these now litter fields where pipes have been disturbed by subsequent deeper ploughing and drainage works, and this material is sometimes mistaken for sherds of ancient pottery, or roof tile from some long-lost buildings. Where they remain intact, these old drains can still do their job. You may still find water trickling out of old clay drains that poke out of the sides of field edge ditches.

Other large-scale enclosures in the seventeenth, eighteenth and nineteenth centuries involved land drainage on an epic scale, and with considerable state and Crown interest and vast private investment. Schemes to drain and enclose the marsh-land of the Somerset Levels were begun by the region's abbeys in the medieval period. A further scheme was promoted by King James I and then picked up with a consortium led by Dutch engineer Cornelius Vermuyden in the seventeenth century; more extensive reclamation and enclosure took place there in the late eighteenth century and nineteenth century.

Before tackling the Somerset Levels, Vermuyden had previously been appointed by Charles I to drain the low-lying, marshy Hatfield Chase in South Yorkshire. At the time, this was the single largest drainage and reclamation scheme ever undertaken in England. Vermuyden, now knighted, went on to an even grander scheme in the great Fenland region of eastern England, which includes substantial parts of Cambridgeshire, Lincolnshire, Norfolk and a bit of Suffolk.

Walloons and Huguenot refugees from the Netherlands and France accompanied Vermuyden in Yorkshire.

They later settled on the Duke of Bedford's newly drained land around the village of Thorney, in the Fens, and names in the locality such as French Farm and French names on headstones in the village churchyard recall their presence there. For a time in the seventeenth century, French-speaking services were held at the village church, which incidentally originated as a medieval abbey church.

Long drainage dykes were cut to replace formerly meandering rivers, and marshland was turned into good grazing land and excellent arable land. You might think that all the villagers, clustered on small islands within the vast wetlands, or in the villages bordering these regions, would have welcomed the disappearance of the treacherous and malaria-infested swamps. But like their prehistoric and medieval ancestors, they found many useful resources in the wetland environment; this was their common. They quickly realised that it was becoming inaccessible to them as the land was 'improved' and becoming the private property of the investors who had funded the drainage works. Local riots and the smashing of newly constructed banks and sluices took place alongside many years of petitions and legal disputes.

It was not only marshland that was enclosed by parliamentary acts, but also upland moorland in places such as Yorkshire and Derbyshire, heathlands across southern England, and even former royal forests that had retained unimproved scrub and woodland. All such rural 'waste' land was targeted as England grew and industrialised.

PARKS, GARDENS AND ESTATE VILLAGES

The sixteenth, seventeenth and eighteenth centuries saw the construction of many grand country houses and palatial stately homes across England. Many of these were developed on the sites of newly dissolved monasteries, old medieval manors and castles on the edge of villages; but castles and fortified residences were no longer necessary or fashionable. Where they could afford to do so, old landed gentry rebuilt their old manor houses in the new architectural styles. Wealthy courtiers and merchants acquired country estates as retreats from their town houses within expanding and ever more crowded cities, and built grand new residences.

This was a new type of living for the super-rich. These houses were not built with defence or farming practicality in mind, but were all about comfortable living, entertaining, extravagance and display. No expense was spared in achieving the most lavish and fashionable effect possible. Many of the larger and more ambitious places constructed or greatly extended in the sixteenth century and early seventeenth century, especially those within a few days' ride from London, were built by courtiers with the aim of hosting and impressing and gaining favour with royalty. They were partly investments towards attracting royal titles, lucrative state posts and commissions. These became known as 'prodigy houses'.

Sir Christopher Hatton's vast Elizabethan building projects at Holdenby House and Kirby Hall in Northamptonshire bankrupted him, and both houses are now fragments of what they once were. The Cecils built Hatfield House in Hertfordshire and Burghley House on the Great North Road near

Stamford, which is one of the largest and most impressive Elizabethan grand houses to survive. Audley End in Essex, Knole in Kent, Longleat in Wiltshire, Barrington Court in Somerset and Bramshill House in Hampshire also display the new scale and splendour typical of the era.

None of these places and their equivalents, nor their smaller and slightly less ambitious cousins that were built in every corner of England, were complete without formal gardens and a surrounding park. The parks often took in vast areas of landscape and incorporated much former open-field cultivated land. The park was then enclosed by banks and fences (park pales) or a wall, put into permanent pasture and grazed by the landlord's own sheep, cattle and herds of deer.

The construction and running of large country houses and their estates was often a significant boost to local rural economies, and provided employment for generations of villagers. Country house estates often included one or more estate villages and outlying farms, all of which were property of the lord.

It is perhaps hard to believe that the growing interest in the aesthetic qualities of country living and the creation of these exclusive new grounds, rather than plague and hard commercial factors, caused the demise of many of these villages; but entire villages were run down and removed in order that villagers and village life did not interfere with the high life. Old aristocracy and new gentry landlords had the power and money to evict and buy out tenants, and to level homes and farms that impeded enjoyment of their surroundings. There was not much that villagers could do to stop them.

The construction of the magnificent stately home Castle Howard, created by Vanbrugh and Hawksmoor for the 3rd Earl of Carlisle, was begun in 1699. It replaced an earlier residence, Henderskelfe Castle, with an associated village. No trace of the old village of Henderskelfe remains; it was swept away to create gardens for the south vista of the palatial new house. There is now a massive ornamental pond and fountain in what was once the heart of the village and a seventeenth-century plan map held by the estate archives is the only record of Henderskelfe's location and its layout.

At Kirby Hall, near Corby in Northamptonshire, it is possible to look out of the big bay windows of Sir Christopher Hatton's state suite and, in the right light, see traces of a former village. The village of Kirby was already slowly dwindling away when it was enveloped in Kirby Hall's grounds, but the remaining buildings and the church were finally demolished when the Jacobean gardens were laid out. The hollow of the village's main street, which once led down the slope towards Kirby Hall, can be seen, along with the low turf-covered foundations of some buildings and property boundaries.

Next time you wander around the grounds of one of England's great country houses, have a close look at the pasture of its parkland. The chances are you will find the telltale undulating ridge and furrow of former open fields that became parkland, or even the humps and bumps of former village buildings.

Perhaps the most remarkable example of the removal of an entire community to make way for a park was undertaken by Joseph Damer, Baron Milton, later the 1st Earl of Dorchester. During the 1770s, he set about buying out and bullying out the residents of Middleton in Dorset, which lay uncomfortably close to his newly acquired country house, Milton Abbey. Middleton, also known as Milton, was a sizeable place for the period, more a small market town than a large village, comprising over 100 houses. It was medieval in origin and had grown outside the precincts of an abbey that dated back to well before the Norman Conquest.

Damer rebuilt and greatly extended an earlier mansion based around the surviving buildings of the abbey complex, which was situated alongside the huge abbey church. But Damer's human neighbours in Milton were too close for comfort; busy Market Street and the properties lining it backed right on to his garden. Damer had paid for the foremost landscape designer of the era, Lancelot 'Capability' Brown, to lay out highly fashionable new grounds and Milton was a nuisance in the way.

The residents protested and tried to frustrate Damer's ambitions as much as they could. One in particular, a solicitor, refused to budge. The tale goes that Damer opened the sluice to one of the abbey's old ponds and flooded him out, but was then sued and lost. Eventually, however, the new lord got his way and Milton was entirely cleared, except for one cottage, its place being taken by pasture, banks of trees and a large lake. The designed landscape that was created around Damer's mansion, Milton Abbey, is now revered as one of Capability Brown's best.

Damer was not at all popular, but he did something that not many earlier landlords involved in settlement clearance even contemplated. He built a brand new village to the east of the lake, well away from his grounds. Damer did not rehouse everyone from the old town in his new village; he had no obligation to do so and his priority was accommodating his estate workers and tenants. The new village was given an old sounding name, Milton Abbas (Latin for abbot; there was already a village of Milton Abbot in Devon), but it was not a reconstruction of the old village. It was laid out and built in a style compatible with the fashionable new aesthetic aspirations of the mansion and parkland.

Milton Abbas was built in a little valley, which had been further engineered to accentuate the gently curving serpentine shape so beloved in landscape design of the era. The new village was a picturesque row of uniform houses along one long street, and each house had a green area at the front and a garden backing on to wooded hillside at the back. The houses were built economically from cob, which was plastered and whitewashed, rather than the more expensive timber, brick or stone. They were thatched, rather than tiled. Some thought that the location of the new village and the quality of the housing there was much better than the former town, which had a boggy stream running through it.

The houses looked large, certainly much larger than many villagers enjoyed at the time, but each house was in fact divided into two, or sometimes four, separate units for separate households. There were instances of severe overcrowding in Milton Abbas. However, Damer ensured that the almshouse of the town was dismantled and rebuilt in the new village to house the elderly poor, and a new village church and vicarage were built. Baron Milton did not build a pub (that came later) and he forbade his tenants to set up their own drinking dens and places of entertainment in the new houses. He did not want this perfect picture of rural life to be spoilt by poor behaviour.

Damer was one of many landlords of his era and later who replaced an old historic village with a new estate village. Their motives were a mix of extreme high-handedness and genuine attempts to improve ancient, squalid village living conditions. Even at the time, this attracted both admiration and scathing comment:

The man of wealth and pride
Takes up a space that many poor supplied;
Space for his lake, his park's extended bounds,
Space for his horses, equipage, and hounds:
The robe that wraps his limbs in silken sloth,
Has robbed the neighbouring fields of half their growth;
His seat, where solitary sports are seen,
Indignant spurns the cottage from the green:
Around the world each needful product flies,
For all the luxuries the world supplies.
While thus the land adorned for pleasure, all
In barren splendour feebly waits the fall.[4]

---

[4] Extract from *The Deserted Village*, Oliver Goldsmith, 1770.

Usually, however, village desertion and clearance was not carried out in a single dramatic sweep on the scale or time frame managed by Damer. At Kelmarsh Hall in North-amptonshire, not far from Market Harborough, Colonel Lancaster contemplated the view across his gardens and park-land towards the elegant church of St Denys. The view could be much improved, he thought, if only that old ramshackle farmstead wasn't there. So he pulled it down. This was not the 1550s or 1750s, but the 1950s.

Colonel Lancaster and his wife Nancy were interested in creating a harmonious aesthetic indoors and out. Nancy owned Colefax and Fowler, the upmarket decorating firm, and though American by birth was at the forefront of creating the English Country House Style. She was known to bring furniture that looked too new and weather it outdoors to give it a 'shabby chic' look. As a gardener she was associated with creating 'garden rooms', or quaint enclosed compart-ments within larger gardens. The gardens produced fresh flowers and produce for the household. But the imperfec-tions of antiquity were only celebrated and tolerated so far; old rural charms could be further enhanced by demolition and deft planting.

Nancy had first moved to Kelmarsh Hall with her second husband Ronald Tree before the war and had begun the restoration of house and garden then. They moved on and divorced. It is said that Nancy married Colonel Lancaster, by then the owner of Kelmarsh Hall, only so she could get back there to carry on the work she had begun. They divorced in 1953.

The once sprawling medieval village of Kelmarsh had shrunk long ago and had been replanned as tidy, terraced estate cottages beyond the grounds of Kelmarsh Hall during the nineteenth century. The old farmhouse and farmyard was the last standing remnant to go. This is an unusually protracted example of the shifting and total clearance of a village. Nevertheless, many cases of village desertion and clearance were drawn-out affairs, a gradual dwindling away, rather than sudden eradication.

The new Kelmarsh estate houses were small, terraced, one-and-a-half-storey buildings built of local limestone and ironstone and some brick-built cottages. Estate villages such as Milton Abbas and Kelmarsh have quite different styles of construction, materials and appearance, but they share some characteristics that most purpose-built estate villages share. The most obvious one is a general uniformity, or at least cohesiveness, in architectural styles used for the cottages and other buildings.

Estate village buildings may well draw on elements of the local traditional (vernacular) styles and materials, but they were usually architect-designed. Their features often reference earlier eras of architecture and they consciously project a sense of estate identity, and a sense of heritage. They may have coats of arms and monograms built into them on stone tablets, or outlined in brick, to confirm their association with the estate and its owner. A single colour scheme is often adopted for woodwork.

The clearance of the old village from the park at the Harewood House estate in Yorkshire was accompanied by the construction of new village buildings just outside the park boundary, unlike at Castle Howard in the previous century, and at Kirby Hall before that, where no new villages were planned. Renowned architect John Carr of York designed both Harewood House, whose construction began in 1759, and the new village.

Its layout was based on neat, regular terraces of uniform, symmetrical stone-built houses at the junction of two main roads. A small ribbon factory, school and vicarage were planned for the village, but the old medieval parish church remained in the park. The former estate workers' cottages in the new village still belong to the current earl and countess of Harewood's estate.

Houghton Hall, in Norfolk, was home to Sir Robert Walpole, Britain's first prime minister. The village of New Houghton, an eighteenth-century replacement for the old medieval village that was removed from the parkland of Houghton Hall, is strikingly regular and uniform. The single village street (called entirely accurately, but unimaginatively, 'The Street') is lined by regularly spaced two-storey, semi-detached cottages. They are identical in size, form and colour: whitewashed brick, with black, glazed pantile roofs.

Blaise Hamlet near Bristol, however, was created around 1810 with a wildly different aesthetic vision. This group of nine cottages based around a small green was built for retired employees of John Scandrett Harford, a Quaker banker, who lived in nearby Blaise Castle House. Harford hired leading architect John Nash to build his new house and new estate village. Nash opted for romantic, picturesque, individual forms and styles for each cottage.

The use of thatch, stone rubble, stone roof slates, clay tiles, large Tudor-like brick chimney stacks, a pigeon loft gable and leaded windows, suggests Nash was aiming for a solidly traditional character. But some of the cottages look like the stage set from a fantasy film, supposed to represent some mythical old time and village in England. You know, the films featuring dwarfs and dragons. The style of Nash's cottages is in stark contrast to his stately classical Buckingham Palace, terraces of London town houses, Blaise Castle House itself, and for that matter his flamboyant, lavish Royal Pavilion at Brighton. The effect is even quirkier now that Blaise Hamlet is surrounded by modern housing estates.

Estate villages and estate buildings with eclectic, whimsical touches were built in many places from the early nineteenth century onwards. Clovelly in Devon is a famously attractive coastal village, loved by tourists; it is also an estate village. It has been owned by only three families since the thirteenth century and it is still privately owned. No matter how much visitors fall in love with Clovelly village life, they cannot buy a house there, as they are for rent only.

During the late nineteenth century and early twentieth century, the lady of the manor, Christine Hamlyn, renovated, modified and rebuilt Clovelly's old cottages in a mix of different vernacular-inspired styles. The effect is deliberately varied rather than uniform, but all in proportion and harmonious. She had her monogram and the date of renovation displayed on each building, but this was her only concession to estate 'branding'.

The Queen's estate at Sandringham includes thirteen villages that existed long before the place was bought by the royal family in 1862. There are a great variety of old estate cottages in the villages, but many of the Queen's tenants live in houses with doors that share the same duck egg paint scheme.

CHAPTER 5

EXPLORING EARLY
VILLAGES

Lone, detached, abandoned and ruined churches are the most obvious indicators of lost, deserted, shrunken and shifted medieval villages, but there are other key signs to look out for. Though many village sites once cleared were eventually levelled and absorbed into the surrounding cultivated land, or came to be built on once again, many survived fortuitously, because no subsequent intensive use was ever found for them.

Their undulating and rough ground, often strewn with rubble from the foundations of demolished buildings, was typically only useful for grazing. If you look closely enough at these places, the subtle undulations caused by the remnants of boundary banks, walls, ditches, roads and streets, now covered with turf, can be traced. Even the sites of individual buildings can be picked out by slightly raised and parched turf over remnants of foundations, or by the rectangular platforms and levelled terraces on which buildings once sat.

Not far below the topsoil lie the rubbish pits, post holes and detritus left by everyday life over hundreds of years. Generations of villagers lie in unmarked graves in lost churchyards. Only archaeological excavation can reveal the layers and complexity of changing village forms as buildings are built, demolished and rebuilt. Often, however, much of the basic structure of a deserted village and some phases of its development can be seen as patterns on the surface.

Over the last few decades the survival of many ancient village sites has been assisted by their designation as Scheduled Monuments, and consequent protection against ploughing and development.

ANCIENT MONUMENTS

The Ancient Monuments Protection Act 1882 was the first piece of United Kingdom legislation whose purpose was the preservation of ancient structures and buildings for the sake of their archaeological and historical interest. The Act was promoted by John Lubbock, a scientific polymath, banker and Member of Parliament, who had long tried to get protective legislation on to the statute books. The 1882 Act introduced the concept of a list or 'schedule' of specific monuments to which it applied.

Initially the schedule comprised only twenty-six monuments in England and these were all prehistoric in date, including places such as Avebury, Silbury Hill, Stonehenge and the Rollright Stones. These types of monument reflected the growing interest in the scientific archaeological investigation of the prehistoric past. Lubbock himself had introduced the terms 'Palaeolithic' to describe the earliest Stone Age and 'Neolithic' to describe the later Stone Age. He was later made the first Baron Avebury, which we can see is not a mere coincidence.

The Ancient Monuments and Archaeological Areas Act 1979, a descendant of the 1882 Act, is still the main protective mechanism for archaeological sites and monuments in the UK. The list or schedule of protected monuments in England has grown to around 20,000 of the best examples of their type, the majority of which are in rural locations. Prehistoric monuments, settlements, Roman forts, villas and villages of both periods, such as Grimspound and Chysauster, are designated as scheduled monuments. Medieval castles, manorial sites, monastic sites and entire deserted village sites, such as Hound Tor, Gainsthorpe and Wharram Percy, are also designated as scheduled monuments. More recently, nineteenth- and twentieth-century industrial and military sites have been designated as scheduled monuments.

Modern edition 1:50,000 and 1:25,000 Ordnance Survey maps note the locations of many archaeological sites, including deserted village sites. These are accompanied with the village name, where that is known emphatically. Archaeological sites ceased to be added routinely to Ordnance Survey maps many years ago (there are too many), so this source provides only a very selective coverage. Many more former village sites can be found in the National Heritage List for England (NHLE), which records all nationally designated (scheduled or listed) historic buildings and monuments, registered parks and gardens, and registered battlefield sites (www.historicengland.org.uk/listing/the-list/).

An online search of the NHLE on terms such as 'deserted medieval village' and 'deserted settlement' will produce hundreds of examples across England. Searches can be refined by county, district, parish and place, and several other criteria. Looking at the NHLE entries for Registered Parks and Gardens will reveal notes about villages, hamlets or farmsteads that were cleared to create or remodel parkland around a stately home, or that still form part of an estate.

Local Historic Environment Records (HERs), which used to be knowns as Sites and Monument Records (SMRs), are an even more comprehensive source of information for lost settlements in particular localities. These inventories of archaeological sites, discoveries and excavations are most often maintained by county councils and unitary authorities (www.algao.org.uk/news/guide-historic-environment-records-hers-england). They are used to inform advice for development planning, and also to assist archaeological research and local history studies. HERs record all known archaeological sites and finds, and many historic buildings, not only those recognised by a specific official designation, such as scheduling or listing.

Many HERs now offer basic online searches by geographic area, place names, period and various themes. Norfolk Heritage Explorer (www.heritage.norfolk.gov.uk/) and Keys to the Past for County Durham and Northumberland (www.keystothepast.info/) are two good examples of searchable online HER information. Both also include a lot of useful contextual information, such as summaries of the history of parishes and villages. The basic records held by many HERs that do not have their own individual online search systems are available through the Heritage Gateway. This portal allows simultaneous searches across more than sixty local and national heritage databases (www.heritagegateway.org.uk/gateway/).

Even where an old settlement has been completely levelled by ploughing and buried, there can still be some physical traces on the surface. Ploughing often cuts into buried archaeological remains and turns up spreads of building rubble, broken roofing tiles, sherds of pottery and other artefacts. Simply walking over a field and noting where this material is clustered can locate ancient farms, hamlets and villages, some perhaps never discovered by anyone before.

Local archaeological societies and research projects often reveal an immense amount of information about long-forgotten settlements without ever excavating. The structured collection of finds on the surface of a ploughed field using grids and transects (known as 'fieldwalking') is a great way to find archaeological sites, and get some exercise.

Geophysical surveys use specialist technical equipment and data analysis to identify below-ground archaeological remains. There are various geophysical techniques. Electrical resistance survey (or resistivity survey) relies on buried archaeological features generating variable electrical resistance in the soil. Magnetometer survey measures anomalies in the background magnetism of the earth caused by buried archaeological features. Ground-penetrating radar (GPR) measures the differential penetration and reflection of high frequency, electromagnetic waves. Seismic survey measures variations in the way that sound travels through ground.

Joining a local archaeological society or research project is the best way to learn about and get involved in these techniques. Metal detectorists who join clubs and report their finds through the Portable Antiquities Scheme benefit from a free artefacts identification service, and also make an important contribution to understanding the past (www.finds.org.uk/).

It should be remembered that all land in England is owned or controlled by someone or some organisation. Even land that is freely open to public access is usually subject to laws, by-laws and stipulations about what may or may not be carried out there. Ad hoc digging never goes down well. Always get a landowner's permission to enter land, and also check the status of the land. It is illegal, for example, to remove objects from, or to damage, any scheduled monument without obtaining specific consent issued by Historic England (www.historicengland.org.uk/advice/hpg/has/scheduledmonuments/).

Many ancient artefacts, not only those made of precious metal, now fall within the terms of the Treasure Act 1996, and by law must be reported when found (www.legislation.gov.uk/ukpga/1996/24/contents).

Much more new evidence awaits discovery. Next time you are walking around a village or in surrounding countryside, take a close look at that pocket of pasture surrounded by arable land or housing. Why has it survived? Was it reserved as a green or common, do its highs and hollows result from quarrying, or does it retain traces of former habitation long since gone? It is always sensible to report any finds you think may be significant to the local Portable Antiquities Scheme Finds Liaison Officer, or to the local Historic Environment Record. Who knows, you may have found evidence of a lost village or part of the history of a village that nobody has noticed before.

LOST VILLAGES FROM ABOVE

It has long been known that many archaeological sites that are invisible or undecipherable on the ground can be seen clearly, or are more readily understood, from the air. The availability to archaeologists of aeroplanes and aerial photographs from the inter-war years onwards has transformed our understanding of the past. As a pilot, I am fortunate to be able to enjoy this revealing, often astounding, perspective on landscape history. But you don't need to fly or use a drone to explore villages from above. The English countryside has been comprehensively photographed from the air for decades.

In addition to aerial photographs held by local Historic Environment Records, national aerial archives retain millions of aerial photographs. An increasing number of these are now available online. Have a look at the *Britain From Above* website (www.britainfromabove.org.uk/), which gives access to nearly 100,000 (of well over 1 million) aerial photographs taken by the Aerofilm company between 1919 and 2006.

The Historic England Archive contains over 4 million aerial photographs (www.historicengland.org.uk/images-books/archive/collections/aerial-photos/), and the Cambridge

University Collection of Aerial Photography contains nearly half a million photographs dating from 1947 onwards (www. cambridgeairphotos.com/). Google Earth and other browsable map websites also now provide comprehensive vertical aerial photography coverage spanning several decades.

The earthworks of deserted and shrunken settlements appear far more obvious and coherent when viewed from above. They are most visible when the grass that covers them is short, and the sunlight is low and rakes across them. This highlights the bumps and puts shadows in the hollows, which accentuates the patterns of undulations. As the sun moves, or as you fly around the site, different aspects of the earthworks will show more or less clearly.

Entirely plough-levelled villages and other settlements can reveal themselves as striking marks in ripening crops ('cropmarks'), or in variable shades and textures of ploughed soil ('soilmarks'). The cropmark effect is produced by the amount of moisture and nutrient in the soil layer that the crop's roots are drawing from. The effect is best seen in cereal crops: each single stalk and ear of wheat or barley responds to the conditions beneath the soil. If the cereal plant is growing over an ancient rubble foundation or a stony surface, it will be stunted when compared to its neighbours on better soil, and will ripen quicker. If it is growing on a buried pit or ditch that retains moisture, it will grow taller and stay greener for longer during the ripening season.

Each cereal plant therefore acts rather like a pixel, or dot on a computer screen, and each dot helps to build a picture of what is below the surface. When the crop is under stress in times of drought, or as it nears ripening, the cropmark contrast is turned up. So green lines and circles in a ripening crop indicate old buried ditches, and the ring ditches around prehistoric houses or round barrows. A stripe of stunted crops across the same field might indicate a Roman road or old stony track; parchmarks in mown grass under stress regularly reveal the outlines of buried roads, walls and buildings.

Soilmarks, patches of different coloured soils on the surface fields, are produced by buried features that the plough has disturbed and brought to the surface. The rubble, tile or lime mortar of buried buildings that have been disturbed by ploughing may contrast with the general brown colour and texture of soil in the field. An old large pit or pond filled with organic material might show as a dark splodge among lighter coloured soil.

The cropmark and soilmark effects are easy to spot in the right conditions, but sometimes they take a bit of interpretation, because natural geological features and modern disturbance can produce similar effects and shapes to buried archaeological remains.

Another aerial technique whose results are becoming increasingly available from a variety of sources is Lidar. This works rather like radar. Beams of light, rather than radio waves, pulse at the ground from equipment carried by an aircraft. Capturing the position and speed of them bouncing back provides an extraordinarily accurate model of the contours of the surfaces they have contacted. Lidar doesn't see things that are not present on the surface, but in being able to detect a few centimetres difference in height in millions of spots a metre or so apart, it detects undulations on the surface of the ground that would not be seen with the naked eye.

Again, the pattern of undulations can indicate very subtle things like the last surviving few centimetres of house platforms, or the remnants of a burial mound long thought to have been ploughed completely away. Making sense of Lidar is all about processing the raw data returned by the aerial survey to create digital models of surfaces. It is then possible to shine digital 'suns' from different angles on the digital surface models, and reveal features that were not highlighted from a single angle. This is much like looking at earthwork sites under different sunlight conditions.

Even better, Lidar works on ground beneath trees and other vegetation in areas that have been impenetrable to traditional aerial photography and ground survey. Lidar can't actually see through leaves, branches and stems, but enough light beams can go through the gaps between them to register on the ground beneath and create a digital model.

OLD MAPS

Many villages have acquired a lot of new development in the last hundred years or so and it can be difficult to trace historic village features in the structure of today's villages. Old maps provide a very helpful bridge between a village as it appears today and its early forms. Not only can you look at an old village map and find buildings and other features that have since disappeared, but you can find evidence of even earlier features, such as the remnants of ancient property boundaries, greens, market places and lanes, that were still fossilised in the structure of villages when first mapped, but have since been masked or entirely lost.

The earliest estate maps with village plans appeared in the late sixteenth century and seventeenth century. Some landlords were keen to have mapped surveys of their estates in order to help their management, purchases and disposals, and no doubt to help settle property and enclosure disputes. Detailed depictions of villages, however, are rare in this period.

In county and regional maps of the era, villages tend to appear only as stylised symbols. That remained the case for the best part of 200 years, until maps were drawn up to accompany Enclosure Acts and the Tithe Commutation Act of 1836. Tithe maps showed each parcel of land in a parish with a reference number that referred to an entry in the list of 'tithe apportionments'; each entry identified the owner and tenants, the measurements of the land parcel, and its name. The maps were very detailed, recording small plots of land and individual dwellings. Most English parishes had tithe maps.

Even more systematic mapping of villages took place as the Ordnance Survey began mapping the whole of Britain. In the middle of the nineteenth century, a base mapping scale of 1:2500 was agreed upon. Old maps are often things of beauty, but the first two editions of Ordnance Survey 1:2500 county series maps are beautiful, incredibly accurate and very detailed. They are a wonderful starting point to examine the historic layout and character of a village, its buildings and many features of its surrounding landscape.

Original historic maps are held in many different places, such as private estate collections and museum and library collections, County Record Offices and archives, the National Archives and the British Library. The latter has one of the largest map collections in the world, and holds a comprehensive collection of Ordnance Survey maps. Digital historic maps, which have been georeferenced to the modern map grid, are also available through various online sources and available to purchase. Overlaying historic maps on their modern equivalents, or on vertical photography, is always illuminating.

When using historic maps to investigate a village, even those that are the result of a meticulous, measured survey, you do have to think about why the map makers had been commissioned, what exactly they had been asked to depict, and what things they might have left out. Map making is part science, part art, part pragmatism and part politics. No map can be taken for granted as a comprehensive depiction of a village at any one point in time, and all maps are out of date the moment they are completed.

VILLAGE NAMES (OR THE IMPORTANCE OF BEING MILTON ERNEST)

Village names are an endearing characteristic of rural England. They are often quaint, frequently quirky and some-times downright silly. Unlike the names of some modern car models and children, however, the names that ancient people gave their villages, their streets, fields, woods, streams and rivers, are not abstract but meant something to them. These meanings are usually decipherable by us today. They provide tantalising glimpses of what people in the past thought notable enough to distinguish one place from another.

Let's get some silly names out of the way first. See if you can guess their origins without looking at the footnotes. Beer, Swine, Bunny, Eagle, Lover and Great Snoring[5] all imply that the village was so named because of its association with a particular or peculiarly notable thing. That thing seems pretty clear in each case. There are some surprisingly derogatory and angry sounding village names. Who would like to live in Bicker, Seething, Yelling, Great Heck, Slaughter, or just plain Nasty?[6] There are also places that sound like the whimsical creations of wags in the village pub, such as

---

[5] Beer (Devon, 'woodland grove', Old English), Swine (Yorkshire, 'creek' or channel in this instance, but *swin* names often mean swine or pig, Old English), Bunny (Nottinghamshire, 'island where reeds grow', Old English), Eagle ('wood where oaks grow', Old English), Lover (Wiltshire, perhaps a corruption of 'lower', and it appears to be relatively modern), and Great Snoring (Norfolk, 'settlement of the followers of a man named Snear', Old English).

[6] Bicker (Lincolnshire, 'place by a marsh', Old English and Scandinavian), Seething (Norfolk, 'settlement of the followers of a man named Sitha', Old English), Yelling (Huntingdonshire, 'settlement of the followers of a man named Giella', Old English), Great Heck (Yorkshire, 'hatch or gate', Old English), Slaughter (Gloucestershire, 'muddy place', Old English), Nasty (Hertfordshire, from 'eastern enclosure', Old English).

Middle Wallop, Matching Tye, Pidley and Wetwang.[7] The latter sounds a bit rude. No tittering at the back please. Even 'Tittering' sounds like it could be a village somewhere in southern or eastern England. It isn't, but there are similar village names, and the meanings of these names are not what they seem. English village names, whether odd or apparently mundane, are products of people moving in from elsewhere and bringing different languages and perceptions to bear on existing, ages-old settlements, or attempting to differentiate their newly created villages. People have invented, assimilated, interpreted and mangled the names of these places over hundreds, sometimes thousands, of years.

ANGLO-SAXON ATTITUDES

The majority of place names in England are firmly 'Old English' or Anglo-Saxon (410 to 1066) in origin. These are not names that native Britons would have used to describe their settlements and landscapes throughout prehistory, but instead reflect the domination of the groups of Angles, Saxons, Jutes and others who settled here following the collapse of

---

[7] Middle Wallop (Hampshire, 'valley, wall or ridge with a spring', Old English), Matching Tye (Essex, 'settlement of the followers of a man named Maecca', Old English and 'tye' meaning common pasture, a later, Middle English term), Pidley (Huntingdonshire, 'woodland clearing of a man named Pyda', Old English), and Wetwang (Yorkshire) is a field where justice was dispensed (Scandinavian), not a 'moist penis', as defined by Douglas Adams' and John Lloyd's alternative dictionary *The Meaning of Liff.*

Roman governance in the early fifth century. These north-west European groups and their ancestors left a richly descriptive legacy of place names, but they were also quite comfortable with economising when naming their settlements, or perhaps occasionally they ran out of inspiration.

Have you ever wondered why there are so many Nortons, Suttons, Eastons and Westons in England? The *ton* element just means a farmstead or village and the prefixes are simply north, south, east and west. You can now guess what Middleton means. But even these straightforward, common names pose questions. Farmstead to the north of what exactly? Were the Anglo-Saxon colonists renaming existing Romano-British settlements in these locations, or places they had newly founded?

Anglo-Saxons liked referencing local topographic features, firmly locating a settlement by its surroundings. Orwell is a spring by a pointy hill, ridge or bank (*ord* and *wella*, a spring in Old English). Anywhere ending in 'ey' or 'ea' is likely to be an island, or to have been an island in Anglo-Saxon times (Thorney – thorn tree island; Mersea – island of the pool). Names including *ley* and *leigh* derive from woodland, or more specifically clearings in woodland (Langley – long clearing; Farleigh – clearing with ferns). *Dons* and *duns* are hills (Haddon – hill of heath or heather). *Hursts* are wooded hills (Ashurst – hill wooded with ash trees) and *marsh* is, well, a marsh. The prefixes *Stan*, *Stam* and *Stain* (Stanbridge, Stamford, Stainton, etc.) indicate natural stony ground or describe man-made stony features, such as metalled roads.

Another favourite Anglo-Saxon place-naming theme was to include a personal name, most probably a pioneering head of household or group of settlers. The so-called *ingas* names are among the earliest Anglo-Saxon place names. Wittering is the settlement of the followers or family of a man called Wither. Itteringham is the homestead (*ham*) of a man called Ytri. So if the Titta, who gave his name to the village of Titley (a woodland clearing in Herefordshire) had instead been among the first Anglo-Saxon settlers in southern or eastern England, we might indeed have a Tittering.

Despite doing a pretty thorough job of overwriting ancient British names across the land, the Anglo-Saxons sometimes acknowledged the earlier history of places. Village names that include *street*, *streat*, *strete*, *stret* or *strat* invariably lie on Roman roads. The main Roman roads were formal, metalled, unwaveringly direct highways that stood out in an Anglo-Saxon world of meandering, shifting muddy tracks and byways. These Roman roads, or what remained of them, clearly distinguished the places that grew up alongside them.

I wonder whether the Anglo-Saxon inhabitants of Streatley ('road in the woodland clearing'; Bedfordshire) or Stretham ('homestead on the road'; Cambridgeshire) looked down on those of Earith ('landing place on a muddy river bank'; Cambridgeshire) and Eastleach ('eastern estate on stream flowing through boggy land'; Gloucestershire)?

Villages and towns that comprise or incorporate *chester*, *cester*, *caistor*, *castor* or *caster* (*caestre* in Old English) refer to old Roman forts and walled towns. Ruinous defensive circuits of walls, ditches and towers at these places would have been significant sites to the Anglo-Saxons, even if they had lost their original purpose and importance long before. The site of the Roman town at Ancaster in Lincolnshire, for example, probably later belonged to an Anglo-Saxon named 'Anna'.

The inclusion of *burgh* or *borough* in a name also indicates a fortification or defended settlement, but these were often contemporary with the Anglo-Saxons who named them. Bamburgh, Northumberland (originally *Bebbanburge*), for example, is the stronghold of a lady named *Bebbe*. Bamburgh also illustrates how village names can mutate over time. The accepted modern spelling of village names can be quite misleading.

Surely nothing could be simpler than Duxford? Perhaps 'ford where ducks congregate'? Encouragingly enough, this south Cambridgeshire village straddles an ancient stream and has a ford (and sometimes ducks). But wait, the first recorded version of the name, in the tenth century, is actually *Dukeswrthe*. *Worth* names indicate some kind of enclosure, a piece of land enclosed by an earthwork bank, hedge or fence, and in this case it belonged to an Anglo-Saxon man named Ducc.

So, it is always wise to look at the very first recorded version of a place name, rather than follow your nose, however tempting that might be, particularly with Beer or Lover. For a huge number of villages, the earliest written form of a village name is provided by the Domesday Book. Nevertheless, even this authoritative source is not without problems for place-name scholars, historians and archaeologists.

The Norman commissioners sent out to survey the villages and scribes sometimes misheard and mangled the

English place names. So the Domesday Book is not quite as ruthlessly comprehensive or consistent as its name and fame suggest; there are omissions, mistakes and ambiguity. If you are very lucky, the village you are exploring may have been mentioned in a much earlier, Anglo-Saxon, charter and this may better reflect the earliest form of the place name.

The historical importance and influence of subsequent waves of colonists is given away by another widespread distribution of distinctive village names. From the ninth century onwards, groups of Danes, Norwegians and Swedes, who were formerly content to be smash-and-grab raiders 'The Vikings', began to settle permanently and control land previously held by Anglo-Saxons.

SCANDINAVIAN STYLE (*NINTH CENTURY TO 1066*)

The area known as the Danelaw, the new homeland of the Scandinavian settlers in England, occupied the land north of a boundary drawn along the Thames as far as Oxfordshire, which then turned and meandered up to Chester. This was the arrangement arrived at in 884, when neither the Wessex Saxons (West Saxons) under Alfred nor the Scandinavians under Guthrum could achieve outright victory in their protracted power struggle. The distribution of Scandinavian village names reflects the deep cultural and linguistic influence of these settlers in this northern and eastern part of England. The Danelaw was finally conquered and England was almost entirely united under Wessex rule, but the areas settled by Scandinavians remained distinctive.

Place names ending in *by* are farmsteads or villages named by Scandinavians. Barkby, for example, is the place of a man called Borkr or Barkr. Places ending in *thorpe* are lesser places, such as outlying farms or hamlets. 'Api' gave his name to Apethorpe in Northamptonshire, which couldn't have been as grand as Corby (village belonging to Kori) not far down the road.

Again, the Scandinavians also drew inspiration from nearby built and natural features to name places. The presence of *kirk* or *kir* in a name indicates a church. Kirkbys and Kirbys can be found all over the north of England. Kirkandrews and Kirkoswald in Cumbria helpfully give the saintly dedication of the churches concerned. *Car* (or *ker*) endings in the Danelaw usually indicate a marsh (Redcar, Cleveland) and *thwaite* is a woodland clearing (Bassenthwaite, Cumbria).

Even in the Danelaw heartlands, however, there are plenty of examples of old Anglo-Saxon village names that survive alongside the newer Scandinavian names. Scandinavian rulers evidently did not ruthlessly sweep away all trace of the Anglo-Saxon people, their villages and their language.

Just east of Nottingham, one of the five great boroughs of the Danelaw, the village of Granby (the farmstead of a Scandinavian man named *Grani*) can be found right alongside Sutton (Old English south farmstead), Elton (Old English personal name, *Ella*), Barnstone (deriving from another old English personal name) and Langar (Old English for a long pointy bit of land), which suggests that the Scandinavian invaders and settlers either could not, or chose not to ethnically cleanse this part of Nottinghamshire.

In fact, Granby, surrounded by these established settlements, suggests that Scandinavian settlers were almost
apologetically inserting themselves there into a steadfastly
and densely settled Anglo-Saxon landscape. That doesn't
quite fit the uncompromising Viking image.

Nor do village names that mix Anglo-Saxon and Scandinavian elements, such as Barlby in North Yorkshire, 'Bardulf's
village'. Bardulf is a solid Anglo-Saxon or Germanic personal
name, but the *by* is firmly Scandinavian; it suggests some kind
of compromise and assimilation rather than total domination.

This village name might have sounded as incongruous to
the locals then as 'Dave Smith's Italian Restaurant' sounds to
us today. However, it is more likely that hybrid names like
this indicate the intermingling of two cultures and traditions
to such an extent that people could comfortably compound
previous names, or terms from a different era and mother
tongue, to create a new place name. A new hybrid version
of the English was being formed and in much of the country
people would have gradually become much less conscious of
the ethnic and political implications of their villages' names.

But a big political and social change was on the horizon,
handily punctuated by the most famous date in English
history: 1066.

NORMAN NOMENCLATURE
(*1066 ONWARDS*)

The Norman Conquest and its aftermath brought about
radical changes in society. Norman French greatly influenced the development of the English language. However,

there are not as many Norman village names in England as we might expect. The Normans were not only effective conquerors, administrators and innovators, but they were also great assimilators when they needed to be. They had to be in England, because they were relatively few in number; only enough to exert military control and replace the Anglo-Saxon and Anglo-Scandinavian aristocracy. Even this regime change was not immediate and total, and this is reflected in the fact that they did not change many existing village names.

The Normans gained control of an already well-organised, well-populated and relatively intensively farmed country. Simple pragmatism prevented them renaming everywhere and everything they mastered, which after a decade or two was virtually everything, virtually everywhere in England. The population at large did not speak their overlords' language and it was pointless trying to make them do so, as generations of French teachers have discovered since. In fact, the descendants of the original Norman aristocracy eventually began speaking a newly mixed English language, Middle English, which was probably partly induced by the sort of sheer exasperation that is familiar to French officials and shopkeepers today. Documents continued to be written in Latin and French.

Norman misinterpretation of Anglo-Saxon and Anglo-Scandinavian names gave rise to unintentionally altered village names, but the Normans largely left existing English village names alone, even where they entirely replanned the settlements themselves. There were limited reasons and opportunities to create entirely new places with shiny new

Norman names. However, when a new Norman castle, abbey or village was established, there was often a blank canvas, so we have places and villages such as Belvoir (beautiful view) in Rutland, Beaulieu (beautiful place) in Hampshire, and Montacute (pointy hill) in Somerset. Beaumont (beautiful hill) in Essex must have been given a full Norman makeover. Its Old English name was Fulepet – 'foul pit'.

The Norman barons and manorial lords, and those who inherited manors later in the medieval period, also appended their names to existing places. The villages of Orton Longueville and Orton Waterville, which derive from the existing Anglo-Saxon 'upper farmstead' or 'farmstead near a ridge' (*ord*, *ton*), was divided into separate manors and appropriated by the Norman de Longuevilles and de Watervilles respectively. Ashby de la Zouch (Leicestershire) and Ashby de la Launde (Lincolnshire) were just plain Ashby (Scandinavian village where ash trees can be found) in the Domesday Book, before the two Norman lordly families got hold of them. This practice extended to ecclesiastical lords. Weedon Bec (Northamptonshire) and Tooting Bec (formerly Surrey) were acquired by the powerful Bec Abbey of Normandy.

One of my favourite examples of a medieval magnate's name resonating down the centuries is 'Vauxhall', an old village later subsumed into London, which originated as 'Falkes Hall' in the thirteenth century. Falkes de Breauté was one of King John's chief hard-man enforcers. Incidentally, his motif, a griffin, is captured in the Vauxhall car badge in recognition of the place where the motor company was founded.

Milton Ernest, a village in Bedfordshire, is an Old English 'middle farmstead' combined with the name of its sometime lord. In the medieval period, this surname could appear as Ernies, Erneys, Ernes, Ernyes, Hernes, Hernies, Hernis, Herneys, Harneys, Harney, Herneys, Orney, Earnest or Ernest. The addition was needed to distinguish this village from the other Miltons in the region and across the country.

These manorial names stuck and persisted long after the original barons and lords of that name had ceased to have anything to do with a village.

MODERN VILLAGE NAMES (*NINETEENTH CENTURY TO THE PRESENT DAY*)

The industrial 'barons' of the modern era were responsible for creating entirely new villages and village names. Saltaire, a mill and industrial village constructed in the middle of the nineteenth century, is a combination of its owner's name, Titus Salt, and the Yorkshire river on whose banks the place was built, the River Aire. Later in the Victorian period the Cadburys, of chocolate fame, founded Bournville village for their workers. The place was named after the local river, Bourn, combined with the genteel-sounding French for town or city, *ville*. This French word is related to vill, village and villa, and originally meant farm.

The Lever Brothers' factory village of Port Sunlight was named after one of its key products, Sunlight Soap. The village of Stewartby in Bedfordshire sounds like a pre-Domesday Book Scandinavian settlement, but in fact was named in the 1930s after the London Brick Company's directorial dynasty, the Stewarts.

The country's rapidly expanding post-medieval population has produced many new settlements whose names sometimes reflect events at the time of their inception, or features around which they developed. Waterlooville (Battle of Waterloo), Peacehaven (First World War), Ironbridge (world's first cast-iron bridge), Virginia Water (an eighteenth-century lake) are prime examples.

In the past, new parishes and villages might have retained the name of the original larger parish from which they were formed, together with a notable feature such as the dedication of their church. Many new villages and parishes were formed on reclaimed land around The Wash in the east of England, giving rise to names such as Sutton St Edmund, Tydd St Giles, Tydd St Mary, Tydd Gote, Walpole St Andrew and Walpole St Peter. Other names reflected where the village was situated, such as Sutton Bridge and Walpole Highway. Gote probably derives from the old word for sluice.

Names of new offshoot villages might also reflect the physical characteristics or different size of the villages, such as Long Sutton. 'Great' and 'Little' are very common indeed in front of village names, and 'Magna' and 'Parva' can be found behind them. Norman, medieval and later village founders would sometimes simply put the dull but accurate 'New' in front of the old village name (New Buckenham, New Bolsover) or 'Market' or 'Castle' or 'Abbey', or anything else that helped to distinguish them.

Burnham Market is one of several Burnhams close together near the north Norfolk Coast, all named from the little River Burn. The remaining ones are Burnham Deepdale,

Burnham Thorpe, Burnham Overy Town, Burnham Overy Staithe and Burnham Norton. The former Burnham Sutton, Burnham Ulph and Burnham Westgate were absorbed into Burnham Market.

Modern planners and developers have often tried to give traditional-sounding names to their new settlements in an attempt to weave them into the fabric of their localities. Sometimes these don't sound quite right. Not far from where I am now writing this, the entirely new communities of Northstowe, Cambourne, Hampton and Alconbury Weald are now on the map and growing.

Northstowe is not north of an existing place called Stowe. Cambourne is near the old village of Bourn, without an 'e', and not near the River Cam. It is not crooked as far as I know, which is one ancient meaning of 'cam'. It is split into the new villages of Great Cambourne, Lower Cambourne and Upper Cambourne, which at least sound like historic offshoot villages. Hampton (split into Hampton Hargate, Hampton Vale, Hampton Hempsted) is a common old village name, but in this case is not associated with anything locally. Alconbury Weald is close to the old villages of Alconbury and Alconbury Weston, but 'Weald' (woodland or forest) is usually 'wold' in this region (for example, nearby Leighton Bromswold).

PREHISTORIC SURVIVORS

Despite the linguistic onslaught of Romans, Anglo-Saxons, Scandinavians, Normans, industrialists and modern developers, some early British place names have survived. It is incredible to think that some names spoken by prehistoric people long before the Romans arrived are still in everyday use. Celtic place names are more frequent in the west of the country and they are ubiquitous in Cornwall. Cornish is part of a group of Celtic languages that includes Welsh and Breton (though not Scots, Irish or Manx). Until the eighteenth century, people who spoke Cornish and nothing else could still be found in the county.

Anybody who has navigated the long journey to a holiday in Cornwall will have noticed the instant change in the spelling and sound of village names once they have crossed the River Tamar. This border between Cornwall and Devon (or border with England as some Cornish people claim) must have been a bridge too far for most Anglo-Saxon speakers, although some Old English names do occur here and there in Cornwall.

In Cornish, *Tre* meant farmstead. So Tremaine is 'farm by the stone' and Treneglos is 'farm of the church'. The numerous *porth* names are harbours. *Bos* (Boscastle) is a dwelling. The Cornish *pen* usually means headland, but is often a hill elsewhere in Celtic Britain. *Pol* is a Cornish pool (it is *lynn, linn* or *lun* elsewhere in ancient Briton) and *ros* is a heath or moor.

The very earliest English place names that we have go way back into the mists of prehistory; some could be more than 3000 years old, predating the Iron Age. Rivers in particular have retained their ancient British names. The meanings of a few rivers such as Cam (crooked), Ouse (water), Tamar and Thames (possibly 'dark one', or just river) and Trent (maybe 'the trespasser', meaning liable to flood its banks) can be reconstructed with reasonable confidence, but the meaning of others, such as Colne, Nene and Humber are now lost entirely. Rivers naturally lend their names to villages and towns that grew up along their banks, but of course this in itself does not imply the great antiquity of those places.

Local folklore often provides entertaining but entirely wrong accounts of the derivation of village names. Thankfully place-name research over a long period of time is distilled in authoritative sources such as *The Oxford Dictionary of English Place Names,* or in online resources such as the University of Nottingham Institute for Name Studies *Key to English Place-Names* (kepn.nottingham.ac.uk/). In these sources you will also find the meanings of the strange village names that I mentioned earlier in the chapter.

CHAPTER 6

VILLAGES OF INDUSTRY

The vast majority of medieval English villages relied almost exclusively on agriculture to survive, and most still depended on agriculture or entirely revolved around agriculture well into the twentieth century. The English agricultural industry went through a revolution, or a series of revolutions, from the seventeenth century to the nineteenth century, and this changed the character of the landscape around villages, and villages themselves.

Even in medieval times, however, there were villages that became renowned for other industries, such as the production of woollen goods or quarrying. As the industrialisation of the country progressed in the eighteenth and nineteenth centuries, many more villages were shaped by particular industries, and many villages were newly founded to serve them. They often have unique features that give clear clues as to their history.

FISHING VILLAGES

Since prehistory, people have lived in coastal settlements and have fished and traded by the sea. Fish, fisheries and fishermen are mentioned throughout the Domesday Book. Neverthe-less, coastal fishing village communities are not listed with quite the frequency that you might expect of a small nation surrounded by the sea, at a time when fish was known to be a significant part of the diet. This might be a consequence of the notoriously different approach to the Domesday survey taken by the various commissioners in certain areas, but it also reflects the fact that many places had not yet developed a large fishing industry.

Only in late medieval and Tudor times, with the wider availability of more capable boats and substantial invest-ment in better harbour engineering, could many coastal settlements start to grow into specialist fishing villages. These large fishing villages were a very common feature of the English coastline more than a century ago, and some still carry on the industry today.

Clovelly in Devon, along with being an old estate village, has a proud heritage as a fishing village. Its Domesday Book entry indicates a sizeable community of thirty-seven house-holds, putting it among the top twenty per cent of villages in England ranked according to size. Smallholders, villagers and slaves are listed in Clovelly. Ploughs and plough land, meadows, pasture, woodland, sheep, cattle, goats and pigs are itemised; but there is no mention at all of fish, fishing or fishermen.

The parish church with its Norman origins is situated inland, half a mile away from the present village, near the mansion of the manorial lords, Clovelly Court. We can be pretty sure that the main focus of the original settlement was inland and principally concerned with farming. It is difficult to believe that no fishing was carried out there in the earliest times, but the sea is treacherous and the site is not ideal. It wasn't easy to keep and launch small boats in the limited space available on the exposed shore at the foot of the cliffs.

Clovelly's rise as a fishing centre was boosted by the construction of a pier or harbour wall to give some shelter and protection to its fleet of small boats. This was built by the lords of the manor, possibly initially as early as the four-teenth century, but certainly during the sixteenth century, when the lord George Carey spent the then huge sum of £2000 on it along with 'divers cellars and warehouses'. This structure, which has been extended, heightened and strength-ened to become ever more robust since then, made Clovelly one of the few safe harbours along this stretch of coast. A sizeable fishing fleet of more than fifty small boats operated from there during the nineteenth century.

Robin Hood's Bay in North Yorkshire enters the written records in the fourteenth century. It is not clear whether a village actually existed there on the edge of the bay at the time, or why the place got its name, but both its name and the first documented reference to Robin Hood's Bay hint at the sort of lawlessness that the village would become famous for later in its history.

Sometime between 1324 and 1346, the irate Count of Flanders wrote to King Edward III to complain that Flemish boats, together with their fishermen and catches, had been hijacked and taken to Robin Hood's Bay. References to the place in the sixteenth century, when it belonged to Whitby

Abbey, confirmed that by then there was a substantial village there. It was reported to comprise fifty cottages by the shore with a fleet of twenty boats and benefited from a dock or a beaching place a mile long. In the sixteenth century, men of Robin Hood's Bay are said to have come to the rescue of a small English ship that was being pursued down the coast by a Scottish ship. The Robin Hood's Bay boats carried archers to fight off the Scots.

Most of the later references to the village, however, concern somewhat less noble enterprises. The village was notorious for smuggling, or 'free trading' as it was called euphemistically by the locals. This was one of many fishing communities in the eighteenth century that supplemented an income from the sea that was highly precarious with one that was highly nefarious.

The former minor, marginal status of Robin Hood's Bay as a settlement is given away by the fact that it remains part of the ancient parish of Fylingdales to this day. The original medieval parish church, which served a widely scattered predominantly inland community, lay a mile away from Robin Hood's Bay (or Baytown as it is known locally). This original church was rebuilt in 1822, but was already in an anachronistic situation. A new Anglican church was finally built in the village in 1870, closer to the heart of the now fully grown coastal community. Had the village of Robin Hood's Bay been the most important and dominant place in the locality in early medieval times, the original church would have been built there in the first place.

Again, one clue about the Cornish village of Port Isaac's relatively late development as a large fishing centre is the far distant location of the medieval parish church of St Endellion. Until Tudor times, Port Isaac was just another place in the parish of scattered farmsteads, manors and hamlets. There is no mention of fishing there in the Domesday survey. The first reference to a fishing community is much later in the medieval period: 1338. The massive expansion of fishing, trade and the village itself, however, was helped by the construction of a harbour wall or breakwater in the sixteenth century. The foundations of the original structure can now be seen only at low tide, and a modern replacement guards the entrance to the harbour.

Most of the streets in Port Isaac's historic core probably originated in the sixteenth century as the place developed as a premier fishing centre and exported locally quarried slate. The village grew ever more densely packed with buildings with the success of the slate and pilchard export enterprises. Port Isaac became an international port and thrived as such until the end of the nineteenth century, by which time it was a very crowded, busy place.

When the pilchard shoals were sighted, the whole village had a role to play in landing and preparing the fish. They were caught in vast numbers and pressed for oil and salted in 'fish cellars' before being exported to Catholic Europe. Fish cellars dating to the nineteenth century, which replaced older versions, can still be seen in the village today; the largest of these, comprising ranges of low, stone barn-like buildings around a small open courtyard, is still in use for preparing and selling fish.

Port Isaac, though hugely grown from its medieval origins and by far the most important settlement in the parish over several hundred years, did not get its own dependent Anglican chapel in the village until 1884. This became the new parish church in 1913. Over the centuries, the villagers had probably become thoroughly tired of the mile and a half hike to the Church of St Endellion. There had long been two Methodist churches in the village, which may also be an indication of Port Isaac people voting for their preferred form of worship with their feet.

Fishing was a very hard and dangerous business. It still is, but in the past there were no weather forecasts to help fishermen evade potential disaster. Clovelly lost eleven of its fathers, sons and brothers in one storm in 1821, and another twenty-one men from the locality were lost in a storm in 1838. Port Isaac's neighbour, Port Quin, is said to have dwindled away as a village because of one disastrous storm that wiped out its fishermen. The Penlee lifeboat disaster of 1981 reminded the modern world of the devastation to coastal village families that seafaring can bring. The entire volunteer crew of the lifeboat stationed near the village of Mousehole in Cornwall, eight local men, was lost bravely trying to rescue the crew of a floundering cargo ship.

These fishing villages and many like them were very tough, rough and ready places, and quite run-down until finding new niches as centres of genteel tourism and leisure from the last years of the nineteenth century onwards. Clovelly, Robin Hood's Bay and Port Isaac cling to the rocks, and their buildings line the sides of ravines that run steeply down to the sea. The streams that gouged out the ravines still flow in conduits and culverts through Robin Hood's Bay and Port Isaac, but Clovelly's once foul-smelling trickle was largely diverted from the main street and covered up after a cholera outbreak in 1861.

Buildings in these villages were crammed into every available space near the shore. Narrow, steep streets and alleyways wound their way between them, and the narrowest thoroughfare in Port Isaac is appropriately called 'Squeeze Belly Alley'. Family life and fishing life was all packed in together in the small cottages and narrow alleys: drying nets and drying fish, guts, blood, household slops, livestock dung, smoke, washing, mending, dealing and hundreds of children running around in it all. These were certainly not the pretty, clean, seaside villages that delight tourists and holiday home-owners today.

In all these villages, topography, disappearing fish stocks and changing diets across society conspired to constrain further village growth from the nineteenth century onwards. The erosion of the cliffs on which sat Robin Hood's Bay periodically took away many of the village buildings until the construction of a concrete sea wall in the 1970s. This is now reaching the end of its designed lifespan. Erosion also ate away a lot of the relatively flat and dry land where boats could be hauled up out of the sea. These days there isn't much space to store, manoeuvre and launch boats at Robin Hood's Bay; they have to be towed across the sand and rocks to be launched and recovered when the tide and sea conditions are just right.

People in Clovelly still have to use wooden sledges to bring items up and down the steep street to their houses, as no vehicles are allowed in the village. Donkeys once helped with this work, but they now amble up and down the steep 'Up Along/Down Along' street solely for tourists.

Little harbours and difficult landing places in small fishing villages could not cope with ever-larger trawlers from the late nineteenth century onwards, so as fishing industrialised, fishing villages lost out to towns with better natural advantages, such as Whitby in the case of Robin Hood's Bay, and St Ives, Penzance, Fowey and Falmouth in the case of Port Isaac.

Huge investment in massive engineering works to create docks and integrated rail infrastructure in order to get huge quantities of fish quickly to market was justified only in some select places. Grimsby, on the North Sea coast near the Humber, represents the ultimate transformation through the centuries from an average-sized village in 1086 (with a mill, but no fishing mentioned) to a port and fishing town in later medieval times, to the world's premier fishing and fish processing centre in the first half of the twentieth century. By this time, it was home to the world's largest fishing fleet. The port of Grimsby always dealt with other goods, and though the fishing fleet declined, together with its sister port at Immingham, it remains a very busy international port.

PORT AND RAIL VILLAGES

The little village of Sunderland Point on the north-west coast of England is an unlikely place to look for evidence of Britain's growing global trading networks in the eighteenth century and links to the transatlantic slave trade. However, it was there that a port for the City of Lancaster was established by Quaker entrepreneur Robert Lawson. The River Lune upstream to Lancaster was difficult for large ships to navigate, but the exposed Sunderland Point near the mouth of its estuary was adapted as their first port of call.

There was only a farmhouse or two there prior to the early eighteenth century, but Lawson built warehouses and a wharf or retaining sea wall from sandstone rubble. Merchants offloaded sugar, cotton and exotic hard woods like mahogany to be used for furniture making by Lancaster craftsmen. Sunderland Point was very convenient in some respects, but not in others. It is separated from the mainland by tidal marsh and cut off by the sea twice a day, limiting traffic. Lawson went bankrupt and the Commissioners of the Port of Lancaster went looking for a new site.

Sunderland Point was soon eclipsed by a new dock, and became known disparagingly as 'Cape Famine' by passing trade. Today, the village comprises two terraces of houses facing the shoreline (First Terrace and Second Terrace) and a handful of others. The origins of some of the terraced houses as converted eighteenth-century warehouses is apparent from their austere facades and lofty proportions. Lawson's wharf is still there, with its single flight of stone steps leading down to the shore, but only a few small leisure boats now operate from the locality.

In 1779, the Port Commissioners found a new site on the opposite bank of the River Lune near a hamlet called Glasson. Here they obtained a licence to build a quay and any other dock infrastructure they thought they might need. The quay was equipped with a small, quaint lighthouse, and they went on to build a wet dock, complete with a dock gate so that larger ships could remain floating at berth, and warehouses.

Canals played a crucial role in the development of many villages. The first canals in England were excavated by the Romans, and in medieval times similar canals that served both drainage functions and river traffic stimulated agriculture and trade in several places.

However, the great canal building age really began in the eighteenth century. It was expensive, slow and hazardous to cart bulk goods, such as coal, by road. The ability to move vast quantities of industrial materials reliably all year round justified the enormous investments and efforts in planning and constructing canals. By 1850, nearly 5000 miles of inland waterway had been constructed in Britain, much of it focused on linking the new industrial centres in the Midlands and North of England with the growing west coast sea ports.

The opening of Glasson Branch Canal in 1825 accelerated the growth of Glasson Dock. It provided a reliable waterway for goods to Lancaster, south to Preston and elsewhere inland via its junction with the Lancaster Canal. The Branch Canal terminated in a large canal basin separated from the wet dock by a lock gate. A dry dock was built for shipbuilding and repairs at Glasson in 1837, and from 1883 the port was served by a railway line. Alongside the docks and canal basin, rows of terraced houses were built for workers, together with a pub or two, customs house, lock-keeper's cottage, a new church and a vicarage.

The old Glasson was completely transformed. There is no building in Glasson Dock earlier than the late eighteenth century and the old industrial port and canal infrastructure, including the little lighthouse, still survives in remarkably complete form. Glasson Dock still thrives as a port for small freight ships.

The medieval village of Shardlow in Derbyshire underwent an extraordinary canal-inspired transformation. The River Trent from this point, near the middle of England, is navigable all the way to the east coast, via the Humber. During the seventeenth century, a significant port developed near the village, but things really took off in the late eighteenth century when the Trent and Mersey Canal was built. The idea was to link the major west coast port of Liverpool with the major east coast port of Hull in a great loop extending south into the Midlands. Shardlow was at the base of this giant canal loop and was already well connected to the river and road network of the time.

It became the place where goods heading into or out of the middle of England were transferred between ships and large barges on the Trent and narrow boats on the canal. This is known as trans-shipment, and Shardlow became a premier centre for the practice. Various boat haulage, boat-building and supporting businesses were set up in the place. No less than twelve canal basins were constructed, with warehouses, stables, offices and workers' houses. The population of the village grew from 200 in 1780 to around 1300 in 1841. Shardlow was talked of as 'Rural Rotterdam' or 'Little Liverpool'.

Similarly, Stourport-on-Severn in Worcestershire was established around the same time and became the major canal-side distribution centre for the West Country. Built on a greenfield site near a small hamlet, it quickly grew to become a village and on to become a small town. Many villages in the late eighteenth century found themselves on or near the route of canals and developed with the economic boom that this new transport system encouraged. Places such as Shardlow, however, suffered stagnation and decline when the next revolution in transport arrived: railways.

Like the canals before them, the construction of steam railways accelerated Britain's growth as the world's premier industrial powerhouse. From 1830 onwards, with the opening of the Liverpool and Manchester railway, the rail network for passengers and goods went on to reach to all corners of the British Isles. At the greatest extent of the rail network, in the first decades of the twentieth century, around 20,000 miles of rail line were in operation, linking large cities and small villages alike. Many formerly isolated villages found themselves connected and transformed in radical new ways.

Halwill, in Devon, was only one tiny village in a landscape of small dispersed settlements in an area north-west of Dartmoor, until 1879. In that year, a new railway station opened about a mile from the old village at the junction of three railway routes. A new village, Halwill Junction, grew to become by far the largest village in the area. It remains so, despite its station having been closed as a result of Dr Beeching's infamous rationalisation of the British rail network in the 1960s. The presumably wryly named housing development 'Beeching Close' near the former station site recalls the village's past, along with the 'Junction Inn' public house, which now caters to villagers rather than rail passengers. Sections of former track bed near the village have become a nature reserve and a cycleway.

The similarly hitherto out-of-the-way medieval village of Melton Constable in Norfolk expanded to become a new 'railway town' in the 1880s; it was on the junction of four railway lines. A significant locomotive works developed there that was sometimes called the 'Crewe of North Norfolk', after the famous railway centre in Cheshire. When the lines closed, Melton Constable reverted back to being the rural village it is today, albeit a large one that has an unusually urban industrial character for the region.

Many settlements across England developed around new railway stations, depots and works. Villages finding themselves bypassed by a railway line, but with a station, halt or crossing nearby, often expanded towards them, or became newly 'polyfocal' with new rows of railway workers' cottages and business premises springing up along approach roads. Hundreds of English villages had easier access to an integrated transport system in the 1950s, via the railway network, than they have today.

COTTAGE INDUSTRY

Cottage industry was born in medieval times when village households began to produce textiles not only for their own needs and to sell to neighbours, but as part of a network of households who all supplied their goods to a merchant. The wool industry in Lavenham and other villages and towns in Suffolk worked this way. The clothiers supplied wool to their outworkers in the neighbourhood, then collected the finished woollen cloth and found markets that bought in bulk.

Bibury in Gloucestershire and its neighbourhood, like many places in the Cotswolds, was renowned for its wool production and weavers. A former medieval monastic wool store in the parish, Arlington Row, was converted to a row of weavers' cottages in the seventeenth century. They are now an attractive part of a famously picturesque and much-visited group of Cotswolds villages.

Weaving and spinning work was carried out by villagers in their homes, around household chores and the other work. Spinning wool on a simple drop spindle, a little stick with a weight at one end that could be twizzled to draw out and twist wool into yarn, was something that could be carried out by anyone, even while doing other things like minding cooking fires, livestock and babies. Spinning wheels and looms, powered by feet and hands, demanded more attention, but again the pace was set by the operator. They could stop and start when they wanted.

The village of Ruddington, near Nottingham, represents the further, post-medieval development of a cottage industry in many other places in that region and across the country. In the mid-nineteenth century, half the households in Ruddington were engaged in textile production. Stockings were big business. Framework knitters used weaving contraptions that allowed them to work a hundred times faster than knitting by hand. They turned their hand, and adapted their machines, to produce not only woollen goods, but also cotton goods and lace.

However, they did not work independently. Villagers had to buy the raw materials and hire the machinery from the Master Hosiers. Their houses, also often rented from Master Hosiers, were adapted as workshops, with large 'weavers windows' (made up of an array of glazed panels, or 'lights') to let in sufficient natural light to work. Workshops with ranges of adjoining cottages for workers were also built by some entrepreneurs. A few of these cottages and workshops survive in Ruddington and one complex now houses the Framework Knitting Museum.

In the Saddleworth district of the Peak District, north-east of Manchester and Oldham, there is also plenty of surviving evidence of the extent of the cottage, hand-loom weaving industry. Cottages in the village of Delph and its neighbourhood have the characteristic, long 'weavers windows' on the upper floors, and the living accommodation for several families was sometimes integrated in one building together with the 'loomshops'.

In this village and its neighbourhood, these combined cottage and workshop buildings are sometimes three or four storeys high. With their arrays of long windows on each floor, they look rather like small factories.

FACTORY VILLAGES

During the eighteenth century, some textile entrepreneurs realised that huge efficiencies could be made by greater centralisation of the cottage industry workforce and the further mechanisation of their work. Richard Arkwright is credited with introducing the true factory system of production, not only to England, but to the world. Arkwright was not the first to bring people together in a single large building to work on a mechanised production line; this had been tried during the early eighteenth century in Derby silk mills.

Arkwright, however, was the first to succeed in bringing the various elements together in a way that persisted and translated to other areas and other industries. He matched large-scale, water-powered mechanical production techniques with a dedicated industrial workforce, who lived in purpose-built industrial housing. Arkwright, a barber and wig maker from Lancashire, developed a 'water frame', which harnessed the power of waterwheels to create cotton yarn. He needed flowing water and so came to Derbyshire's Derwent Valley, which has an abundance of it, and began building his first cotton mill at Cromford in 1771.

Another larger mill on the site soon followed, but Arkwright realised that he couldn't assemble a large enough workforce from the sparsely populated locality. Furthermore, working in shifts around the clock meant it was more efficient to have workers living quite close to the mills, not ambling in every day from far-flung corners of the neighbourhood. If workers missed the start of their shifts at Arkwright's mills, they were locked out for that day and lost an additional day's pay besides.

Arkwright set about building cottages near his factory at Cromford and placed newspaper adverts to attract people from far and wide. This was a totally new way of working, driven by the factory clock and the relentless pace of the mill machinery, but Arkwright offered consistent pay and accommodation at a time when many villagers lived very precariously with the ebbs and flows of seasonal work. He encouraged families to move to Cromford and employed men, women and children in his mills. In fact, in the early 1800s it was reported that his workforce comprised 150 men, 300 women and a whopping 700 children. Child labour commonly made up a large proportion of early textile factory workforces.

The houses Arkwright built in North Street, Cromford for his workers were quite comfortable when compared to the living conditions that many people endured at the time. He equipped them with weaving lofts lit by weaving windows on the first floor; there were to be no idle hands in any of his workers' households. The newly industrialised village at Cromford doubled in size over a twenty-year period.

In addition to the engineering works necessary to ensure a consistent supply of water to his factories, Arkwright invested in the infrastructure of the village itself. He built an inn and established a Saturday market, and offered annual prizes to attract traders. For example, Arkwright proudly advertised an eight-day clock with a mahogany case, worth £9, as a prize to the trader who sold the greatest amount of beef and veal.

A fair was established and eventually the village was furnished with a school and its own parish church; villagers had previously used the parish church at nearby Wirksworth. Arkwright purchased the manors of Cromford and Willersley in the 1780s and built a sizeable home for himself, Rock House, overlooking his factories. This was followed by a much grander new residence, Willersley Castle, on a hillside overlooking the Derwent Valley.

Arkwright was among the first of a new breed of industrial barons, who were as proud to oversee estates of factories and factory villages as the old landed gentry were to look out over landscaped grounds and estate cottages. He inspired many others at home and abroad. Soon after Arkwright's Cromford factories were in full flow, the Greg family built the vast Quarry Bank cotton mill and mill village at Styal in Cheshire. The ambition and scale of the Gregs' 1780s project was helped by the lapse of Arkwright's water frame patent, and again rows of terraced workers' housing were built near the mill.

Arkwright's Cromford cotton mills found other uses in the later nineteenth century as rival cotton production expanded hugely in the north-west of England, much closer to the sea ports that brought in the raw material. The new mills were powered by coal and steam, not water. Industrial towns grew around them, and Manchester became 'Cottonopolis', the first industrial city in the world.

Cromford remained a village. The Arkwright Society rescued Cromford Mills from dereliction in the 1970s, and the mill complex now houses a heritage centre and various businesses. The village, shaped by Arkwright, continues to thrive. Both mill and village at Quarry Bank in Cheshire are now owned by the National Trust, and residents, visitors and staff enjoy very different lifestyles at the Gregs' new model factory and working village.

These early industrial villages, with their rows of terraced houses close to the factory, provided the basic template for the unrelenting streets of back-to-back terraced houses in the rapidly expanding industrial towns and cities. But they also inspired a new generation of enlightened industrialists, who looked back to village life as inspiration for a better quality of life for their workforce.

MODEL INDUSTRIAL VILLAGES

The rapid expansion of manufacturing during the nineteenth century saw country folk across Britain flock to towns and cities in search of regular, relatively well-paid jobs in new steam-powered factories. Invariably they encountered horrendous overcrowding in poor housing with awful sanitation. The ancient city of Nottingham, for example, had not expanded much beyond the circuit of its medieval town walls. It had become a lace-making boom town, but its growth was severely limited by an inability to acquire surrounding land for expansion.

Nottingham, formerly described as a garden city, with urban orchards and grand town houses in extensive grounds, began to suffer from severe overcrowding as every available space was built on. Surrounding common land was finally enclosed by an Act of Parliament in 1845 and the city could spread out. Even today, however, a sense of that historic internal development pressure can be seen in the Lace Market area, where high-rise lace workshops are packed among the maze of narrow medieval streets, giving them a curious canyon-like feel.

In many of England's manufacturing towns and cities, civic authorities, manufacturers and landlords failed to keep pace with the migration from the countryside. They could not satisfactorily house their expanding urban populations and struggled to provide the necessary clean water, sewers and amenities to ensure a reasonable quality of life. There was often little opportunity to expand the urban factories, and some industrialists took matters into their own hands.

Titus Salt's construction of a brand-new mill complex on the River Aire, near Shipley in west Yorkshire, replaced the five mills he owned in Bradford and gave him the opportunity to create a new model industrial village for his workforce. The village Salt built on a greenfield site from 1851 onwards was only a few miles north of Bradford, but was a million miles from its severely overcrowded slums.

From the outset, Salt's village was planned with superior, stone-built houses and a great range of amenities. A hospital, a school, an adult educational institution (with a reading room and library, concert hall, billiard room, science laboratory and gym) were built. There was a park and a boathouse on the river, and workers and their children were encouraged to join brass and drum bands. Saltaire is a very regimented village, based on a rigid grid plan of streets and terraces of houses, but its uniformity is softened by a hierarchy of different house sizes and architectural flourishes that reflected the occupational seniority of their tenants.

William Hesketh Lever, a few years later, dispensed with uniformity entirely and cherry-picked virtually every style

and period of English architecture to create his model industrial village of Port Sunlight. Lever selected a marshy site on
the east shore of the Wirral Peninsula in the north-west of
England for his new soap factory and workers' housing, and
began building in 1888. Adopting the Arts and Crafts principles that were beginning to become highly influential at the
time, Lever employed thirty architects to design his village
buildings.

The Arts and Crafts movement was all about traditional
materials, craftsmanship, and homely, bespoke, picturesque
architecture. In this new industrial village, reproduction
medieval-style timber framing sits side by side with Tudor,
Jacobean, Flemish brickwork, solid stone and elegant Queen
Anne-style frontages. It was a polar reaction against urban
industrial housing and the mass production of building
materials, and therefore a somewhat ironic legacy for a
company that went on to become the ubiquitous global
industrial titan, Unilever.

Lever himself was not entirely soft-centred about the
village he was creating for his workers. This was not about
philanthropy, he said; this was about sound business sense.
Workers living in comfortable homes in a good environment
with plenty of amenities would be committed and loyal.
Lever called this 'profit sharing', but rather than put profits
directly into the hands of his workers, who he believed
were in danger of squandering it on booze and frippery, he
promised to invest in facilities.

The growing portfolio of amenities in Port Sunlight
included the Lady Lever Art Gallery, the Gladstone Theatre,

schools, a hospital, a church, an open-air swimming pool, various social clubs and institutes, a women's dining hall and a temperance hotel. Port Sunlight was planned with acres of parks and gardens, and the buildings were set out spaciously, not crammed together. Even terraces of houses were separated from each other by generous open space.

Lever didn't stop at Port Sunlight. He acquired Thornton Manor, a grand Elizabethan-style house built in the 1840s, a few miles away in the centre of the Wirral. He set about rebuilding the Domesday and estate village of Thornton Hough in a comfortable 'ye olde' style, again furnishing it with amenities, and finishing its transformation as a model village that had began under a previous industrialist. At Port Sunlight, however, Lever had created an extraordinary, almost fantastical new place, a garden village that not only inspired other industrialists, but set the tone for the new garden cities (such as Letchworth and Welwyn in Hertfordshire) and hundreds of garden suburbs that followed.

Chocolate makers the Cadbury Brothers moved their factory out of central Birmingham to a greenfield site around Bournbrook Hall, south of the city, in 1879. In 1893 they bought land next to the factory and then planned and built a surrounding model industrial village, naming the place Bournville. The village adopted some Arts and Crafts styles, and like Port Sunlight, was furnished with facilities intended to improve the physical health, spiritual health, educational aspirations and general wellbeing of their employees.

Joseph Rowntree, also a chocolate maker, built his model village New Earswick, near York, from 1902 onwards. Like the Cadburys, Rowntree was a Quaker, and the development of their factory villages and Salt's Saltaire was underpinned by strong, Victorian Christian moral principles. None of them had the one institution that virtually every historic English village had previously benefited from – a village pub.

Other modern manufacturers created their own styles of factory villages. Trafford Park Village was created for employees of the British Westinghouse Electric Company near its factory between the Manchester Ship Canal and the Bridgewater Canal around 1900. The company was part of an American group and the village was laid out on a grid with typically American street numbered names – Third Avenue, Fifth Street, etc. The village, which was some distance from the outskirts of Manchester, was built to be self-contained with amenities such as shops, eating rooms, a dance hall, cinema, schools and a church. Some of these buildings still survive amid what rapidly became the world's first, vast, modern industrial estate.

'Austin Village' was built at Longbridge, Birmingham in the First World War to accommodate the motor manufacturer's expansion into aircraft and tank production. In the late 1920s and early 1930s, Francis Henry Crittall built the elegant modernist, art deco village of Silver End in Essex, near the factories that made his famous metal window frames. The new village buildings were the perfect showcase for his products.

MINING AND QUARRYING VILLAGES

Richard Arkwright's cotton industry at Cromford was not the first major industry in the area. Lead had been mined and smelted in the region since Roman times. In fact, Arkwright used the constant supply of water running out of drainage 'soughs' for old lead mines for his first waterwheel-powered factories, rather than the raging River Derwent. The lead mining industry there was incredibly important and its products travelled far and wide. It supplied lead for many church roofs in the medieval period, church and house window panes were held in place with lead, and it was the material of choice for plumbing. Lead balls were also the standard ammunition for soldiers' and hunters' muskets and pistols.

The Derbyshire lead industry began to decline in the late eighteenth century due to worked-out seams and cheaper imports. Though the lead industry there helped sustain village and town growth, it did not produce distinct new villages; lead mining was carried out alongside farming and other businesses largely from existing settlements.

The iconic, tall ruined engine houses and chimneys of Cornwall are not the only legacy of the region's mining industry. Tin was the most famous product of the county, but copper, lead and silver were also mined there. Around a quarter of Cornwall's entire population was employed in mining by the nineteenth century, and in areas of dispersed settlement not known for towns and villages, growth was phenomenal. St Just, a small town of under 3000 people, trebled in size in ten years from 1841, and neighbouring hamlets such as Bojewyan Stennack, Botallack, Boscaswell, Carnyorth, Trewellard, Nancherrow and Kenidjack became sizeable villages filled with mine workers.

Other extractive industries, some with short-lived heydays, also gave rise to village growth. Alum, a fixative for textile dyeing, was quarried on a large scale along the North Yorkshire coast. The production process for alum required quarried shale rocks to be burnt to extract a liquor, to which human urine had to be added. So important was the alum industry that urine was collected from Newcastle and London and shipped to the region.

The little port village of Staithes prospered from alum production at the nearby Boulby Works from 1650s to the decline of the industry in the nineteenth century. There are old alum stores overlooking the harbourside in Staithes village. Who who would have thought that the character of the picturesque coastal village (familiar to millions as the quaint backdrop for the BBC children's series *Old Jack's Boat*) has been partly shaped by exporting chemicals and importing urine?

PIT VILLAGES

It is difficult to overstate how important the coal industry was to Britain's growth as the industrial centre of the world. Wood, or more specifically charcoal, fuelled the first part of the Industrial Revolution, but coke (purified coal) propelled it on into the nineteenth century. In the middle of the nineteenth century, steam engines were developed that could efficiently use unrefined coal. From that point on, it seemed that every machine that moved or manufactured something, or heated something, was powered by coal. Just before the start of the First World War, nearly one tenth of the entire male workforce in Britain was employed in the coal industry, well over 1 million workers.

The yields were also staggering. Over 280 million tonnes of coal was extracted in 1913. You might think that any industry on this gigantic scale would be dominated by a few big companies, but in fact at this time there were over 1400 different colliery companies and around 2500 mines. Historically each individual company focused on a particular locality and drew on its villages and townsfolk for labour. As the demand for coal grew, the industry took in more people and land.

The incredible transformation of large areas of the countryside and the character of regions that modern industrial coal mining ushered in is exemplified by 'The Dukeries' area of Nottinghamshire. This was named from the four principal ducal seats in the area, surrounded by their country estates: Worksop Manor (Dukes of Norfolk), Welbeck Abbey (Dukes of Portland), Thoresby Hall (Dukes of Kingston and Earls Manvers), and Clumber House (Dukes of Newcastle). There and in neighbouring Derbyshire (and in places such as Yorkshire and Northumberland), landed gentry promoted coal mining and sold or leased their estate land and mineral rights for the purpose.

The Dukeries region was utterly changed early in the twentieth century from its formerly deeply rural historical character as mines were opened, railway and road infrastructure built to ship coal, and spoil heaps mounded up. New mining communities greatly expanded old villages, such as Clipstone, Edwinstowe and Bilsthorpe. The former village of Ollerton expanded to become a town. Thoresby Hall was sold, threatened by mining subsidence, then saved, and is now a hotel. Clumber House was devastated by fires and finally pulled down in the 1930s, and Clumber Park was bought by the National Trust in the 1940s. It too has suffered from mining subsidence.

More recent perceptions of the coal industry have been dominated by the effects of the complete nationalisation of the industry in 1947. All the old companies were swept away, the industry began to look superficially similar in every pit and coal-mining region (though never to the miners themselves), and then it declined. The end came rapidly in the 1980s and 1990s. Though a handful of mines kept going, the coal industry was effectively consigned to history, and quickly became an irrelevance in too many people's minds. Working coal mines ceased to be a common feature of the English landscape, and it is barely remembered how widely distributed they were.

The extent of the industry across the coalfield landscapes of the East Midlands, West Midlands 'Black Country' and north of England is most easily brought to mind; but there were also coal mines in the Forest of Dean in Gloucestershire, Somerset and Kent. 'King Coal' once ruled much of England. Everywhere, however, the last traces of the industry are now being removed, or disguised by landscaping and tree planting.

The few remaining headstocks, surmounted by winding gear, are usually seen as the most striking markers of a former coal mine, but there is a far more widespread living legacy. Colliery towns and villages ('pit villages') developed around every coal mine in the country. Just like earlier industrial villages, some expanded from an earlier historic village core, but other villages were created specifically to house colliery workers. They were planned with a range of amenities as largely self-contained communities.

Before the nineteenth century, Ashington in Northumberland was merely a cluster of farms. Coal mining had taken place in the locality since the medieval period, but from the 1860s onwards industrial-scale mining developed rapidly. The mines were highly productive and the Ashington Coal Company set about attracting employees to work them. Miners were drawn to the area not only from across the region, but from as far afield as Cornwall and Ireland.

Housing development in the area went hand in hand with pit development. The first colliery village houses were stone-built, but then back-to-back, brick-built terraced housing (the 'pit rows') took over to create the familiar dense, urban industrial housing pattern of gridded streets. A few thousand homes were built and Ashington became known as the 'largest village in England' and the 'biggest pit village in the world'. The area developed its own 'Pitmatic' dialect, which is distinct from the urban 'Geordie' of nearby Newcastle.

Some people still argue about whether Ashington is a town or a village, but now with a population of around 30,000 and a town council, I think that argument could have been put to bed a while back. Ashington accrued the sort of facilities and amenities expected of a thriving colliery settlement: chapels, schools, co-operative shops, a hospital, a rail link, miners' institutes for welfare and entertainment, allotments, brass bands and sports facilities. Over the years Ashington's sports clubs in particular have nurtured professional talent well out of proportion to the size of the place. The famous local foot-balling dynasty of the Milburn and Charlton families has been complemented by some notable cricketers, latterly England's Steve Harmison and Mark Wood.

The development of new pit villages allowed some creativity in new 'place-making' design, while borrowing from old village features. The Bolsover Colliery Company in Derbyshire began building Creswell model village in 1895. The village is based on a very large, elongated octag-onal green, fringed by two concentric octagonal circuits of terraced houses. The same company also built the village of New Bolsover, two concentric circuits of terraced houses, open on one side, around a square plan green. New Ross-ington in South Yorkshire, begun in the second decade of the twentieth century, was planned more spaciously, as a large circular green with fringing concentric circuits of houses. The effect produced by these places is a bit like a cross between an old green-based village and a Georgian town square or circus, but with an industrial feel and scale.

Pit villages were close-knit communities utterly depen-dent on an industry that could be very cruel indeed; accidents were all too frequent in coal mines across the country. At Creswell, eighty miners were killed in a single disaster, an underground pit fire, in 1950. Easington Colliery in County Durham, a coal-mining community grafted on to the old medieval village of Easington, lost eighty-three men in an underground explosion in 1951. An avenue of eighty-three trees leads to their memorial.

The closure of the collieries had devastating and profound impacts on the communities that served them, and though many pit villages have bounced back and found new life, some effects will resonate for years to come.

Even if traces of the mines themselves have disappeared from view, very often the entrance to a former mining village is marked by a monument to its heritage. A large winding wheel, or tub (stubby tilting containers that were coupled to run on small rail tracks underground), or modern sculpture can often be found on grass verges and roundabouts.

AGRICULTURAL VILLAGES IN AN AGE OF INDUSTRY AND REVOLUTION

A rapidly expanding industrial workforce, whether in cities or villages, could not feed itself. Industrialisation relied on farming villages, and so even villages a long way from the industrial centres were affected by their growth; agriculture itself had to became an industry, and rural communities became part of this industry. The path to the development of modern farming villages was every bit as extraordinary as the development of industrial villages.

The early years of the nineteenth century, immediately following the end of the Napoleonic Wars, were traumatic for the agricultural villages of England. The effects of widespread enclosure, the dispossession of access to common land, was causing severe hardship for those who had no land of their own. Rapid industrialisation and the concentration of manufacturing in specialist factory villages, towns and cities was wiping out the cottage industries formerly distributed across the countryside.

The huge cost of defeating Napoleon, effectively fighting a war across the globe, had depleted government reserves, increased taxation and had wrecked the economy. The new Corn Laws, which introduced trade tariffs and restrictions to protect British food production, greatly increased the price of bread, a vital staple for much of the rural population; fending off starvation became much harder.

Even nature, once again, had conspired to make things much grimmer in the countryside. The 'Year Without a Summer', 1816, was precipitated by a massive volcanic explosion in Indonesia. Volcanic ash in the atmosphere compounded the generally cooler conditions of the 'Little Ice Age', which had been ongoing since medieval times, to dramatically lower global temperatures. In Britain and across Europe, persistent rainfall and lack of sunlight caused failure of harvests and severe food shortages.

Luddite riots saw desperate hand weavers smashing up machines in the new textile factories of Lancashire, Yorkshire and Nottinghamshire. From 1830, 'Swing Riots' spread from Kent across southern and eastern England. Named after 'Captain Swing' (a made-up figurehead, contrived with an injection of gallows humour), farm labourers smashed the new threshing machines that had robbed them of hand-threshing employment.

Some of the character of dissatisfaction and insurrection across rural England is epitomised by the sorry saga of the

Pentrich Rebellion. In June 1817, a few dozen rural workers from the villages of Pentrich and South Wingfield in Derbyshire equipped themselves with pikes, scythes and guns, and marched off with the aim of mobilising disaffected villagers from across the North and Midlands. They believed that tens of thousands of others were poised to join them. The intention was for this massive force to assemble in Nottingham, which would become their regional base, then march down to London to overthrow the government.

The would-be revolutionaries were not aware that an informant was among them. The Derbyshire villagers got within a few miles of Nottingham, where they were scattered by twenty mounted troops from the city barracks.

The punishments for involvement in this and other local rural rebellions were swift and severe: imprisonment, executions and transportation to Australia. The reprisals fuelled bitterness that resonated down the years. The case of the Tolpuddle Martyrs became a much more famous focal point for mass protests in the provinces and in London. Half a dozen labourers from the small village of Tolpuddle in Dorset had been found guilty of secretly promoting a trade union for farm workers, and had been sentenced to transportation in 1834. The public and parliamentary success in obtaining their pardon and return from exile inspired the wider movement for workers' rights and unionisation.

As we have seen, from the eighteenth century onwards some major estate owners and industrialists undertook comprehensive, large-scale new village developments in the countryside. Very many more built small numbers of houses for workers in existing villages. Cottages for labourers were built here and there by farmers, brewers and millers on an ad hoc basis. Many villagers were tenants, and for many the house came with a job; losing employment as a farm labourer often meant instantly losing the family home. Few villagers could afford to buy their own house or buy a plot of land and build their own house.

However, against the backdrop of general dependence on landlords and industrialists, there were some early independent radical attempts to redefine villages and rural living completely. During the first half of the nineteenth century, Robert Owen and his adherents attempted to establish new village communities on co-operative, utopian principles. Owen had made the successful textile mill settlement of New Lanark in Scotland famous for an enlightened approach to workers' welfare.

The factory and village had actually been established by Richard Arkwright in partnership with Owen's father-in-law, David Dale. When he inherited the factory, Owen effectively operated it as a sort of social enterprise, investing profits back into infrastructure, amenities, welfare and education. The mill finally ceased production in 1968. It is a remarkable place, set in a picturesque Scottish valley, which has been rescued from dereliction and regenerated with a mix of heritage trust and commercial uses. The former cotton workers' housing is now managed by a housing association and the site is designated as a UNESCO World Heritage Site.

New Lanark provided inspiration for the later industrial villages described above. It also gave rise to experiments in communal, co-operative living by Robert Owen and his followers elsewhere. Instead of being built and run by an industrialist or landlord, these new farming and industrial villages would be built, owned and governed by their communities. They would be financed and sustained by the products of their own labour and any remaining profits would be shared.

Owen went to America where he established a new utopian community in Indiana. After returning from America, he bought Queenwood Farm in Hampshire, renting much of it out to generate income for a new community in the neighbourhood. He built a grand mansion, optimistically named Harmony Hall, to house the community, but the commune was a complete failure. Short of funds and riven by arguments and poor discipline, it quickly dissolved. In 1845 Harmony Hall became a Quaker School.

In fact, the handful of Owenite and copycat settlements that were founded in the wake of New Lanark all failed within a year or two, usually due to inexperience and internal disagreements. Committees of idealists had failed to match the technical expertise and business acumen of industrial entrepreneurs and farmers.

A few traces of the short-lived Owenite village near Manea, in the Cambridgeshire Fens, have recently been investigated by archaeological excavation. William Hodson, a farmer and radical, provided around 150 acres of his own land to set up the colony there in 1838. The community numbered around 100 people, and its members wore a green uniform and had their own newspaper, *The Working Bee*.

They set about building a village complex based around a large quadrangle, comprising cottages, a school, meeting rooms, kitchen, workshops and a windmill.

A quarry pit and brick kilns were constructed to make these buildings, but nobody else wanted the community's bricks or farm produce. No money came in, and just over two years from its foundation, the community dissolved. Apart from the flooded quarry pit, which was subsequently enlarged by commercial brickmaking, nothing is visible of the colony now. However, buried beneath the soil are scant foundations of buildings and the detritus left by inhabitants.

Infinitely more successful were the Land Settlement Association co-operative communities that were established nearly a century later. The LSA was a government scheme to resettle unemployed workers in the countryside, but it also drew on charitable funding. Settler families, often from the industrial North and Midlands, were given a new cottage, five acres of land, some livestock and a bit of agricultural tuition. From 1934 to 1939, twenty-five of these new rural communities were established across England, from Hampshire in the south to Cumbria in the north, and from Suffolk in the east to Gloucestershire in the west.

Astonishingly, by the time the LSA scheme was finally wound up in the 1980s, these places were said to be responsible for producing around forty per cent of all England's home-grown salad crop. They can still be identified today by the arrays of identical houses, large, allotment-like plots of land and acres of greenhouses.

The County Farms Estates are another influential, but not well known, start-up settlement scheme for would-be farmers. The plight of landless tenant farmers during the agricultural depression of the late nineteenth century was championed particularly by the Liberal MPs Joseph Chamberlain and Jesse Collings, who popularised the rallying slogan (and minimum solution) 'three acres and a cow'. The result was a series of Acts of Parliament that allowed county councils to buy up smallholdings and rent them out cheaply. During and immediately following the First World War, further Acts were passed specifically to favour the establishment of smallholdings for ex-servicemen.

From the 1920s until the 1970s, county councils owned farms, collectively, amounting to over 400,000 acres of agricultural land. It is about half that now, but around fifty county councils (or equivalent local authorities) still own and rent out county farms. Farmhouses across a county farm estate are often marked out by common paint schemes and signs, with similar dates and styles of construction signalling their common ownership, much like private estate properties, though usually much plainer with no architectural flourishes.

CHAPTER 7

BUILDING VILLAGE CHARACTER

Whether development of a historic village was structured and largely carried out in a single phase, or happened more gradually and haphazardly in episodes over a long period of time, all villages gain their own particular character. Individual character is not just a reflection of why a village originated and how it developed, but what it is built from. It is the combination of forms, materials and styles changing over time that give us charming, picturesque, neat villages, and untidy, striking and tough-looking villages. The wide variation in village heritage and character across the country is what makes England's villages so special.

Looking closely at the buildings in a village, the materials they use, their form and their date can give a good picture of how a village has changed over time. It is possible to get a feel for the various factors that influenced its growth and development, the periods when it boomed and periods of decline. Village buildings that were originally constructed for one use long ago may have found new purposes since, but some evidence of their former life usually remains to be spotted.

When exploring the history of a village, knowing the dates of individual buildings really helps. The problem is that only a few buildings in a village are likely to display their date of construction for all to see. Public and institutional buildings such as the village school, village hall and alms-houses will almost certainly be adorned with a date. Some of the older and more prominent private houses may also have a date displayed on them, either as a record created by their original builders, or retrospectively by proud later owners who have done their own research. The construction of particular buildings may be mentioned in family and village histories, or buried away in archives. Most buildings in a village, however, will not be dated quite so easily.

There are some written guides. The *Buildings of England* series of volumes first produced by Sir Nikolaus Pevsner (and known as 'Pevsners' in the trade) provide a commentary on significant historic buildings, county by county, parish by parish. For each building included, they give a date based on documented evidence and architectural styles, note archi-tects where known, and give a brief commentary on the main features. They are a useful tool for exploring places, though they tend to deal only with a few principal buildings in a village. The descriptive text often has a pithy, judgemental comment or two from the renowned professor of art and architecture.

Some buildings in almost every village in England are likely to be 'listed'. That is to say that they meet the required level of architectural and historic significance to be legally designated under the Planning (Listed Buildings and Conser-vation Areas) Act 1990. Grade II listed buildings have been determined to be of special interest; these comprise around 92 per cent of all listed buildings. Grade II* listed buildings are of more than special interest, and Grade I buildings are of exceptional interest. The latter comprise only about 2.5 per cent of all listed buildings.

All listed buildings have a published description and this will include a known or estimated date of construction and will often include descriptions of major addition and alteration phases. It is easy to look up list descriptions online at the National Heritage List for England. However, a list description is not a definitive history of a listed building. The origins of the 'list' lay in Second World War London. It was crucial to list and note especially important historic buildings that should be left standing and repaired, rather than simply demolished if damaged by enemy bombs. Wider surveys followed across England. Initially, inspectors toured the country, reference books and notebooks in hand, adding worthy buildings to the list.

Ideally they would make a comprehensive inspection of a building, inside and out, and then write a full description. Such was the pace of work, however, that buildings could be listed purely on external appearance, basically from what could be seen from a quick walk-by or cycle-by assessment. Consequently list descriptions, especially the older ones, can be quite cursory, only a few words, so they do not represent the last word on the history of a listed building.

More recently, thematic surveys have identified the best examples of particular types of under-represented buildings, or concentrated on areas whose buildings are particularly under threat, or buildings that are connected with important national events and anniversaries. For example, thousands of war memorials in villages and towns were assessed and listed as part of the commemoration of the centenaries of the beginning and end of the First World War.

Historic England (formerly known as English Heritage, but properly named the Historic Buildings and Monuments Commission for England) carries out the research, does the assessments and makes recommendations to the Secretary of State for both listing and scheduling. Broadly speaking, any building that dates before the eighteenth century and survives in anything like its original form will almost certainly be a candidate for listing. Buildings that date from the eighteenth century up to the middle of the nineteenth century are also likely to be candidates for listing.

After that, however, things get much more selective. A building constructed within the last few decades has not really had a chance to stand the test of time and prove its importance. Listing is not a historic building beauty contest, nor is it a popularity contest. Historic England publishes a series of selection guides for particular building types, which add to the basic principles and criteria for listing outlined by the Department for Digital, Culture, Media & Sport. Special interest organisations and members of the public can also put forward candidates for listing. This can now be done online by submitting a request and sufficient supporting information to Historic England.

There are now around 400,000 listed buildings across England, representing a vast array of historic building types and regional characteristics. Originally the list was packed with the obvious candidates such as stately homes, medieval churches and ancient manor houses, but as the range of what is considered to be important heritage has expanded, so too has the type of building and structure on the list. It is not too unusual to find that a village postbox and telephone kiosk are listed buildings, if they are suitably old and rare examples of their type.

Importantly, dwellings that are still lived in can be listed at all grades. Historic buildings can also be designated as scheduled monuments if they are deemed to be of national importance, but not if they are currently used as homes. Scheduling is highly selective and is usually reserved to protect ruined and disused ancient buildings, monuments and structures, rather than those still in use.

However, most old buildings in a village will neither be listed nor scheduled. Further information about particular historic buildings, both listed and non-listed, may be available in the local Historic Environment Record. The fact of the matter, however, is that most historic village buildings do not have any official notes written about them, so if you want to start to explore a village, it helps to be able to 'read' the architecture of its buildings. This means understanding how building materials, styles and fashions have changed over time.

TIMBER

Trees suitable for producing timber for construction grew across most of England in ancient times. Knowing the particular qualities of specific tree species and how to use them to best effect was a key part of village life for thousands of years. From the earliest prehistoric times, the majority of English homes were made from timber, but building styles changed under Roman rule and some new building materials were introduced.

The Romans had the labour (mostly forced labour) to quarry and prepare building stone and they could mass-produce bricks and tiles. However, despite widely employing masonry construction for their higher status homes and public buildings (such as villas, bathhouses, amphitheatres and temples), most Romano-British people would still have lived and worked in buildings that were either wholly or partly timber-framed. Stone rubble may also have been used for footings, or low walls on which a timber superstructure was built.

Archaeological excavations across England have revealed plenty of evidence of buildings of this type. A full-scale, high-status Roman home of this hybrid construction type was experimentally built at the site of the Roman town of Wroxeter in 2010. Wandering around this building gives you a very good idea how Roman villas, farmsteads and other buildings were put together and their finished appearance. But real Roman timber work only survives in buried, wet archaeological contexts, and usually belongs to structures such as wells, bridges and wharfs, which were wet to begin with. In a very few places, excavation has revealed the preserved timber remains of Roman timber warehouses, barrack buildings and houses, but don't expect to find preserved Roman woodwork on most archaeological sites, or embedded in standing village buildings today.

After the Romans ceased to administer Britain and their centralised economy broke down, it would have been extremely difficult to finance and construct new stone buildings on any scale, or even repair those that were still standing. Building in stone generally required much more preparation, a greater range of trades, a bigger effort for haulage, and therefore a much larger investment in time and money than building in timber. Many parts of England simply do not have good, easily quarried sources of building stone.

The incoming Anglo-Saxons therefore pragmatically built in timber, because wood was still in relatively plentiful supply across England. These Germanic peoples, who were well used to working with the woodlands of north-west Europe, found timber a more convenient construction material for their smaller-scale buildings and settlements. Apart from some major churches and some defensive works, and a few surviving fragments of Roman buildings, most English villagers from the fifth to the twelfth centuries would not normally encounter any substantial stone or brick buildings.

Sadly, but inevitably, these early timber buildings, once everywhere, are now known only through archaeological excavation. The preserved timber remains of buried Viking houses have been excavated in York and elsewhere. However, only at the Church of St Andrew at Greensted, in Essex, will you find Anglo-Saxon period structural timbers in a standing village building, or any building, anywhere in England.

In the centuries after the Norman Conquest, grand cathedrals and minsters were built or rebuilt on a massive scale.

Former timber and earth castles became the massive stone edifices that can still be seen today, and new stone village churches sprang up everywhere. Nevertheless, everyday buildings in most parts of the country were still timber-framed. Medieval England was largely built of wood, straw, reed and mud.

It wasn't just any wood though. Oak was the best building material for constructing timber frames, though other wood (such as chestnut, ash or even poplar) could be used for structural work, and other species (such as elm, beech and hazel) were used for elements such as rafters, joists and floorboards and infilling panels between the main frame. As the centuries rolled on, localised sources of good timber diminished, so smaller timbers and inferior soft wood was increasingly used for building. Even in the medieval period, fir timbers were shipped to England from the Baltic, and the use of fir increased from the late seventeenth century onwards as fewer large, suitable English trees were available.

Timber-framed buildings are by no means uniform in form and style across England. There is much regional variation. 'Cruck' frames look like the most primordial form of timber framing and are associated with the earliest medieval buildings, though the construction method lasted throughout the sixteenth century. Cruck buildings are formed from pairs of huge, curving timbers (*cruck blades*) that meet at an apex to create an arch, a bit like those arches made from whale jawbones that can be seen as monuments in some former whaling towns. Sometimes cruck frames rise from the ground, sometimes they are propped on low walls or stone supports projecting from high in a wall, and more than one jointed timber can be used to form a cruck blade.

The rest of a cruck-framed building is constructed off the basic tunnel of arches formed by the paired cruck blades. Therefore cruck construction is usually hidden from external view. Occasionally you can see it in gable ends, though often you have to go into a building, and preferably right into the roof space, to find emphatic evidence of cruck construction. Cruck buildings may once have been far more widely and evenly distributed across England than they are now, but today they are almost exclusively found in the west half of the country, the south-west and the north-east.

Timber frames that primarily employ vertical posts and horizontal beams to form box-like structures, rather than an arch-like cruck frame, can be found right across England. 'Box frame' or 'post and truss' buildings are formed from bays defined by the spacing between the principal load-bearing posts. These posts support main triangular roof trusses on the latter type. The basic timber frame can be braced by straight diagonal and curving timbers. Lesser timbers called studs (vertical timbers) and rails (horizontal timbers) form the panels between the main structural posts and beams.

In the west of the country, and in some parts of the south-east, the panels formed by timber studs between the structural frame tend to be square in shape. Across the south-east and East Anglia, however, the panels between timber studs are very narrow. This is called close studding. Close studding is not confined to the south and east of England. It can also be found in the west of England and in the north alongside square-panelled buildings. The panels in a timber-framed building are infilled with smaller vertical timbers (staffs or staves), around which thin, pliable lengths of wood (wattle or spilt laths) are woven. This is then daubed with mud and straw and covered with a lime plaster. Sometimes brick (brick nogging) or even stone can be used for the panel infill rather than wattle and daub.

There is a lot of debate about the original external appearance of medieval and early modern timber-framed buildings. It seems fairly certain that accentuating timber framing by painting timbers black and the panels between them white is largely a nineteenth-century invention. Nevertheless, some timber framing was very showy indeed and was obviously intended to be seen very clearly. The external appearance of the grandest timber-framed buildings in villages in the north and west of England, with their chevrons, herringbone, cusps, quatrefoils, up-swinging and down-swinging curves, took public-facing overachievement in timber-work panels to another level entirely.

The wealthiest timber building owners took other opportunities to display purchasing power and timber craftsmanship. External posts, brackets, 'barge boards' (wide planks under the eaves of gables), window and door surrounds, were often covered with intricately carved designs. Even plain close studding using robust timbers demonstrates that ample money was available to purchase plenty of the best quality wood.

Inside medieval and post-medieval houses, beams and joists had their downward-facing sharp corners taken off to create angled edges (flat chamfers) that were kinder on the eyes and on bumped heads. Carpenters would also carve more elaborate curved and multi-faceted chamfer shapes, and carve elaborate decorations into the surfaces of beams, brackets and bressummers (load-bearing beams) above fire-places. The most lavish designs could include floral patterns such as vine leaves and Tudor roses, mythical creatures, biblical and legendary figures.

The most elaborate woodworking indicates the highest status rooms, either those that were more public-facing, such as halls, or the best private chambers of the household. Servants' quarters, kitchens and back rooms of all kinds have much plainer woodwork. The pinnacle of this kind of lavish decorative wood carving, inside and out, was in the sixteenth century.

The external timbers of the Guildhall of Corpus Christi in Lavenham, built around 1530, are carved with detailed geometric designs and figures, and the interior joists and beams of the ceilings in the best rooms are deeply roll-moulded. The building used and wasted far more oak than was necessary structurally, which sent the message that money was no barrier to the merchants of Lavenham in achieving the best possible effect.

The earliest medieval timber-framed buildings are far more plain. They usually have large panels between timbers and often large upward and downward curving bracing timbers across panels. In many cases entire facades, both timbers and panels between timbers, would have been washed over with a lime-based coating to fill gaps and improve weathering. Alternatively, especially as the quality of timber declined, timber-framed buildings were rendered with thick coats of lime-based plaster, like a generous covering of icing on a cake. The plaster was not always a natural cream colour, but may have had earthy pigments applied to make it brownish, yellowish or reddish.

In Suffolk and Essex, this plaster cladding is often decorated by patterns in relief in a technique known as pargetting. All sorts of designs, from simple swirls, combed lines and dots, to vines, floral arrays and even cartoon-like scenes were applied like decoration on an iced cake. The seventeenth century was the heyday for pargetting, but it was replicated later and is still occasionally carried out on plastered modern buildings in the region.

Sometimes fake stonework joints were etched into wet plaster to make an old, timber-framed building appear more expensive and up to date. Weatherboarding (thin horizontal timbers joined together on edge, or slightly lapped over each other) and vertical hanging clay tiles also could be used to clad timber-framed buildings. These were especially popular wall claddings in the south-east of England. Many timber-framed buildings were later reclad in brick, or even rendered in cement in a misguided attempt to make them more resilient and modern-looking. Sometimes it is possible to see fragments of a former timber frame suspended in brick cladding, no longer really supporting the structure of the building.

Jetties (overhanging storeys or gables) are a common feature of historic timber-framed buildings. Recladding in

brick, plastering and modernising their appearance generally, often included bringing forward the line of the timber
frame under-storey to align with the jetty above. This created
a new, uniform facade which was more fashionable in the
eighteenth century. Over time, the lower timber structural
elements of timber-framed buildings may suffer decay, or
come to be replaced by substantial alterations and rebuilding,
leaving the upper part of the original timber building perching
on more modern fabric beneath. This can lead to the curious
phenomenon of finding a medieval roof *in situ* happily sitting
on top of a substantially Georgian or Victorian house, which
has been built beneath.

Even when it is entirely hidden from view, a timber-
framed building enveloped in later cladding can be given
away by its external appearance. Timber shrinks and warps
as it ages and this can pull the frame well out of true, creating
a crooked-looking building. It is usually in no danger of
falling down; in fact, the timber frames can become stronger
with age as the timber shrinks and the joints between timbers
tighten. The contortions a timber-framed building has gone
through over time will often show in the warping and bulging
of its plastered or otherwise clad walls.

The appearance of the apex of roofs is another clue to
hidden, ancient timber framing. If the ridge line sags before
rising up again at regular intervals (much like telephone
wires between poles) it may indicate that the building has
stout, old main roof trusses, which have stood firm while the
lesser timbers (rafters and purlins) between them have flexed
and bowed.

Looking at the timbers close up also gives a clue as to the age of a building. Before machine saws and mass production of timber, large tree trunks had to be either split with wedges or cut by huge hand saws. One method was to suspend the tree trunk over a deep, long trench. One person stood in the pit and drew the saw through its down stroke, the other stood on top and pushed and guided the path of the saw. Some towns and villages still have a Sawpit Road (Lane, Close or Hill) that recalls this feature. It was laborious to saw timber before mechanical saws, so it was often roughly shaped and dressed with axes and adzes sufficient to achieve a basic function.

This is particularly the case where there was little spare money or little point in showing off woodwork, such as in agricultural buildings, or where timber was intended to be covered anyway. Thin, weedy, wobbly-looking timber studs now displayed on the front of an old timber-framed house may indicate that it was originally intended to be fully plastered.

The Industrial Revolution ushered in waterwheel- and steam-powered sawmills so timbers could be finished in the more uniform, square or rectangular sections that we are used to seeing in builders' merchants and DIY stores today. Generally speaking, if the surfaces and cross-section of timbers in a village building look square-sectioned and regular, they are likely to be eighteenth century or later. If a timber beam or post is large and a bit wobbly, it is likely to be older.

Quite a lot of fakery has been employed since the late nineteenth century to make timber beams look older. Chipping lumps out of a sawn beam, as an afterthought to rusticate it, never achieves quite the same authentic look produced by a carpenter who has tried efficiently to make an irregular piece of wood acceptably fit for purpose.

'These houses look like they are about to fall down. Do people actually live in them now?' I was asked once by an incredulous American tourist, as he peered into somebody's living room, only to see the occupants sitting on their sofa watching a very large, up-to-date flat screen TV.

We were in Lavenham in Suffolk, which has the best collection of ancient timber-framed buildings that you will find anywhere on the planet. Only it is not a collection, which implies the buildings are museum pieces. These timber buildings are as much part of the living fabric of the place now as they have been for centuries; and are more desirable than ever as homes, fetching eye-watering prices.

A good quality, timber-framed building will last for many centuries if it is looked after properly. The medieval Knights Templar, who built the magnificent barns at their Cressing Temple estate centre in Essex, did a splendid job. They were clearly building for longevity. However, they could not have imagined that these buildings would not only outlive their illustrious order, but would still be thriving in the twenty-first century. The Barley Barn was built around 1220 and is thought to be the oldest timber-framed barn in the world. The Wheat Barn is only a little younger, dating to around 1280.

These barns, situated between the villages of White Notley and Cressing, are among the ancient Wonders of the

World in my view. They are historical and archaeological monuments in one sense, but even more importantly they continue to function as purposeful buildings, hosting a wide variety of activities and events.

New 'green' oak timbers naturally age to a lovely silvery colour over the years. Internal timbers become blackened where they have been exposed to the smoke of open fires; in roof timbers, this is a clue to the presence of a hall that was open to the rafters. Ancient oak timbers often look worm-eaten, decayed and cracked on the surface, but they actually harden and become more resilient with age. Their hearts become almost impenetrable even to modern saws, and burrowing beetles can't get far into them. I have seen ancient, original timber needlessly removed and replaced because it looked a bit shabby on the surfaces, when in fact its load-bearing capacity had hardly been reduced at all.

Old timber-framed buildings, at least those that have stood the test of time, tend to have been well over-engineered by their original builders. Theoretically it is possible to get a massive crane and pick up a traditional timber-framed building from one single point of suspension and place it down somewhere else without it falling apart. It would hang together much better than a stone or brick building, because it has been designed and built as a giant, interlocking 3D jigsaw. In fact, this theory has been tested occasionally, because some large, historic timber-framed buildings have been jacked up and moved as one piece, or have been dismantled into manageable sections and re-erected elsewhere.

The problems occur when timbers get perpetually damp and cannot breathe. If timber has been clad in something that traps moisture, like a cement covering, then rot will set in. Despite their inherent resilience, it is extremely rare to find substantial remains of timber-framed village buildings dating to earlier than around 1400. Most that survived fires and decay were swept away in a period from the later sixteenth century to the later seventeenth century, which came to be called the 'Great Rebuilding'. The landscape historian W.G. Hoskins coined the term, and though the causes and effect of this apparent building boom have been questioned (and its much later arrival in the north of England has been pointed out), substantial timber-framed buildings of this era are much more common than from earlier periods.

Many timber-framed buildings of this era were themselves swept away by more fashionable brick buildings in the eighteenth century and nineteenth century. In fact, perversely, the survival of lots of timber buildings in a village can hint at a period of stagnation or decline from the seventeenth century onwards. They can indicate that there was little money to undertake new development and rebuilding and that people simply made do with the old buildings they already had.

We now think of English villages with an abundance of timber-framed buildings as very special indeed; exploring them is a delight. Places such as Lavenham and Kersey in Suffolk, Pembridge and Weobley in Herefordshire, and Smarden and Biddenden in Kent, give an impression of transporting you back to sixteenth-century or seventeenth-century

England. The first English villages in America would have looked similar.

Timber-frame construction became much less used for homes during the eighteenth and nineteenth centuries and was generally reserved for lower status buildings like barns and sheds. Stone and brick were preferred for higher status buildings. But it has never died out. There are many modern homes and other buildings that take a new approach to a very old tradition.

STONE AND EARTH

There is a tale told about the formidable early geologist Dean William Buckland (died 1856). It is said that one very dark night riding back to London from the country, he and a friend became hopelessly lost. Buckland dismounted his horse, scooped up some earth, sniffed it and exclaimed 'Uxbridge!', after which they were able to navigate back to London. You do not need Buckland's finely tuned geological nose to appreciate changing local character. With a bit of understanding about English regional building traditions and materials, it should be possible to arrive blindfolded in many historic villages, take the blinkers off, look around, and almost instantly know in which part of the country they are located.

The geological bedrock of a region has a huge influence on the character and appearance of its villages, not only because it forms the basis of the landscape and environment in which a village has functioned, but also because until modern times, most village buildings were constructed from the materials that were readily to hand in the neigh-bourhood. Ancient environments that persisted through geological time spans dictated how bedrock was laid down in the first place. Subsequent erosion and deposition have determined where rock outcrops, or is redeposited. In very broad terms, bands of bedrock tend to run south-west to north-east across England, the oldest in the west overlapped by the youngest towards the east.

Limestones were laid down in the north-west of England over 300 million years ago. Millstone Grit, a hard sandstone over 300 million years old, is found in the Peak District and Pennines in the north of England. Granite, very hard igneous rock formed in the molten earth core, pushed up through sedimentary sandstones and siltstones to outcrop in Devon and Cornwall around 295 to 270 million years ago.

A belt of limestones and sandstones (the oldest of which are around 250 million years old) extends from Somerset, through Northamptonshire, and up towards York. Sand-stones are also found in the north-west. Adjacent and south of this limestone and sandstone belt, a band of Jurassic clays, around 150 to 170 million years old, runs through Oxfordshire, Bedfordshire, Cambridgeshire and up to Lincolnshire.

A great mass of chalk, laid down as a sediment in warm Cretaceous seas 66 to 100 million years ago, extends from Dorset, across to Kent, up through Norfolk, and into east Yorkshire. The chalk rubble used to build the prehistoric burial mounds around Stonehenge is related to the White Cliffs of Dover, the white band in the famous stripy cliffs at

Hunstanton in Norfolk, and the 'Drinking Dinosaur' rock formation at Flamborough Head.

Bedrock in many parts of England is overlain by much younger 'superficial' deposits of mixed rubble, clays, sands and gravels, which have been churned and pushed by glaciers to their final resting places. Gravel and sand has also been deposited by fast-flowing rivers, whereas fine silt and clay was laid down by slower-moving water in lakes, estuaries and periodic incursions by the sea. Stagnant watery environments give rise to peat and moss, which grows organically from dead vegetation. These superficial geological deposits generally make for poor buildings in their own right, but can be mixed usefully with other materials as aggregates and infill.

Around 2000 years ago, communities on the Land's End peninsula turned their back on the long-established prehistoric tradition of building largely timber-framed roundhouses and instead used the abundant and easily accessible hard local stone to build new stone houses. Entirely stone-built villages like Chysauster and Carn Euny were constructed. Only in the most stone-rich areas of England, such as the moors of Devon and Cornwall, upland Cumbria and Northumberland, were substantially stone-built prehistoric and Roman period native houses and villages built.

The very widespread use of local stone and occasional use of more exotic, imported building stone in Roman buildings across England has been attested in the archaeological excavation of thousands of villas, bathhouses, forts and temples. No totally complete and roofed stone Roman buildings survive in England, though there are some impressive standing masonry structures. The villas at Chedworth in Gloucestershire, Lullingstone in Kent and Bignor in West Sussex, and the walls of forts in places such as Portchester in Hampshire, Pevensey in East Sussex and Burgh Castle in Norfolk, give a good impression of how accomplished the Romans were in constructing stone buildings.

These coastal forts of the Saxon Shore, as it was known, acted as ports, supply depots, garrisons and settlements and were heavily defended from the increasing attacks by raiders from north-west Europe by a strong wall circuit. The walls at these places still stand several metres high, nearly to their full original height. The Romans had a very strong mortar called *opus signinum*, which was pinkish in colour and had ground-up clay tile fragments and other inclusions thrown in to strengthen the mix. Bands of thin ceramic bricks or tiles were often employed as levelling courses, and they give a pleasing decorative banding effect.

The village that was built on the rocky headland at Tintagel, in Cornwall, was exceptional in many ways, but so far it is unique in having evidence of substantial stone buildings of early Anglo-Saxon period date. Elsewhere, apart from a few defensive structures, the only stone-built Anglo-Saxon buildings were churches. It is notable that many of the earliest Anglo-Saxon churches are associated with former Roman sites, whose ruins provided handy 'quarries' of building material. Later in the Anglo-Saxon period, shortly before the Norman Conquest, stone churches became more common, but timber was still preferred for most Anglo-Saxon buildings.

The Normans were much keener on building in stone, and were able to transport it considerable distances for their prestige building programme in the decades after the Conquest. Castles, cathedrals and abbeys showed off the Normans' architectural flair and solidly reminded the English that they were here to stay. Creamy white limestone was shipped from Caen in Normandy and used alongside the best stone that the English regions had to offer.

The British Geological Survey states that historically around 3000 different natural stone types have been used for building in the United Kingdom. Some of the stone was very specific to a small area, lending its villages a very distinctive character. Other types were broadly similar across regions, or across the country. The wonderful golden and yellow-silvery glow of Cotswold villages in the sunshine is closely replicated in villages in parts of Northamptonshire and Lincolnshire, because the local ironstones and limestones in these places have similar properties. You could almost get away with swapping some buildings between villages such as Castle Combe in Wiltshire and Collyweston in east Northamptonshire without many people noticing.

The granite used to build churches in Cornwall, such as the fifteenth-century parish church of St Neot, was not quarried but simply hauled off the moors and split and cut into unusually large blocks. Granite was not a stone that was easy to cut in pre-industrial times, so it was worked as little as possible; only in the nineteenth century were granite quarries opened in Cornwall and Devon. Their granite was widely used in the region for industrial buildings and structures such as bridges, harbours and lighthouses, where its unyielding qualities were particularly valued.

Back in Tintagel, the village's Old Post Office is built of the local stone and slate, just like the nearby Anglo-Saxon period buildings. The Old Post Office is in fact a small medieval manor house dating to the late fourteenth century. It started as a simple three-room, single-storey dwelling, with one room used as a livestock barn, but it was extended and given a stone slate roof in the sixteenth century.

Barnack stone, named after the village near Stamford on the Cambridgeshire, Northamptonshire and Lincolnshire borders, was 'freestone'; that is, it could be cut in any direction without fear of exposing bedding planes to weathering. It was durable, highly prized and used extensively for architectural features and dressings, such as quoins, in buildings across the wider region and further afield. The Barnack quarries were largely worked out around 1450, and the quarry pits and spoil heaps of the former quarries, 'The Hills and Holes' as they are known locally, can be seen adjacent to the village. Barnack's parish church is a fine example of the use of this local product, and has a rare, early eleventh-century Anglo-Saxon stone tower.

Many traditional sources of building stone are no longer available today. Hundreds of small quarries were worked out or became economically non-viable as cheaper mass building materials came on to the market. Many old quarries have become landfill sites or have been built on, or have become important nature reserves, as at Barnack. Ancient mounds of excavated spoil or water-filled quarries that have not been touched for years can generate interesting wildlife that can't be found elsewhere.

You will find overgrown large hollows, pits and scoops from former quarrying in the landscape around many villages. Even stone quarries that remain open today may not be capable of producing the best building stone any longer. A mason, scrutinising a newly exposed seam of stone that we hoped to use for the repair of a historic building, once said to me despairingly, 'They got the best stuff out in medieval times.' Many quarries now blast stone out with explosives and crush it up for hardcore, rather than painstakingly excavating it and cutting it to make building stone.

Some parts of England have poor building stone, or stone that is hard to extract and limited in supply. Good building stone was imported to one place from another in pre-industrial times, but this was difficult, time-consuming and expensive. In those circumstances, stone would be used sparingly, for the most prominent buildings, and those required to be particularly durable.

The absence of good building stone in many areas of England, particularly parts of the Midlands, East Anglia and the south-east, partly explains the persistence of timber framing traditions in these regions well into the seventeenth century. Stone imported into these areas was used highly selectively. That is why an otherwise timber-framed village might have only one or two stone-built structures or buildings, such as a church, castle or bridge. These regions also adopted brick building earlier than others, before the end of the medieval period.

Many villages are characterised by other materials that were employed when neither good stone nor good timber were abundant. Well into the nineteenth century, many villagers across England were quite used to constructing houses, barns and boundary walls from a mix of earth, straw, pebbles and animal dung. 'Cob' construction did not require much structural timber, and might use only some rubble stone foundations apart from this unpromising sounding mix. Cob walls had to be thoroughly covered with plaster to keep them weatherproof, otherwise a householder would see their home being eroded away by the rain and ultimately find themselves with a great big pile of mud, sticks and poo, rather than a house. If looked after properly, however, cob buildings will last for hundreds of years.

The thick plaster covering means that it can be difficult to spot an old cob building. However, cob walls have to be very wide, they are usually not entirely straight, and if any plaster is missing, the material beneath will be immediately obvious. Cob buildings are often thatched because they are not well suited to supporting very heavy stone slate and tiled roofs. Devon has the largest concentration of cob buildings, but they can still be found in many other parts of England.

Clunch (chalk blocks) makes an adequate construction material where no better stone is available, but is vulnerable to erosion by the elements and is best when protected with plaster or used internally. However, lots of chalk clunch walls have lasted for hundreds of years in village buildings in the south and east of England. Seams of flint are often exposed in chalk deposits, and this makes for a paradoxical mix of flint cobbles and chalk rubble in walls: the almost indestructible alongside the highly vulnerable. Knapping flint nodules into small square blocks became an industry and a fine art in Norfolk especially; they were used for areas of walling and in chequered panelling alongside stone and brick to great decorative effect.

If there was no other consistently good stone to hand, village builders would use any stones and pebbles lying around. Picking large stones from the path of the plough and piling them at the edge of fields was one of those activities that kept idle village hands occupied if there was little else they could do. Fieldstone rubble, a random mix of stones of different shapes, sizes and geological origins brought from all over the place by glaciers and ancient rivers, can be seen in otherwise stone-impoverished areas as a filler material.

Even churches that have very fine stone tracery for windows and doors, and precisely cut and dressed stone blocks in vulnerable and showy areas (such as corners and parapets) may have large areas of walling made of fieldstone rubble. There would be no attempt to cut and shape it, and lesser effort put into trying to achieve regular courses. Beach cobbles and pebbles are used in the same way in coastal village buildings.

The effort taken to quarry, cut, transport and shape quality building stone means that it is often recycled for use in other buildings (or indeed the same building) when its original purpose has gone. You will find large amounts of reused building stone in churches that have been significantly remodelled over the years. You will also find good stone reused in buildings and walls in villages that once had a castle or an abbey. Redundant and ruinous grand buildings were often bought and sold simply as quarries for their building stone and timber, or robbed by villagers when nobody was looking.

Clues to spotting reused stone from earlier buildings include seeing good quality ashlars (regular, smooth-faced rectangular blocks) that originally would have been joined by thin beds of mortar in regimented interlocking courses, instead used in very loose courses, or haphazardly tumbled together as if they were rubble. They might find themselves jumbled alongside varied, irregular stones of other types bedded in thick mortar joints. It is common to find fragments of decorative stone that once formed parts of windows or doors lumped in among the rest.

Field walls did not necessarily need a mortar to bond the courses of stone (drystone walls), but walls for buildings generally needed some kind of bonding material, even if this was simply clay or earth. Lime mortar was made from a mix of lime, sand and water, sometimes with other natural additives. It is made from burnt limestone, and this was also used in agriculture as an alkaline dressing for fields. Lime manufacture was once very widespread across the country, and place names recalling lime kilns can be found in many English villages.

Lime mortar was used almost universally until the introduction of cement mortars from the start of the nineteenth century onwards. Lime mortar tends to be a creamy colour.

Cement mortars are generally much harder, greyer and less permeable. They work much less sympathetically with historic stonework, both aesthetically and mechanically. Cement doesn't allow moisture to escape through joints between masonry, so it pushes through the masonry itself, weakening it from within. Misguided repointing with cement mortars has ruined many historic buildings of old stone and brick construction.

BRICK

Brickmaking was introduced to Britain by the Romans. They made tiles or thin bricks for walling, tiles for roofs, and box-sectioned pipes for heating systems. Prehistoric communities in England could make excellent pots from fired clay, but never bothered to make bricks. The Anglo-Saxons were also uninterested in making bricks and tiles, but they did salvage and reuse these Roman products in some of their masonry buildings.

The Anglo-Saxon village church at Brixworth in North-amptonshire incorporates reused Roman brick, and quarrying old Roman buildings was a habit that continued into the Norman period. The Norman tower of St Albans Cathedral is built of brick obtained from the ruins of the adjacent Roman town of *Verulamium*. St Botolph's Priory in Colchester, built from around 1100, uses a huge quantity of Roman brick recycled from the ruins of *Camulodunum*.

Not far from Colchester, the Church of Holy Trinity at Bradwell-juxta-Coggeshall also reuses some Roman tile in its flint and pebble rubble walls, but this village church is especially important for incorporating some of the earliest bricks made in England after the Roman period. In the middle of the twelfth century, a brickworks was established nearby for Coggeshall Abbey. The thin bricks it produced can also be seen in quoins and window surrounds of the Church of St Nicholas in the hamlet of Little Coggeshall. This church, built around 1225, was the former gatehouse chapel of the abbey.

Building in brick didn't catch on widely across England until after the medieval period. It was used only in a few regions, and then only for prestige buildings. Villagers in north Lincolnshire, near the Humber, would have looked on with interest as the new brickwork of Thornton Abbey gatehouse went up in the 1380s and surely must have been impressed with the results. Villagers in Tattershall further south in the county would have seen Ralph Cromwell's magnificent brick castle take shape in the 1430s. Forty years later, the village of Kirby Muxloe in Leicestershire gained Lord Hastings' brick castle.

More early brick buildings were found in towns and cities, but on the whole, they would still be seen as a novelty in English villages over the course of the next two or three hundred years. In stone-rich areas, early brickmaking didn't offer huge advantages over continuing to use local stone. In areas where the timber-frame tradition persisted, bricks would be used only to make chimneys, and clay tiles would be increasingly used for roofs to lessen the risk of fires.

Bricks, like stone, were bulky and heavy goods to transport before the age of canals and steam. Happily, however, the raw material suitable for brickmaking, both clay bedrock and clayey superficial deposits, can be found across much of England. Therefore when huge brick building projects were required, such as for the new grand country houses of the sixteenth, seventeenth and eighteenth centuries, pits would be opened for that purpose as close as possible to where they would be used. Temporary brickyards would be built alongside the pits.

The extracted clay was allowed to weather in heaps to break down the clumps, and then stones had to be picked out; adding just enough water made a clay paste that was suitable for pressing into wooden moulds. The bricks then had to dry out before being stacked with combustible material in large 'clamps' which were then fired.

The whole process was a bit hit and miss: too much water, the bricks would deform before firing or explode during firing. Stones in the clay could heat up and crack a brick from within. Too much heat and the bricks would discolour and fuse together; too little heat and the bricks wouldn't fire properly and remain too soft. Even though the unfired ('green') bricks started off the same size, the variations in the clay and inclusions would lead to variable shrinkage when fired. It was impossible to achieve even heat throughout the clamp and there was a lot of wastage.

The character of the pre-industrial age brickmaking process means that the earliest English bricks generally are small, thin and irregular in shape, and variable in their shades of colour. If you look closely, you will find stones in them. Because early bricks were not consistent in shape and size, they would be used rather like small, rough blocks of stone, laid in courses separated by thick mortar bedding and joints.

Most early brick was red in colour, which was a product of iron oxide in the clay. Variable amounts of iron oxide and variations of heat in firing produced different shades, including a very dark red 'blue' brick, or over-fired ends of bricks. These were sometimes specially selected to make diamond-shaped patterns (diaper work) in walls. A lack of iron oxide, or the inclusion of chalky material, produced a white or yellowish brick. The Gault Clay of the chalky area that runs up towards eastern England produced yellowish bricks.

A pattern of bricklaying called 'Flemish bond' was introduced in the seventeenth century. This required bricks to be laid in courses of alternate headers (the end of the brick) and stretchers (the length of a brick). The next course was offset so that a header always appeared over the centre of the stretcher below. Prior to that English bond, whereby alternate courses of headers and stretchers were laid, was considered to be the optimum method. It was very strong, but consumed a lot of bricks.

There were other bonds, such as English garden wall bond, which saw several courses of stretchers used between header courses. Rat trap bond used bricks on edge, which covered more space but was not strong. Stretcher bond just comprises courses of stretcher with no headers. These bonds were considered inferior and primarily used in lower cost cottages, outbuildings, agricultural buildings and garden walls. Looking at the pattern of brick courses in the wall of a village building can tell you something about its status. In many buildings the best bricks and bond was reserved for the public-facing front, while cheaper bricklaying was used at the sides and back. Stretcher bond is used everywhere today, and this is just one reason why modern brick buildings don't look anywhere near as elegant as the brick buildings at the height of the craft in the eighteenth century and nineteenth century.

From the eighteenth century onwards, architects and homeowners wanted regular bricks, laid in very neat, tightly jointed courses. During the early eighteenth century, legislation was introduced to regularise the size of bricks, setting minimum acceptable sizes. Then in 1784, a brick tax was introduced that increased the cost of each brick. Resourceful brickmakers decided to get around this by drastically increasing the size of their bricks so that fewer were needed in a building. This trend lasted into the first few years of the nineteenth century and therefore these oversized bricks can help to date a building.

Improvements were made to the brickmaking process over time, most crucially in the introduction of different, specialised and efficient kilns. After the middle of the nineteenth century, railways were able to transport vast quantities of bricks around the country. There was a huge demand for brick within the growing towns and cities, and efficient mass production concentrated in fewer, larger brickyards lowered the cost of bricks. Mass-produced, machine-pressed bricks produced from the late nineteenth century onwards were precisely made, with crisp edges and uniform in consistency and colour. These new production methods took much of the cost, but a lot of the character, out of brick buildings in English villages.

It wasn't only the colours and textures of brick that varied throughout English regions, but also brick building styles. For example, circular brick oast houses for drying hops, with their conical tiled roofs surmounted by movable cowls, characterise many Kent villages. The crow-stepped gables and rounded scroll 'Dutch' gables in the east of England reflect the proximity and influence of the Netherlands. In the Victorian and Edwardian period, there was a revival of earlier brick building styles that matched the fashion for reinterpreting old English architecture generally. Notable new village buildings, such as schools, chapels and village halls, were built from new brick in these retro fashions.

Brickyards are noted on old Ordnance Survey maps and remembered in village street names such as 'Brick Pit Lane' and 'Brick Kiln Lane'. Like the remains of small stone quarries, partially back-filled former brick pits can still be seen as hollows in the ground in land around many villages.

ROOFS

From prehistoric times, throughout the medieval period and beyond, vegetation was used as a roof covering for village buildings of all types. Reed thatch, turf, long straw thatch and heather thatch carried on being used for some lower status buildings, such as humble cottages and barns, long after other materials became available. These types of inherently permeable roof coverings usually required a steep-pitched roof to ensure that rainwater would run off as quickly as possible.

The Romans introduced clay roof tiles. A distinctive inter-locking combination of flat tiles (*tegula*) and semi-circular sectioned curved tiles (*imbrex*) that can be seen on Italian buildings today, the parallel rows of curved tiles run down the roof slope. Roman tile fragments litter many Roman settlement sites. The Romans also used natural stone slates that were available in some English regions. These were heavy materials and required substantial roof structures and walls. Stone flagstones and slates were also used again from medieval times onwards in the same regions. They were first used in substantial village buildings, such as manor houses, and then became more commonly used in other buildings as time went on.

Just like building stone and brick, the regional and local geological character and properties of the stone dictate the character of the roofs. The heavy, grey sandstone flag-stones of village buildings in the Pennines contrast with the smaller, lighter, golden-coloured limestone slate roofs found in the Cotswolds. The grey slate from the Delabole quar-ries in Cornwall contrasts with the light sandstone slates of Gloucestershire, Herefordshire and Shropshire.

Lead has been widely used as a roof covering for church roofs and other major buildings since the medieval period. It can be laid in great flat sheets, or moulded around corners, and detailing. It is a very versatile and resilient material that can last for hundreds of years if not abused. Clay tiles were reintroduced in the medieval period, and replaced thatched roofs as first-choice material on timber-framed homes in the south and east of England in the sixteenth century. Small rectangular tiles were pegged in place in regular, overlapping courses.

Early rectangular 'plain tiles' are not flat, but are gently cambered in both directions. Like stone slates, old plain tiles have much colour variation and give roofs a characterful textured effect, quite unlike the unnervingly smooth, monochrome synthetic tiled roofs of the modern era. Pantiles, with a curving S-shaped profile, were introduced to England from the Netherlands in the seventeenth century and remain popular along the eastern side of England and Scotland.

The orangey-red-coloured wavy pantile roofs of North Norfolk coastal villages, such as Brancaster and Cley, are matched by the roofs of North Yorkshire villages such as Robin Hood's Bay and Staithes. These are villages with distinctive regional characters that look quite different in other respects. Pantiles in particular could be laid on much flatter pitched roofs than thatch without fear of leaks. It is often possible to spot buildings in villages that were once thatched but have been re-covered with tiles or slates, because their roofs will have an unnecessarily steep pitch. Sometimes roof structures have been replaced with flatter pitches, leaving higher, pointy gables at either end.

Welsh slate became very widely used across England from the middle of the nineteenth century onwards. This flat, grey rectangular slate can be a real giveaway for the date of construction of a village building, its rebuilding or its extension, especially when seen in combination with other building materials. Old Welsh slate makes for charming roofs, but like mass-produced brick, it is a real indicator of the industrial age replacement of traditional, regional materials by imported materials. Its use marks the beginning of the erosion of much old, localised village character and the loss of traditional craft skills in the modern era.

CHAPTER 8

SOME MORE TYPICAL VILLAGE BUILDINGS

There are some buildings that are found in almost every village. Homes, manor houses, churches and other medieval buildings have been introduced in previous chapters, but here are some more buildings that help define village character after the medieval period, and without which no English village is really complete.

VILLAGE PUBS

For many people, public houses are the heart and soul of village life. Lots of pubs have the appearance and aura of having been part of the fabric of English villages forever, and many of them have indeed been serving their villages for centuries, but first glances can also be deceptive. Some pubs strive to look more ancient than they are in reality, and some establishments that people think of as classic old English pubs are largely a product of the nineteenth century and early twentieth century.

In fact, lots of pubs claim highly dubious dates of origin. It is almost as if publicans have picked suitably ancient-sounding centuries at random for one-upmanship on neighbouring establishments. There are several claims on the title 'England's Oldest Pub'. Perhaps the most ambitious claim I have seen is that one particular village pub has been serving beer since AD 560. It hasn't. The present pub is mostly seventeenth century in date, and although the building has earlier origins, there are no documents or physical evidence that could possibly extend its opening hours back nearly a millennium and a half.

Today's English pubs are really a formalisation and hybrid of their alehouse, tavern and inn ancestors. Some pubs occupy very old buildings that did not originate as pubs, but there are also some very old village pubs.

Brewing intoxicating beer-like drinks goes right back into prehistory, at least to Neolithic and Bronze Age times when the first farmers produced domesticated cereal crops. Analysis of minute traces of organic residue on the interior of the clay pots made by these people (and often buried alongside them in their graves) has shown that they contained a variety of foods and drinks, but some of these pots had held an ale-like concoction.

More evidence of prehistoric brewing has been identified in charred cereal grains dating back to the middle of the Iron Age, around 400 BC. Microscopic bubbles in the structure of discarded grains indicate they were in the process of fermentation, rather than being prepared for breadmaking.

Given the specialised nature of the brewing process, and the importance of getting the end product just right, it is possible that brewing was a job entrusted to particular individuals or families in a prehistoric community. Despite whatever outrageous claim a publican or brewery company may make next, however, there is no evidence of prehistoric pubs in England.

The Romans introduced wine to Britain and wine shops soon sprang up to serve military bases and towns. These shops or stalls were called *tabernae*. We probably get the word 'tavern' from this, although the Roman term actually embraced commercial premises offering a wide range of retail functions and services. The Roman inns (*mansio*) in settlements on the principal roads would have served invigorating beverages to weary travellers. No doubt the shows put on at amphitheatres and theatres went down better with some liquid refreshment too.

Romano-British people also routinely drank alcohol at home. The majority of the Romano-British settlement sites that I have excavated or visited have produced some sherds from delicate little pottery wine cups (and occasionally fragments of glass goblets) representing the aspirational, nouveau-Roman side of native alcohol consumption. However, the Romans found that Britain was much better at producing cereal crops than vines, so they quickly adapted to producing and drinking ale. All Roman sites reveal plenty of evidence of large, beaker-like drinking vessels that were intended for knocking back larger quantities of alcohol. Some beakers were decorated with hunting scenes, witty slogans and even pornography.

The Romans gave England the first firm evidence of premises that sold alcohol, and they also gave England its first named brewer. Excavations at the Roman fort of Vindolanda, near Hadrian's Wall in Northumberland, have revealed astoundingly rich glimpses of life in a Roman garrison at the edge of an Empire, in the form of preserved wooden writing tablets. Painstaking excavation, conservation and analysis of their content has revealed many fascinating insights into military and family matters.

The most famous Vindolanda tablet is a birthday invitation from a military wife to her friend. The lines that Claudia Severa wrote in her own hand almost 2000 years ago are probably the earliest example of female writing in Latin known anywhere in the world. Other tablets concern more mundane administrative matters, but are no less informative. One contains a memo from one military officer to another asking for orders and adding that his garrison has run out of beer, so please could more be procured.

Another tablet lists some of the people carrying out key roles for the garrison such as vets, medics, a shield maker, and a man called Atrectus, who was a brewer. We don't know whether Atrectus was a soldier or a civilian attached to the garrison and based in the adjoining civilian village (*vicus*), but the tablet records that he owed money to the local butcher.

When the Roman Empire ceased to rule Britain, early in the fifth century, the archaeological and historical evidence suggest that few of its institutions survived for long. Roman inns, theatres, wine shops and military brewers would have shut up shop never to reopen. Nevertheless, it is difficult to believe that the remaining Romano-British population managed through those disruptive times without some form of alcohol. Even if they had forgotten how to make it, the incoming tribes from north-west Europe brought with them their own sturdy brewing tradition.

One of the ancient ancestors of the English village pub is the Anglo-Saxon hall, sometimes called a mead hall or feasting hall. In the epic Anglo-Saxon poem *Beowulf*, the powerful chief, Hrothgar, marks his success in battle by building a huge mead hall, ('a house greater than men on earth ever had heard of'), and naming it 'Heorot'. This was the place where Hrothgar mixed with his followers and feasted with them. The hall figures prominently in the story of Hrothgar and Beowulf, and there are plenty of references to drinking not just mead, but ale.

Another Anglo-Saxon poem, *Judith*, which is actually based on a biblical story, paints a vivid picture of a banquet in a similar hall:

> *So they went and settled down to the feasting, insolent men to the wine-drinking, all those brash armoured warriors, his confederates in evil. Deep bowls were borne continually along the benches there and brimming goblets and pitchers as well to the hall-guests.*
>
> *It goes on to recount that Holofernes, the bountiful lord of his men, grew merry with tippling. He laughed and bawled and roared and made a racket so that children of men could hear from far away how the stern-minded man bellowed and yelled, insolent and flown with mead . . .*

> The drunk lord kept the party going and later
> on all the assembled company . . . *lay unconscious,*
> *the whole of his retinue drunk as if they had been*
> *struck dead, drained of every faculty.*[8]

So in the early Anglo-Saxon period, a building type specifically associated with drinking alcohol enters English literature for the first time, quickly followed by the first reference to a 'lock-in' and its consequences. Halls like this were not mere fiction or wishful thinking. Their faint remains have been discovered on archaeological excavations of Anglo-Saxon settlements across England.

The communal nature of feasting and drinking in the Anglo-Saxon halls of lords and kings, and the quantities necessary to supply retainers and guests, suggest that specialist brewers and trading must have been involved, rather than individual household producers. However, these early halls were the lord's domain, so strictly speaking they were private, not public houses, and therefore not quite like the common alehouses that appeared during the same era.

ALEHOUSES, TAVERNS AND INNS

From the seventh century onwards, the laws made by Anglo-Saxon kings mention ale drinking and alehouses. Early attempts to prevent drinking to excess and to curb

---

[8] All extracts from the translation in *Anglo-Saxon Poetry*, S.A.J. Bradley, Everyman.

the popularity of drinking establishments obviously failed because by the late tenth century King Edgar (the Peaceful) was trying to restrict the number of alehouses to one per village. A few years later, the third law code of King Aethelred II (the Unready) included a clause specifically dealing with violence in alehouses. Soon after pubs were becoming a village institution, it seems they were on firm notice to behave; obviously some people couldn't help themselves and were spoiling it for everybody else.

References in later medieval documents show that specialist alehouses selling their product to all-comers were a well-established feature of town and village life, and that they were coming under increasing regulation. References to 'brewsters', female brewers, are quite common, and from the earliest times women have been associated with brewing and keeping alehouses.

Archaeological excavations have shed some light on the environmental and structural evidence for malting and brewing in medieval times, and the pottery from this period also indicates a society that was well used to quaffing ale. The few contemporary illustrations of medieval alehouses suggest that their basic forms were virtually the same as ordinary houses of the period, and like medieval shops and commercial premises of all kinds, they were also homes. Therefore it is very difficult to distinguish distinct alehouses through archaeological excavation and in surviving medieval building fabric.

Brewing ale was also undertaken by monastic communities, for castle garrisons and by the largest households. However, these places also brewed mainly for their own use, not for sale to the medieval public. Monks, servants and labourers would drink ale throughout the week as part of their staple diet. The brewing process created a tasty drink that relieved the monotony of drinking only water, and helped kill off all sorts of nasty things that infested drinking water at the time.

There are plenty of pubs that were later established in already ancient buildings, but only a few known examples of medieval buildings still standing that probably originated as alehouses, or became alehouses not long after construction. At Lamberhurst in Kent, a house known as Ricardes Toft looks unpromising at first glance. Its timber frame is mostly hidden from view beneath much later recladding, but this building may well date back to the fourteenth century and records indicate an alehouse existed here in the fifteenth century. There is a fine (and more obvious) late fourteenth- or early fifteenth-century timber-framed property next door called The Charity, which was once a workhouse.

At West Hoathly in West Sussex, a fifteenth-century private house, known as Duckyls Holt, was an alehouse formerly known as The Batts and later The Tuns. The village's current pub, The Cat Inn, is itself an early sixteenth-century timber frame building, disguised by later cladding. The Rose and Crown Inn at Elham, in Kent, is a late fifteenth- or sixteenth-century building thought to have been licensed as an alehouse in the mid-sixteenth century. Later a coaching inn, it is still a public house, but again its ancient origins are largely hidden by a later facade.

Old ale was just malted barley, water and yeast, but in the fifteenth century the idea of adding hops to the brewing process was introduced into England. Ale then became more like the beer we drink today. The term 'public house' did not come into widespread use until the eighteenth century, and was simply used to distinguish drinking establishments open to all from private houses and clubs. The term 'tavern' was used to distinguish premises that also sold wine and stronger liquor. The distinction was lost when public houses were able to widen their drinks offer, but the word 'tavern' is still found in some pub names, often to help evoke an air of antiquity.

Inns offered all kinds of drink and food, and crucially accommodation and stabling for horses. Again, there are plenty of pubs that use the word 'inn' in their name but that never offered these services. Former inns tend to be more distinctive in form than alehouses and they are therefore much easier to spot and to link with ancient documentary references.

They usually occupy prominent positions in villages on main roads, or what were once main coaching roads. They have former stables and outbuildings at the back and may have extra accommodation wings that form a courtyard complex. Invariably they have a wide carriageway to give access to the yard behind, and often this goes through the building from the street front. Even where this entrance has subsequently been filled in entirely, replaced by a lobby, or reduced in size to create a smaller opening, its former presence can be obvious from joints and scars in masonry.

The Alehouse Act 1828 and the Beerhouse Act 1830 were government attempts to curb the drinking of hard liquor and to increase competition in the brewing industry. For a relatively modest fee of two guineas (£2 and 10 pence, equivalent to perhaps around £130 today), a licence to sell beer or cider, but not any of the hard stuff, could be obtained by virtually anybody. There were not many other restrictions and when the licence fee was later abolished, any would-be village pub landlord could set up in their own home, turning the front room into a 'tap' room and selling as much as they could to fellow villagers.

There were four pubs in our village when I was a child (plus three social clubs) and I knew there had been more from house names such as 'The Fish Inn' and 'Jolly Bankers', which was named from a pub that once stood there. It referred to drainage workers, not city suits. My grandfather told me that he could recall about fourteen pubs. I didn't believe him. Fourteen? Surely this was an old man's fantasy or joke on a youngster. Anyway, he would begin naming them, but after about ten or so he would start to falter and I am pretty sure repeat pub names or include minor variations of the same names (The Chequers, The Anchor, The Globe, The Ship, The Six Bells, The Crown, Royal Arms, Royal Crown, Kings Arms, Kings Head, erm, Kings things . . .).

However, if anything he underestimated the number of drinking establishments in the village. Gardner's 1851 *History, Gazetteer and Directory of Cambridgeshire* lists no fewer than twenty-one victuallers and beer retailers in Sutton. Only the victuallers have pub names listed alongside their names (there are eight). The beer retailers must have operated from more humble premises, and probably only as a sideline to their main occupation; two of the beer retailers were also listed as blacksmiths. Only one brewer is listed, and he was also a grocer and draper. He must have been very busy. All this opportunity to buy pints for a village of only 1,599 souls at the time.

The fact is that in the nineteenth century and early twentieth century, as in much earlier times, quenching your thirst with water drawn from a well or stream was not as pleasant or safe as drinking something that had been through the brewing process. Beer for everyday consumption was not especially strong. A special, even weaker version, known as 'small beer', which was really a by-product of brewing beer, was a staple and even regularly drunk by children.

VICTORIAN AND EDWARDIAN MORALS

Throughout much of their history, most village alehouses and pubs were humble buildings with little to distinguish them from the cottages around them. Pubs changed radically in Victorian times, and though the drivers for this originated largely in urban areas, the country pub scene was also affected. Huge numbers of purpose-built pubs were constructed in nineteenth-century urban neighbourhoods as town and city populations grew and factory workers looked for places to let off steam and blow their weekly salaries. These ranged from small establishments, often on street corners, which served a few rows of terraced houses, to large and elaborate 'gin palaces' on high streets.

At the same time as the pub trade began booming, the temperance movement also grew and lobbied for restrictions on the sale of alcohol. The authorities became increasingly alarmed by the extent of drunkenness in England and its effect on law and order, family life and industrial productivity. America famously introduced total prohibition in 1920, but the British government held back from taking that drastic and largely counter-productive step, relying instead on a series of measures to curb excesses. Legislation from the 1870s onwards sought to deal with problem drinking and troublesome premises by measures such as withholding and revoking licences, preventing them from selling alcohol to children (except for consumption off the premises!), the apprehension of drunks in the street, and punishing horse and carriage drink-drivers.

At the beginning of the First World War, David Lloyd George, then Minister of Munitions and later prime minister, declared, 'We are fighting Germany, Austria and Drink, and as far as I can see, the greatest of these three deadly foes is Drink.' Among the emergency measures introduced by the Defence of the Realm Act 1914 was the restriction of pub opening times to lunchtime and evening. The government dabbled in directly running public houses. The state acquired premises in the vicinity of key defence manufacturers in various part of the country, such as around Carlisle and Enfield (then Middlesex), where munitions were produced, and either closed or refurbished them.

The government even built entirely new pubs. The state-managed pubs were more understated in their external and internal appearance than the Victorian gin palaces, and introduced light and airy spaces with seating around tables, instead of the standing-room-only, dingy snugs of local pubs. The overall effect was sometimes more like a cafe than a pub. Civil servants with fixed salaries (to discourage motivation for generating trade and profits) were installed as managers, and they offered a limited range of high-priced drinks. You could be forgiven for thinking that some of these fun-packed ideas have been adopted by major pub companies in more recent times.

The major breweries and other pub owners responded to Victorian and Edwardian intolerance of their dens of intemperate behaviour by attempting to widen their offer beyond hard-drinking working men. They also began building a new type of 'reformed', family-friendly pub that would appeal to middle-class sensibilities.

These new pubs were often built in the suburbs, but also in villages, typically on main roads where they invited travellers to stop and rest. They were spacious, often including several bars, dining and function rooms, and they were frequently finished in a Tudoresque style with superficial decorative woodwork that mimicked grand, timber-framed manor houses. Many had gardens and plenty of space for parking horse and traps and motor cars. This was an influential design and the large, black-and-white, half-timbered pub that superficially looks ancient, but is in fact only around 100 years old, has become a significant feature of many English street scenes.

Pub designs got more varied and sometimes radically modern after the Second World War, though again many of these new types of pubs were built to serve new suburbs or motorists. Rather than being rebuilt in new styles, successful old village pubs tended to gain extensions or some periodic internal remodelling. Usually this has meant removing and knocking through walls to create larger rooms. Occasionally a few old timber studs of a former partition have been left in place, the infilling removed to allow visual permeability across a large room created from two smaller rooms, and former small internal doors may be widened to become large openings.

Nevertheless, many old village pubs still feel cosier and less brash than purpose-built urban corner pubs and high street pubs, and they are celebrated for this. These sorts of village pubs look and feel homely because they were once people's cottages.

The modern definition and use of the term 'pub' is complicated by the fact that many now emphasise their food and accommodation as much as their drinks. The Campaign for Real Ale (CAMRA) has come up with a definition for a pub that comprises four main criteria. Basically, a pub must be open to all without an entrance fee or membership requirement; serve at least one draught beer, cider or perry (not just dispense bottled beer, unless it is a specialist bottled beer bar); must not require customers to buy food in order to drink alcohol (and must have at least one room not laid out for meals); and must not rely solely on table service to serve customers (i.e., customers should usually be able to order and stand at a bar).

However, this definition requires sub-criteria and three pages of caveats to cover such things as micro pubs (which may have no bar or other serving point), and not necessarily to exclude some hotel bars and leisure centre bars, if the public can drink without having to be members or residents.

PUB NAMES

There are thousands of different pub names, covering a vast range of themes, but many names are repeated over and over again. If you are spinning a drinking yarn and can't quite recall the exact name of the pub concerned, like my grandfather, you could do worse than plump for The Red Lion, The Crown or Royal Oak. These are the most popular pub names. Failing that, try something ending in 'Arms' or 'Head', which are also very common. Many village pub names recall a particular person, place or event with which they might have some association or affinity, and others are much more cryptic. Some pub names, especially in the modern era, are comic and playful, though the puns that pubs use are seldom as bad as those used by hairdressing salons.

It was traditional for early alehouses to display a pole wrapped with foliage as a sign that they were open for business. Later in the medieval period it became a legal requirement for an alehouse to display a sign, and these motifs became the name of the pub. Pubs called The Bush or something similar recall those early decorated poles. Simple objects or symbols, such as a ball or a bell, suspended as a sign, also gave rise to pub names. Pub names that include heraldic symbols such as crowns, lions, harts, swans, cross keys, boars, bears, stars, etc., are common and also usually early in origin, though that does not necessarily mean buildings that now bear these names are ancient. Pubs can be rebuilt, renamed or simply draw on earlier tradition for a name.

Village pub names sometimes include the name of a local aristocratic family. They give an instant clue about land ownership and the location of the dynasties' principal estates. Cavendish and Devonshire (as in the Dukes of Devonshire) can be found in Derbyshire and elsewhere. Fitzwilliam can be found in Yorkshire and near Peterborough. Montagu can be seen in Northamptonshire and Hampshire.

Pub names that commemorate kings and queens, and notable public and military figures are also popular, and may indicate that the village has some association with the person. It might simply also suggest when a pub was built and who was in fashion at the time. Equally a pub landlord or pub company may have drawn on a popular personality cult for marketing purposes. The many 'Royal Oak' pubs reference the then Prince Charles's hiding place after he was trounced by Oliver Cromwell at the Battle of Worcester (1651). Prince Charles eventually came back as King Charles II, but rather than the whole episode being a complete embarrassment, Royal Oak Day became a public holiday as thanksgiving for the Restoration. Celebration and a day off work is a good thing for a pub to be associated with.

Lots of pubs get their names from historic military victories and other notable events. It is not surprising that there are plenty of pub names that commemorate Nelson, his ship HMS *Victory* and the Battle of Trafalgar (1805). More surprising, perhaps, is the number of pub names that commemorate the Battle of Alma (1854), the first major battle of the Crimean War.

Timing is everything. Many pubs were being built during this period, and the allied victory over the Russians, barely remembered by most people now, was very widely celebrated at the time. The heroic but misguided Charge of the Light Brigade and Florence Nightingale (the influential and popular military nurse) are the two subjects from the Crimean War that have most endured in popular culture. There are pubs named after Florence Nightingale. I set myself up to be corrected, but I don't think there are many pubs named after a suicidal dash, prompted by a misunderstanding.

The date of major national events explains other pub names, such as The Great Exhibition (or just The Exhibition), which reference the Great Exhibition of the Works of Industry of all Nations held at Crystal Palace in 1851. Barrels, tuns (brewing vats) and other brewing paraphernalia provide obvious inspiration for pub names. And it is no surprise to find pubs with nautical-themed names in coastal villages (The Ship, Anchor, various ship names, various sea creatures, etc.), agricultural names in the countryside (The Plough, Wagon and Horses), or Railway Tavern, The Locomotive, etc., next to railways.

However, pub names can also provide clues for a local industry, activity or feature that has long since disappeared. There are plenty of Miners Arms and similar across the country, but the Blue Pits Inn at the village of Castleton, near Rochdale, is a more unusual name that reflects former clay quarries in the locality.

Then there are some truly quirky names. It doesn't take too much imagination to guess that The Bees in the Wall could refer to a long-lived bees' nest. But The Badger Box in the village of Annesley, in Nottinghamshire, is a puzzle, unless you happen to know that a former landlord apparently kept a pet badger. The pub named The Bucket of Blood in the village of Phillack, in Cornwall, recalls a grisly tale about the landlord finding a murdered smuggler in the well. Best stick to drinking the beer.

VILLAGE CHAPELS

The history of village churches is so closely connected with the history of villages that you can read much of a village's history in its church, its size, position and condition. Whether a church is present or not in a village is also crucial. Villages that grew later alongside existing settlements in a historic parish, with an existing parish church, might later acquire their own church and form their own new parish. Many villages, however, did not. If these villages grew sufficiently and were an inconvenient distance from the parish church, they might be provided with a chapel that was a sort of satellite venue for the parish church.

Strictly speaking, this sort of building was known as a 'chapel of ease'. A chapel of ease was usually a smaller and less lavish building than the main parish church. The term chapel also refers to additions to parish churches and partitions within them reserved for particular services, dedicated to particular saints, and built in commemoration of their funders. Chapels for private family use can be found in stately homes and for the use of monastic communities and their visitors.

In addition to these chapels, other new places of worship, also known as chapels, were added to the village street scene from the late seventeenth century onwards. These were the meeting houses and chapels of the various 'Nonconformist' Christian faiths, such as the Baptists, Methodists, Quakers and their many related variations. In fact, by the middle of the nineteenth century there were more of these types of chapel in England than Church of England parish churches. Whereas a large village usually had only one church, it might have two or more chapels belonging to different Nonconformist denominations.

The roots of the expansion of alternative places of worship lie in the English Reformation and its aftermath, when Catholicism centred on Rome was rejected in favour of a new Protestant state-sponsored church establishment, the Church of England. In the late sixteenth and seventeenth century, there was constant argument about exactly how to worship and about the freedom to worship outside of the stipulations and infrastructure of the Church of England. Dissent led to expulsions of clergymen and the founding of a variety of different Protestant Christian groups, all with their own ideals and practices. One thing they tended to have in common was a dislike of official religious hierarchy on earth and pomp and pageantry in churches. Many felt that the new Church of England was still too Catholic in many respects.

The first 'meeting houses' used by groups such as Quakers in the seventeenth century were exactly that: private houses.

At the end of the seventeenth century, licences were granted that allowed purpose-built Nonconformist chapels, but these still tended to be built in a more domestic and low-key style than parish churches.

Quakers in the village of Jordans, in the parish of Chalfont St Giles in Buckinghamshire, met in a farmer's barn until building their own meeting house in the village in 1688. The plain brick building with its tiled roof was built in three months. Externally, apart from its larger than usual windows and front door, it looks a lot like a moderate-sized house of the period, complete with a chimney. It is still a Quaker centre. The pop-up pub in the Jordans village hall is called 'The Jolly Quaker', as a slightly cheeky nod to the area's Quaker heritage.

As restrictions on the Nonconformist denominations and their adherents eased during the eighteenth and nineteenth centuries, some of their village chapels also became less restrained in style. Features were inspired by classical architecture, such as columns, pilasters and pediments and even Baroque flourishes were introduced. In the Victorian period, some Nonconformist chapels were built that were inspired by Norman and medieval church architecture. Externally they were almost indistinguishable from new Victorian Church of England parish churches and chapels.

In the nineteenth century and early twentieth century, where rural communities were growing rapidly or new villages were being formed, church authorities of all denominations took the innovative step of building small, prefabricated kit-form churches and chapels clad in corrugated tin. These became known as 'tin tabernacles'. Some still survive and are being used for their original purpose.

The tiny tin tabernacle in the parish of North Bradley stands at a crossroads near the hamlet of Brokerswood. It still serves the neighbourhood, but this was not its original location. It was moved here in 1904 after first being erected in the neighbouring village of Southwick. Southwick had acquired its first tin tabernacle as a chapel of ease to St Nicholas Church in North Bradley in 1881, but this burnt down in 1897, and the tin tabernacle now at Brokerswood was its replacement. Then a new stone church of St Thomas was built at Southwick in 1903 and the replacement tin tabernacle was moved to its current site. The shifting church and chapel situation of a parish comprising several settlements is exemplified here, along with the utility of this particular type of chapel.

VILLAGE SCHOOLS

Education was all 'learning on the job' for most medieval village children. Children quickly became part of the village workforce and only a select few from the upper levels of medieval society had private tuition, or were sent away to a monastery to get some formal education. Cathedral schools were also established for child choristers, but again these were only for a select few. After the Reformation, parish priests sometimes established schools for village children in village churches. Church 'porch schools' simply used the church porch with its inbuilt benches. The largest village church porches had first-floor chambers that could be used for libraries and school rooms.

In the late medieval period, but especially after the Reformation in the sixteenth century, wealthy patrons gave money to establish purpose-built schools. They were often part of a suite of charitable endowments, such as almshouses for the poor, and the new Protestants in particular were keen on this kind of philanthropy. Estate villages were also often provided with schools, enlightened industrialists established schools, and Nonconformist denominations established their own schools.

There were other types of school that catered to different sectors of society. 'Dame schools' were typically run by an elderly lady who taught reading and sewing. Charitable part-time 'ragged schools' for the poorest children were mostly associated with large urban areas. You can imagine that the type of education the children received at these places, the style and capacity of the school buildings, and the facilities they offered all varied enormously, along with how much it cost parents for each child to attend.

In the early nineteenth century, national educational initiatives were set up by various religious and philanthropic organisations. The cumbersomely titled National Society for Promoting the Education of the Poor in the Principles of the Established Church in England and Wales promoted 'national schools' in villages. You might think that with a catchy name like that the idea was never going to take off, but the 5000 or so Church of England state schools teaching today, many of which are village primary schools, are the legacy of this movement. New Church of England affiliated schools are still being built across the country.

'British schools' were the main rival to the Church of England's schools. They were established by a Nonconformist organisation that certainly tried to outmatch the Anglican society's name: British and Foreign School Society for the Education of the Labouring and Manufacturing Classes of Society of Every Religious Persuasion. Both National schools and British schools tended to be fairly simple buildings comprising a single rectangular hall.

Not until the 1870 Education Act did the government encourage local councils to build schools, and not until 1880 was primary school education made compulsory. A huge number of schools were built from this point onwards as the various national and local school societies sought to compete with the local authority 'board school' building programme. The early village board schools tended to be built in historical styles, with features reminiscent of chapels. They had a central assembly hall, around which classrooms were clustered. Infants, boys and girls were segregated and often entered the school building through different labelled entrances.

The Sir John Moore Church of England Primary School in the village of Appleby Magna, in Leicestershire, is a remarkable early village school. It is a beautiful brick building with stone dressings that looks like a country mansion. It was built in 1697 to the design of none other than Sir Christopher Wren, architect of St Paul's Cathedral. Sir John, son of the lord of the manor, had made his fortune in London and became Lord Mayor in 1681. Originally known as Appleby Grammar School, it provided free education to village boys and took in boarders from further afield. The historic school was due to be closed in the 1990s and a new school was going to be built nearby, but it was reprieved when a Heritage Lottery Fund grant was provided for repairs and conversions.

Other historic village schools are also still very much in use, particularly many of the Victorian and Edwardian board and National schools, though the original historic school building may have been enveloped by later class-room developments as the school grew with an expanding village. Some village schools have long been closed, either as numbers of children declined or when replaced by new school complexes. Many disused school rooms have found new uses as homes, business premises and village halls.

VILLAGE HALLS

A village hall can tell us a lot about a village. The most successful village halls reflect the vibrancy of the communities they serve and the range of its interests. They might be fondly remembered for childhood table-top jumble sales and Santa's grotto, teenage discos and a first furtive kiss, amateur dramatics and live music; all perhaps of variable homespun quality. Or maybe badminton tournaments, taekwondo sessions, carpet bowls, flower arranging and produce shows. They host temporary clinics, parish council meetings, film nights, christening and wedding receptions, funeral wakes . . . the list is endless. They are there at the beginning of village life and at its end. They are a parlour or front room into which a village welcomes visitors, and within which a village shows itself. They were the ultimate 'pop-up' venue, long before 'pop-up' was a fashionable thing.

The village hall alone is the one shared place where all villagers and visitors, regardless of background and affiliations, can meet on equal terms to partake in an eclectic, even random, mix of activities, and feel like they totally belong. Purpose-built village halls are a surprisingly recent addition to village life, but the deep-seated need for communities to come together to celebrate, administer and share special events goes right back into the Stone Age.

Prehistoric gatherings, however, were usually outdoor affairs, taking place at special locations in the landscape and at purposely constructed monuments. Prehistoric builders produced buildings of relatively limited span. Their houses could comfortably accommodate an extended family and some animals, but not great tribal ceremonies, even for standing room only. There is no evidence that Stonehenge was ever roofed and clad to protect its users from the midwinter chill of Salisbury Plain!

The Romans introduced various public spaces and buildings to Britain. Basilica and forums were public buildings used for governance and administration, and also commercial activity. They are a sort of cross between town halls and corn exchanges. The best known places of Roman entertainment, theatres and amphitheatres, were also associated with towns. Temples were found everywhere in Roman Britain, but these catered to specific cults and practices. They were certainly not community centres. Romano-British society did not seem to have anything quite like village halls, and in any case the civic infrastructure they built disintegrated with the arrival of the Anglo-Saxons.

Anglo-Saxon great halls (or mead halls) were important community gathering places. They were the centre of Anglo-Saxon kings' and lords' governance, but they hosted similar types of communal activities to those held in later village halls. Feasting, drinking, music, dancing, storytelling and gift-giving. The raids on King Hrothgar's hall, Heorot, by various monsters, and its final destruction by fire, would have been especially shocking to *Beowulf*'s Anglo-Saxon audience, because these were attacks on the very heart of Anglo-Saxon society. The hall was the place that bound the king's folk together and defined them. If Hrothgar's people were not safe in Heorot, where on earth could they be safe?

Norman manorial and castle great halls were far more rigid in construction and in their use. They reflected the social distance between the foreign conquerors and the Anglo-Saxon communities they governed. They were often built in stone and enclosed within walled defences and moats. This tells you much of what you need to know about how well Norman lords got on with their subjects and neighbours.

Not many Norman lords would have been keen on throwing free-for-all parties for their Anglo-Saxon people. Norman and medieval feudal society was built on strict hierarchy and the manorial hall reinforced everybody's place in the world. The lord and his lady sat on a raised platform (*dais*) at one end of the hall, in front of their private apartments. Their servants were called in to sit and eat before them; the lowliest were furthest from the fire and nearest to the door.

As the gentry swapped medieval manors for country houses and stately homes halls changed functions. From the seventeenth century onwards, houses had more private rooms for the family, and servants had their own accommodation and eating areas. The hall became a large reception area for guests and a space for occasional entertaining, not a daily living space where the household and servants came to eat together. Villagers and servants may have gathered in the hall of the squire's house on a few special occasions, when invited, but it was far from being a community venue.

Village communities looked to buildings other than the lord's hall for their gatherings throughout the medieval period and beyond. Churches were usually by far the largest buildings in most villages. They were not furnished with pews until late in the medieval period, which meant they were very adaptable covered spaces, and were expected to host all sorts of parish meetings and events. 'Church ales' (or 'parish ales') were effectively beer and cider festivals that were held to raise funds for the upkeep of the church and for parish charities; but these sorts of events could get way out of hand. It must have been difficult to maintain a sense of sanctity and reverence on a Sunday, when parishioners had been rolling drunk and cavorting in the aisles on Saturday.

The church authorities eventually banned many of the less religious village activities customarily held in churches and churchyards. Sometimes separate buildings were constructed that could host events that were no longer felt appropriate to hold in the church itself. In the south-west of England in particular, separate 'church houses' (or 'church ale houses') functioned as village venues and hostels for visitors. A fine example, built in 1515, survives at Crowcombe in Somerset. It is built of stone and has a hall on the first floor. The original kitchens where bread was baked and ale brewed can still be seen on the ground floor. The building is still available to hire for private and parish functions.

Church houses went out of favour under a more puritanical regime in the seventeenth century and many, like Crowcombe, were converted to almshouses. The beautiful 1530s timber-framed church ale house in the village of Colwall, in Herefordshire, was also converted to an almshouse, before eventually becoming a church hall. Others were sold off to become alehouses, such as the Church House Inn at South Hams, in Devon.

Church halls were built across England, especially from the Victorian period onwards. Many still serve their villages very well, hosting a wide variety of parish events and activities, but unlike village halls, these are part of the church estate and subject to the oversight of church authorities. Many of these church authorities are keen to attract imaginative uses of both church halls and churches. Some churches are themselves now used once more for an impressive array of functions and activities, such as concerts, plays, lectures and toddler groups. Some even house village post offices and shops, and house beer and cider festivals.

However, some church authorities are still mindful of the primary purpose of their buildings and are wary of permitting activities that are too incompatible with the Christian faith. Some churches do not tolerate gambling, drinking, or other potentially disreputable activities. Equally, some villagers find that churches and chapels are venues that still come with too much religious baggage, and not enough heating, for their comfort. Other village meeting places, such as Nonconformist chapels, were similarly too closely aligned to a religious organisation's aims to act comfortably as the go-to venues for all village entertainments.

Political clubs, subscription reading rooms, sports clubs, works clubs, miners' institutes, working men's clubs and women's institutes also catered for members with particular affiliations, interests and genders (the clue is in the names). They were happy meeting places for some villagers, but not necessarily quite as welcoming for others.

Towns and cities in the eighteenth and nineteenth centuries had their assembly rooms, where dances and other fashionable gatherings were held, and theatres. In villages, where purpose-built premises like this were not commercially viable, large barns were cleaned out temporarily to host dances and touring plays. But use of these depended on the goodwill of farmers, barns did not offer the facilities and comfort that people increasingly expected.

By the end of the nineteenth century and into the early twentieth century, many village communities wanted an independent venue that was managed by the village, on behalf of the village, which was open to all and adaptable to a variety of uses and events. Some village communities set about acquiring and re-purposing existing buildings, in others purpose-built village halls were constructed. In some places village halls were provided by benefactors, and in others villagers raised the funds themselves.

Some of the barns traditionally used for village functions later became permanent village halls, such as at Ducklington in Oxfordshire, Blickling Hall in Norfolk, Stanway in Gloucestershire, and Briantspuddle in Dorset. Many other village halls began life as school buildings. If the schools were closed due to dwindling rolls, or larger more modern schools replaced them, the opportunity was often taken to re-purpose them for new community uses. Examples of old schools converted to village halls can be seen at Laxton and at Barnby in the Willows in Nottinghamshire, Woodnesborough in Kent, Weedon in Buckinghamshire, and Cleasby in Yorkshire.

Other buildings adapted as village halls include, ironically, former chapels, houses, various former clubs and institutes, and old army barrack huts. These prefabricated timber buildings were readily available after the First World War and Second World War, and were fairly easily dismantled and transported. Many still soldier on in all sorts of guises more than a century later. The old army hut that served as my cricket team's tearoom and bar was the scene of many memorable (and some mercifully forgettable) nights. My grandma remembered it as the headquarters of her Girl Guide troop during the inter-war years. This venerable social hut lasted until the piano fell through the floor once too often.

Some village halls were built to commemorate the war dead, or to mark a special event. The hall in Horsham, West Sussex, was built to mark Queen Victoria's Diamond Jubilee. Many village halls were built by local grandees. In 1840, the Duke of Bedford, who was not short of a bob or two to spare, built a hall for the village of Milton Abbot in Devon. The charming, original village hall of Benenden in Kent was built in 1908 as a memorial to the first Earl of Cranbrook, a prominent nineteenth-century politician and government minister, who made a nearby country estate his home. Benenden's present village hall (which the Benenden Village Trust proudly considers to be a 'top of the range venue') and other village facilities were funded by gifts from Viscount Rothermere in memory of two sons killed in the First World War.

The eccentric Reverend Massey accidentally built an impressive village hall at Farringdon in Hampshire. Known as Massey's Folly, it took thirty years to build and nobody, including his small workforce of two local labourers, quite knew what the Reverend's original intentions were. The building eventually became a village hall in 1925 after his death.

Francis Henry Crittall, of metal-framed windows fame, built a vast village hall, said to be the largest in the UK, for his factory community at Silver End in Essex. It was equipped with a dance floor, cinema, library, billiard room, card room and health clinic. The hall, like the village houses, is a 1920s modernist building that made very good use of Crittall's own products.

Burton-on-Trent brewing magnate Robert Ratcliff built a fine village hall at Newton Solney, in Derbyshire. Completed in 1926, the hall boasts many of the expected village hall facilities: kitchen, toilets, main hall, meeting rooms, billiard room and an outdoor bowling green. Somewhat bizarrely, it also incorporates an indoor rifle range. Perhaps it reflected the readiness of locals of the time to defend their village at all costs? Actually, it is there because Ratcliff was lieutenant colonel of a local Territorial Army regiment. The land on which the hall was built was originally given as a volunteer practice ground and firing range. The rifle range is still used by the local gun club.

Substantial funds to build village halls were often raised entirely by the villagers themselves. The public appeal for funds to build the village hall at Kelmscott, Oxfordshire, was launched in 1928 and the building was opened by George Bernard Shaw in 1934. Over the last thirty years or so, many entirely new village halls, or extensions to existing halls, have been built after local fundraising and obtaining grants. They are still being built and extended, and it is a measure of their continuing usefulness and place in village life. Village halls across England seem to be enjoying renewed success and appreciation, not just struggling on as relics of Victorian and Edwardian village life.

Modern village halls are built in all sorts of styles and materials. The architecture of older village halls is usually quite conservative and traditional, deliberately evoking earlier times and suggesting ancient origins. Gothic, Tudor, Queen Anne and Arts and Crafts styles are common in halls built during the nineteenth century and early twentieth century. However, some village halls really do date back to much earlier times and originated as other buildings. Small irregular bricks, hewn and tool-worked timbers rather than sawn timber, blocked doors and inserted windows might indicate origins as an ancient barn or house. Former school rooms might retain separate boys' and girls' entrances and dedication plaques. Former chapels may retain their gable crosses and large east windows.

VILLAGE WAR MEMORIALS

The First World War, or Great War, took a terrible toll on young men of all classes right across England, robbing families of loved ones and denuding their communities of talent, labour and vigour for many years afterwards. Around 700,000 who went off to fight were killed.

All but a few English villages sent men and women off to serve their country. Hardly any saw them all safely return. Of around 16,000 villages in England, only fifty-three can count themselves as 'Thankful Villages', a term later coined for those villages that did not lose a son or daughter in the conflict. Only sixteen or so of these villages are 'Doubly Thankful Villages', in that they suffered no casualties in the Second World War either. The village of Catwick in Yorkshire proudly proclaims 'Doubly Thankful' on its modern road sign, with 'please drive carefully' added beneath. Mercifully, the village of Upper Slaughter in Gloucestershire saw no slaughter in either World War, despite sending dozens of men and women off to serve.

Most village cemeteries contain a few war graves scattered among the other burials. The distinctive plain, cream-white stone headstones provided by the Commonwealth War Graves Commission are more numerous if the village was associated with a military facility, such as an aerodrome. In these cases, the service graves are often arranged in a separate military enclosure. However, most servicemen and women died and were buried overseas, so have no resting place or individual marker among their village kinsfolk.

The Cenotaph, an 'empty tomb', at Whitehall in London, was built shortly after the First World War and inspired the desire for dignified physical memorials in thousands of communities across England. In the years following the First World War, most English villages built war memorials that served as a focal point for commemorative services and as a permanent record of those from the village who went to fight and did not return. Nobody could envisage that they would also come to commemorate those killed in a Second World War just over twenty years later, or villagers killed in conflicts since then.

Unlike the headstones supplied by the War Graves Commission, village war memorials were commissioned and funded by communities individually. Consequently they take many different forms and styles. Many are simple, free-standing stone crosses, obelisks or columns on bases or stepped plinths, reminiscent of the medieval wayside, preaching and market crosses that are also found in many villages. Some feature sculptures of servicemen; others are shrine-like alcoves or panels built into walls, or simple plaques erected on older monuments and buildings, such as churches and chapels.

Most village war memorials are in prominent locations, such as a market square or a green, a high street or in a churchyard. They have become familiar village landmarks over the last century. Some villages chose to commemorate with new buildings such as lychgates at the entrance to churchyards, village halls, British Legion and comrades social clubs, or extensions to these buildings.

The list of names inscribed on memorials and plaques, with usually many more relating to the First World War than the Second World War, gives some sense of how badly small communities were affected. It is especially poignant to see the same surnames repeated several times, brothers, fathers, cousins and uncles, and realise that these names represent the devastation of entire village dynasties that often dated back hundreds of years. Many of those who fought and did come back were scarred and led very difficult lives. As a young Cub Scout attending my first remembrance services, I noticed that the First World War veterans were more likely to be missing limbs than those who served in the Second World War, but not until much later did I get any sense of the continuing mental anguish faced by many from both conflicts.

War memorials that predate the Great War are much rarer in villages and are more often found in county towns that had particular associations with army regiments. Nevertheless, it is possible to find tablets and plaques in parish churches and gravestones that record gentry and villagers' participation in the eighteenth-century European and colonial wars, Napoleonic Wars, Crimean War and Boer War. For those who returned from these places, imagine the adventures and horrors with which they could regale their fellow villagers.

The war memorial at Elveden in Suffolk is an extraordinary landmark, familiar to anybody who has travelled along the A11 London to Norwich road. It commemorates the Great War dead of three parishes associated with the Elveden Estate (Eriswell, Icklingham and Elveden) and is situated where their boundaries meet. It was commissioned and funded by the owner of Elveden Hall, Edward Cecil Guinness, supported by local donations. At 39 metres (128 feet) high, it is only a little shorter than Nelson's Column in Trafalgar Square and no less striking in its setting. Lenham in Kent lost forty-two villagers in the Great War. Their grieving friends and relatives carved a giant cross in the chalk hill overlooking the village, where it can be seen to this day.

Memorial stained glass can be seen in many parish churches. Second World War and more modern commemorative themes often depict soldiers in uniform and weaponry, but the Great War designs are often quite traditional, depicting angels and saints. The stained glass of the Church of St Mary at Swaffham Prior, in Cambridgeshire, is something else entirely. It depicts the equipment and scenes of war in great detail. Pictures of Zeppelins, submarines and tanks, a howitzer, a field telegraph tent, a mobile kitchen, Red Cross hospital and trench scenes are presented, along with selected prescient quotes from the Bible.

Beneath the image of a German aeroplane is the text: 'Though they climb up to heaven thence I will bring them down.' Beneath a British tank there is: 'But the man that shall touch them must be fenced with iron.' And a depiction of women working in a munitions factory has: 'Whatosever thy hand findeth to do, do it with thy might.' Even more quirky is a picture of the Statue of Liberty with the quote: 'Nation shall not lift up sword against nation neither shall they learn war anymore.'

Nevertheless, there was not much equivocation in this church about which side had the moral grounds to wage war. The accompanying commemorative plaque states that the windows are dedicated to the men of the village who died 'fighting nobly for God, king and country against the aggression and barbarities of German militarism'. Interestingly the village Nonconformists, who had objected to the village memorial being placed in the parish church, commissioned an alternative memorial.

Hundreds of village war memorials have been cleaned, repaired and designated as listed buildings over the last few years as part of the centenary commemorations of the First World War. Whatever form they take, it is an overwhelming experience to stand at a village memorial alongside veterans on a cold, crisp November morning for the annual service of remembrance, and to hear the names of the village fallen read out.

CHAPTER 9

VILLAGES IN THE MODERN WORLD

Throughout the medieval period and into the early twentieth century, powerful manorial lords, private enterprise, local philanthropy and the efforts of villagers themselves governed village development and the character of its housing. Their ideas, motivation, ambition, vision, preferences, tastes and resources varied, and these are some of the important factors that make each village different from the next. In most villages there is not much evidence of 'nationalisation' or direct intervention by the state until the twentieth century. Apart from the occasional dwelling for coastguards, the police or military officers, the governments of the eighteenth and nineteenth centuries did not provide, or even take much of an interest in, rural housing, or shaping the growth of villages.

VILLAGE HOMES FIT FOR HEROES

All this changed with the Housing and Town Planning Act of 1919 (also known as the Addison Act, after the Minister of Health who authored it) and the Housing Act of 1930 (or Greenwood Act, after the MP who promoted it). Both Acts are most closely associated with city slum clearance and the construction of urban and suburban council estates, but they also had a major impact on rural England and the character of its villages. Government action was necessary because the private sector, devastated by war and its economic consequences, could not provide sufficient affordable housing. The famous 'homes fit for heroes' phrase coined by Prime Minister Lloyd George signalled the intention of the state to provide a war-weary and depressed nation with good, modern living conditions.

Richard Reiss MP, colleague of Lloyd George and Addison in the Ministry of Reconstruction, wrote a book explaining the 1919 Act, called *The Home I Want*. It was publicised by a poster showing a typical 'Tommy' British soldier, tin hat on and rifle slung over his shoulder, pointing towards a pretty cottage among a row of identical cottages in a rural setting. The poster read: 'You cannot expect to get an A1 population out of C3 homes.' The reference was to medical grades used by the British Army to categorise the health and fitness of its troops. A1 was fully fit to serve anywhere, C3 was far from fit for active service. The street of urban terrace housing at the foot of the poster was labelled C3; the pretty rural cottage was labelled A1.

The message could not have been clearer to a population by now well used to army speak. The future strength of the nation depended on good housing. There was also an important subtext. Substandard housing had been recognised as one of the major causes of social and industrial unrest. The war had mobilised and militarised millions of British citizens; and a revolution raged in Russia. The balance of power there had been swung by the sheer number of citizens conscripted into the army who proved willing to defy the authorities and turn their guns from a foreign enemy towards their class enemies and political opponents. The government could not risk ignoring sources of mass discontent.

Some local councils had commissioned and financed housing independently before the 1919 Act, but its introduction put all local councils firmly at the forefront of responsibility to clear slums and compulsorily purchase land, and to plan and deliver new housing developments. Rural councils, like urban councils, had an obligation to provide subsidised, affordable houses for rent. Estates of council houses (local authority housing, or social housing as it has come to be known more recently) became a dominant feature of housing development and growth in towns and villages everywhere across England.

Early council houses for families in villages were relatively large and semi-detached two-storey dwellings, with three or more bedrooms, a living room (lounge), a kitchen/scullery and perhaps a larder (kitchen store room) and an outside toilet. They were set within a generous amount of garden, which was not intended for play equipment (or decking and hot tubs) but to help household economics. Tenants could grow vegetables and perhaps keep some chickens or a pig. The basic requirements for council houses followed government guidelines, but their designs were determined by individual local authorities. Usually the houses were solidly built in brick, and though usually plain and conservative in form and use of materials, they could have hints of vernacular cottage style.

As housing need became more acute and costs rose, cheaper council houses built of precast reinforced concrete were designed and constructed. Probably the best known and most distinctive of this type is the Airey house, named after their civil engineer designer, Edwin Airey. Airey houses have a frame of concrete columns and are clad in slightly overlapping horizontal concrete panels. This is a sort of concrete version of the timber-framed weatherboarding on traditional houses and farm buildings in the south and east of England.

In Airey houses, however, this was not an exercise in reflecting historic, regional building styles; it was simply borrowing a cheap and practical way of kit building and cladding to ensure rainwater run-off. Airey houses were austerity in built form. They met the need for rapid and cheaper house building following the Second World War, when tens of thousands of people had lost their homes.

They were particularly preferred for building in rural areas, since the prefabricated sections could be easily transported and assembled in relatively remote locations without the need for many specialist tradesmen. Airey houses and other prefabricated concrete, local authority housing can be seen in a huge number of villages right across England, such as the village of Wroxeter in Shropshire, at the southern edge of the Roman town. Later examples of local authority house design sought to address issues with the performance of these concrete buildings, and tried to keep pace with modern expectations for better heating, insulation, toilet and bathing facilities.

The earliest village council houses, pre-war and immediately post-war in date, are often situated on the outskirts of villages, where sufficient land was more easily obtained. Rows of old council houses often line approach roads to villages, or are arranged in separate closes and small estates. The linear, crescent or grid-shaped regularity of the council housing developments are easily picked out on maps and aerial photographs.

The uniformity of houses and garden plots is another giveaway, even though most have now been modified to greater or lesser degrees by the personal tastes of their new owners. Gone are the common glazing and paint schemes periodically carried out in batch jobs as council funds permitted. Gone are the restrictions on what tenants were allowed to alter about their homes, or even possess in their grounds. Often at least one house in a group of former council houses still has a small panel built into the principal elevation at first-floor level that displays the date of construction and the initials of the council responsible.

By the 1960s, over a quarter of the population of the United Kingdom rented their homes from local councils, a dramatic increase from ten per cent in the 1930s. By the late 1970s, it was more than a third of the population. Councils, however, were struggling to maintain and modernise their existing ageing estates and build new homes fast enough to meet demand. There had long been wide political consensus that this situation was untenable and that more people should be allowed and encouraged to own their homes.

It was the government of Margaret Thatcher, however, that brought in the Housing Act 1980 with its 'right to buy' scheme for council tenants. Their homes could be bought at discount prices, and within a decade around 1 million council houses had been sold off. Housing associations, not-for-profit social housing providers, have taken on a large amount of the former council housing stock and have built new homes since the 1980s. Around seventeen per cent of English households now live in social housing rented from local councils or housing associations.

The planning system now requires commercial developers to provide a proportion of 'affordable' housing as part of their schemes, and there have been some creative attempts to help people onto the property ladder, such as shared equity ownership. Nevertheless, the provision of affordable houses that enables villages to grow and gives young village families the option to stay within their community continues to pose a major problem in many parts of the country. Very high house prices in the most desirable villages, the lack of suitable opportunities to build more houses in some places, and limited employment prospects have driven many young families away, or have kept them from joining village life in the first place.

URBAN VILLAGES

If you look at old maps of England divided into its counties, you will find some counties that no longer exist in their original form. Rutland and Huntingdonshire were incorporated into Leicestershire and Cambridgeshire, respectively, during local government reorganisation in the 1970s. Westmorland went the same way, absorbed into Cumbria (formerly Cumberland). These were always quite small counties, and in the case of Westmorland sparsely populated and not rich, but they still cling to their historic identities in various ways. Local newspapers, sports associations and business names complement the district council names in recalling their former county status. Rutland actually regained its county status in 1997.

The lost county of Middlesex is another matter. Middlesex (from the ancient territory of the Middle Saxons) in the early seventeenth century was a rural county with the City of London and Westminster tucked into its south-east corner. At this time the map-makers John Norden and John Speed drew Middlesex, like every other county of the kingdom, divided into its ancient hundreds and dotted with villages.

London expanded rapidly from the eighteenth century onwards, and then sprawled phenomenally during the late nineteenth century and first half of the twentieth century. The county of Middlesex persisted as an ever-decreasing fragment of its former rural self and as an urban county until 1965, when it was abolished and the area of the old county came under the administration of the Greater London Council. The historic county is remembered in the name of London hospitals and many other institutions, such as Middlesex County Cricket Club, whose home ground is Lord's in St John's Wood, an area now considered to be in the heart of London.

Some of the old Middlesex hundred names, such as Fynsbury (Finsbury) and Edmonton, are familiar as districts of the capital today. Others, such as Goare (Gore) and Ossulstone, will not mean much to many Londoners these days. More familiar will be some of the old Middlesex village names, such as Golders Green, Hampstead, Hornsey, Crouch End, Highgate, Stoke Newington, Turnham Green and Barnes. Greater London also extended over parts of the old counties of Surrey and Kent, south of the Thames, and Essex to the north and east, absorbing many hamlets and villages as it grew. The process that turned ancient rural villages into urban areas could happen quite quickly.

One of the most famous early council housing estate developments, and at one time the largest such housing project anywhere in the world, the Becontree Estate, engulfed the rural Essex parishes of Barking, Ilford and Dagenham with their farms, hamlets and villages. Begun in 1921, the complete urbanisation of this area was further propelled by the opening of the Ford Motor Company's main United Kingdom factory in 1931, which had relocated from the early industrial estate Trafford Park on the outskirts of Manchester.

If you drive a Ford or anything else through Dagenham today, you will get no sense of the historic landscape or the Essex village whose name is now synonymous with the Ford brand in Britain. You will have to work quite hard to navigate the rigidly structured pattern of streets and rows of uniform housing to find any distinctive landmarks that might lead you to the core of the old village.

However, buried away amid tens of thousands of twentieth-century houses are the thirteenth-century church of St Peter and St Paul, a seventeenth-century vicarage, and the fifteenth-century Cross Keys Inn. These buildings are all that survives of the once thriving and characterful old village; even the current green is not what it seems. It was created in 2000 on the vacant site left by the demolition of old buildings. Dagenham is no longer a village but now very firmly urban, lending its mass and name to the London Borough of Barking and Dagenham.

Another fragment of old rural Essex can be found just under two miles to the north-west of Dagenham's old parish church. Tucked away in the corner of a recreation ground, close to the core of the Becontree Estate, is Valence House. Named after its fourteenth-century owner, and seventeenth century or a bit earlier in its current timber-framed form, it is the successor to a manor house that has occupied this site for at least 800 years. Three arms of the water-filled moat that once completely surrounded the house and outbuildings can still be traced. Valence House has been converted to an excellent museum, but externally it still resembles the moated manor houses that can be seen across deepest rural Essex to the north and east of London.

The complete envelopment of formerly distinct and detached historic rural villages by expanding urbanisation is something that can be seen in all English cities and many large towns. They became urban villages by default; other urban villages have urban origins.

London is sometimes said to be a city of villages and it is true that many of the cores of the old historic villages absorbed by its growth have kept something of their identity as distinct places, even if they are not physically separated at all from the surrounding neighbourhoods. A cluster of old buildings along what was once a village high street, or a medieval church and churchyard amid commuter housing, provide the focal point for this identity, but the idea of 'London villages' is as much about perceptions of community as historical fact and old buildings.

Hampstead is mentioned in the Domesday survey. It was absorbed into London more than a hundred years ago. It is part of a larger borough and not detached from, but continuous with neighbouring conurbation on its south and west sides. It doesn't have a parish council. Hampstead is not 'self-contained' as the dictionary suggests it must be to meet the definition of an urban village; but then again, no villages, whether urban or rural, are really self-contained. Nevertheless, Hampstead Village fiercely protects its title. Its residents have fought hard to retain their village identity over the years, banding together to see off harmful modern development schemes and conserving their heath, characterful buildings and street scenes.

It is perhaps less easy to explain how other London neighbourhoods have carved out a distinct identity and their own niche as urban villages. Many of the places now called 'villages' or regarded as villages were never historic villages and do not seem to have developed many of the characteristics of villages.

Connaught Village is in the heart of London's West End, just north of Hyde Park. It is very fashionable indeed, full of high-end retailers and homes of the rich and famous. It is difficult to work out quite why this area is now called a village. Presumably the new name provided a better image than the previous name of the area, Tyburnia, and its original historic name Tyburn, which was a notorious place of execution from medieval times until the end of the eighteenth century. Whitecross Village is a new name for the area around Whitecross Street, immediately adjacent to the City, where historically there was no village. Abbeville Village is a recent name for an area around Abbeville Road, a Victorian housing development adjacent to Clapham Common.

Nevertheless, from Golborne Road in the west of the city to Broadway Market in the east, and from Brixton south of the river to Primrose Hill to the north, quite different communities have developed a village 'vibe', albeit with much better broadband and many more places to get a takeaway coffee than rural villages.

The distance from a Tube station has been cited as one factor in London neighbourhoods becoming relatively self-contained and developing their own character, independent shops, community spirit, social scene and events. But ultimately these places, however close-knit, are embedded within something much bigger and much harder to manage. At a small villagey event in one part of London, right after being told by locals what a friendly community it was, I was reminded to be careful not to put my bag down for a second, or carry it roadside, because it would be nabbed either by pickpockets or thieves on mopeds. I haven't been to many rural village fêtes where I have had to worry about that kind of thing.

It is interesting that amid one of the largest, most vibrant and successful cities in the world, people are still attracted to the concept of 'the village', and feel very attached to their own urban villages. It reflects the enduring appeal of villages as comfortable and convenient units of settlement that people can relate to. The homes, public amenities, shops, markets, restaurants, pubs and other characteristics of particular London villages are pored over by lifestyle commentators and celebrated as aspirational, or condemned by others as unaffordable gentrification. Developers and estate agents, clearly responding to demand, feel the need to fabricate new villages. Some like East Village, based on the former Olympic Village, are just taking shape.

VILLAGES ON THE TOURIST TRAIL

For most of history the English countryside and its villages have primarily been places of work, and housed only those who lived and worked in them permanently. Villagers enjoyed some leisure time in their village and its surroundings, and some occasionally travelled to nearby market towns or even further afield, but villages were not much visited by others, except out of business or family necessities. Tourism is a modern phenomenon.

From the earliest times until the eighteenth century, much of England was still considered inaccessible and dangerous to travellers. The wilder parts of England were not celebrated by visitors until wars in Europe curtailed grand tours and encouraged people to look for inspiration closer to home. Artists then began to sing the praises of home rural landscapes. Poet William Wordsworth 'wandered lonely as a cloud' in the Lake District in the early nineteenth-century because he grew up in the region. Hunting and shooting trips and country house parties brought guests to select delights of the countryside, but rural England did not host fun and relaxation for the masses until much later.

In the eighteenth and nineteenth centuries, the land-owners' apocryphal cry of 'Get off my land!' could be backed up with some pretty robust measures for poachers, snoopers and livestock worriers. Petty poaching was punish-able by fines and imprisonment, but more serious poaching offences were subject to the death penalty, which was gener-ally commuted to transportation to Australia. Brutal booby traps could be used perfectly legally, and rural museums delight in displaying huge, jagged-toothed mantraps, whose sprung-steel jaws would snap fast on to ankles when someone stepped on them. They must have resulted in very severe inju-ries, if not instant amputation.

Spring guns, similarly camouflaged and primed in the undergrowth, inflicted equally gruesome injuries, as snagging the string or bar attached to the trigger would send a short-range shotgun blast into the hapless prowler. In more recent times, it has not been unknown for farmers of old to aim a twelve-bore blast or two above the heads of trespassers, to help guide them back on to the highway. Anyone who has been caught on a barbed-wire fence, or electric fence, while trying to take that short cut across a field, will tell you what effective incentives they can also be for staying on the desig-nated route.

The growth of tourism and the leisure industry, and the rise of the conservation movement, all of which have occurred only in the last century or so, are among the most radical changes ever to have taken place in the English countryside. Conservation and countryside tourism are interconnected, and to a large degree they are a reaction to the nineteenth-century and twentieth-century industrialisation of both town and country. More recently, they have become hugely significant factors in shaping the future of the rural landscape and the character of its villages.

Pressure groups and conservation organisations such as the Open Spaces Society, Campaign to Protect Rural England and the National Trust originated in Victorian and Edwardian times, but it was not until the middle of the twentieth century that the government began to legislate for the protection of, and access to, the countryside. Many landowners in the past viewed the prospect of various strangers roaming all over their land, wherever and whenever they wanted, as entirely incompatible with running their businesses. After all, people did not expect to turn up at the gates of a factory to wander around, pick at products from the production line, perhaps bed down for the night, and then get indignant if anybody asked them to leave.

The 1932 'Mass Trespass' of Kinder Scout, a moorland plateau and the highest point in the Derbyshire Peak District, is widely credited as a formative event in the movement to widen public leisure access to the countryside. The Mass Trespass is shrouded in folklore and accounts vary about how many people actually took part and exactly what happened where on the day. Nevertheless, the participants were said to be mostly from the Manchester area, and members of the Young Communist League were a driving force, along with an assortment of aggrieved ramblers.

The moorland in question was privately owned and reserved for game shooting. The trespassers did not want to stick to the existing rights of way, but instead wanted the freedom to roam across the moors at will. Some fought with gamekeepers and arrests were made. The radical, organised approach of this act of mass civil disobedience was taken seriously by the authorities and although the wider implications were not immediate, the event was not forgotten.

Even during the desperate drive for rural productivity during the Second World War, and the widespread development of military facilities, there was a growing feeling that the best of the countryside needed more protection. With this came the thought that more people should be able to enjoy more of the 'green and pleasant land' that the whole nation had been fighting so hard to hold on to.

National Parks came into being in 1949, the first Area of Outstanding Natural Beauty was designated in 1956, and National Trails and long-distance footpaths were created. Villages within these newly designated landscape areas were subject to the new authorities and conservation controls they introduced, and many villages now found themselves on the hikers' trail. Established ancient networks of local footpaths, bridleways and tracks were formalised as Public Rights of Way. The Countryside and Rights of Ways Act 2000 finally gave public access to roam over private 'open land' (that is moorland, heath, mountain and down), which is exactly what the Mass Trespass set out to achieve.

The increasing availability of motor cars and motor-bikes throughout the twentieth century opened more of the English countryside and its villages than even the best railway network in the world had achieved beforehand. The development of the internal combustion engine allowed people to reach more remote places independently, and to skip the walking element of their explorations entirely if they wished. The Automobile Association, founded in 1905, had over 700,000 members by 1939 and there were already around 2 million cars on the road by then.

The AA was quick to encourage leisure motoring in the countryside. Immediately after the First World War it published motoring routes with points of interest noted on the reverse and in the 1920s it offered complete touring routes. These could take several days of meandering around the countryside to complete, and cars touring through village streets and narrow country lanes became an increasingly familiar sight.

The Director General of the Ordnance Survey from 1911 to 1922, Colonel Charles Close, also appreciated the rise of this new, mass touring market. The venerable Ordnance Survey was a part-military, part-government agency, part-commercial map-making institution, which produced maps for many serious uses. Their accuracy and clarity were the envy of the world. Close turned the Ordnance Survey's hand to also producing handy pocket maps for the touring public, and a new series of folding maps with attractive cover illustrations were an invitation to explore and get on to the newly beaten tracks.

A century on, the Ordnance Survey's marvellous Landranger maps, produced at a scale of 1:50,000 (or one and a quarter inches to one mile) are still the single most essential piece of kit for any countryside explorer. They are marked with an awesome array of information, not only the roads, footpaths, bridleways and byways needed to keep you on track, but a whole host of interesting things to see and note.

Although lacking the extraordinary detail of the historic 1:2500 scale Ordnance Survey maps, their symbols depict many things of interest to village history explorers, such as deserted medieval villages, former manorial sites, churches, motte and bailey castles and parks. Much of the old historic grain of the landscape can be read in the mapped contours of hills and valleys, the winding courses of rivers and streams, the distribution of existing villages and other settlements, and the routes that link them. It is fun to wander through the past while wandering through the present.

Ordnance Survey maps have long been available in digital form on hand-held Global Positioning System units, smart phones, tablets, and now even on smart watches, but the purists still prefer wrestling with the wind to fold and unfold the paper maps, diligently marking their routes and way points with pencils. Wherever you want to go, or whatever you want to see, it always seems to be on the well-creased folds of the map, or just over the page, but it doesn't matter. This is proper countryside navigation.

Throughout the twentieth century, large parts of the English countryside and many of its villages adapted to unexpected new roles as temporary hosts to walkers, cyclists and motorists. Formerly obscure farming villages became tourist hotspots and remain hugely popular, busy watering holes to this day, changing their character forever.

THE WELL-WORN PATH

In the Lake District, Peak District, Dales, Moors, Broads, Wolds and large parts of the coast, there are villages where for much of the year it must be difficult for locals to go about any business at all, except for work connected with leisure and hospitality. Glimpses of wax jackets or rubber wellies are swamped beneath a tsunami of Lycra and Gore-Tex. People carriers with bike racks and roof racks, not tractors and Land Rovers, rule the roads, and hikers and cyclists clog the lanes. In recent years, formerly grubby local pubs have been revamped to become smart eateries with rooms. Rambling farmhouses built for large farming families host bed-and-breakfast guests, whilst paddocks and pasture become camp sites.

The southern Lake District villages of Coniston, Hawkshead and Near Sawrey exemplify this twentieth-century transformation. These villages were known to a few discerning Victorian visitors long before cars and motor coaches, but in the late twentieth and twenty-first centuries they have developed into almost absurdly busy tourist destinations.

Coniston was served by a rail branch line in the late nineteenth century. In addition to well-heeled visitors seeking the charms of the surrounding countryside, it had attracted influential critic and commentator John Ruskin and painter Henry Robinson Hall as residents. Tourists could take sail and steamboat tours of the lake. However, the main year-round business of the village was copper mining, slate quarrying and farming.

Hawkshead had been a place of some importance in the medieval period, but sandwiched between Coniston Water, Windermere and the lesser known Esthwaite Water, it wasn't really on the way to anywhere and its significance dwindled. Until the last century, its principal businesses were connected with its role as a local market centre and farming. Charcoal burning, peat digging, but above all sheep farming were the main occupations around Near Sawrey.

The incredible transformation of these villages over the last seventy years or so has much to do with increasing public appreciation of the beauty of the surrounding area and increasing ability to travel, but strangely it has also been supercharged by children's fiction. Beatrix Potter's tales of anthropomorphic little animals were the chief catalyst, but Arthur Ransome's children's sailing adventures have also played a part in the global promotion and incredible popularity of the area.

Potter gradually acquired 4000 acres of land, fifteen farms, and cottages in the neighbourhood of Near Sawrey and across the Lake District, all funded by her book sales, courtesy of Peter Rabbit and friends. Her bequest of this land and buildings to the National Trust were instrumental in the conservation of the region, and the formation of the Lake

District National Park in 1951. Beatrix Potter's former Lake District retreat, Hill Top, in the village of Near Sawrey, is now one of the region's top tourist attractions.

Over the last few years, well over 100,000 visitors from many nations have crossed the threshold of this modest seventeenth-century house every year. What few of them realise is that when Beatrix Potter moved permanently to the Lake District in 1913, she actually lived in Castle Cottage across the road. The small and neat but otherwise unexceptional village of Near Sawrey is now all busy lanes, heaving car parks, bed and breakfasts, holiday cottages and queues.

Hawkshead, at the other end of Esthwaite Water, is larger and even more shaped by visitors, with a Beatrix Potter gallery, gift shops, a tourist information centre, an outdoor clothing and equipment shop, tea rooms, restaurants, pubs (with and without rooms), bed and breakfasts, holiday lodges, cottages, a camp site and a caravan park.

Archaeologists and metal detectorists can locate the sites of medieval markets, fairs and places of pilgrimage long since forgotten by finding scatters of lost small change and religious trinkets. Artefacts such as badges depicting saints and small lead flasks (ampullas) that were supposed to contain holy water or oil are common finds at such gathering places. In thousands of years' time, if nothing else remains of Near Sawrey and Hawkshead, scatters of coins from many countries, and trinkets depicting rabbits, pigs and ducks wearing Edwardian clothing, will give archaeologists something to ponder about these particular places of pilgrimage.

Coniston is similarly equipped for tourism as Hawkshead, though instead of a Beatrix Potter museum it has a Ruskin Museum and memorabilia relating to the world speed record-breaker Donald Campbell, who was killed on Coniston Water in 1967. William Wordsworth went to school at Hawkshead, but he wouldn't wander lonely as a cloud in that neighbourhood now.

In fact, such is the success and popularity of these honeypot destinations in the Lake District and in many other places that pressure of visitors on and off road has long been a source of grave concern to the National Park authorities, the National Trust and private landowners. A constant stream of walkers disturbs the wildlife and wears grooves in upland paths, causing serious soil erosion, which is accelerated by rainwater run-off in a vicious cycle. It requires a lot of expensive management to address; without a rest from tramping feet, nature will not repair itself.

The village of Avebury in Wiltshire sits within the famous Neolithic henge and huge stone circle. At around sixteen miles north of Stonehenge, it is part of the modern-day pilgrimage trail that also takes in Silbury Hill, West Kennet Long Barrow, and a plethora of other prehistoric monuments across the region's chalky downs and plains.

On a visit to Avebury several years ago, I was horrified to see the depth and extent of the muddy hollows that had formed around the bases of the standing stones. It was like the sort of trample you see around cattle troughs. Paths on top of the henge's earthwork bank circuits were bare chalk and mud; networks of tree roots sat exposed on top of bare soil. However reverent mine and tens of thousands of others' footsteps were, we were all participating in the slow destruction of the object of our veneration.

Great improvements have been made to visitor management at Stonehenge and the appearance of its surroundings over the last few years. Nevertheless, it is saddening to look at the wide, modern pathway that cuts elliptically across the earthworks of the monument and have to concede, reluctantly, that this was probably the best compromise between allowing vast numbers of visitors a good view of the stones, while preventing them from trampling away delicate buried archaeological remains on the site.

Most rural heritage sites don't get anywhere near the level of daily footfall as Stonehenge and Avebury, but many suffer unchecked visitor erosion and harm through vandalism and unsympathetic use. There are many earthwork castle mottes up and down the country that have great grooves worn into them by people taking the direct route and not sticking to spiralling paths, or sliding down them. Prehistoric hill-fort ramparts are being worn away by mountain bikes, and undulating deserted settlement sites are being pulverised by off-road vehicle enthusiasts. Achieving a balance between conservation, enjoyment and work in the countryside is a conundrum that is being wrestled with across many much less high-profile locations across England.

Lumsdale Valley in Derbyshire was a crucible of water-powered industry. The ruins of historic industrial buildings, partly reclaimed by nature, ponds, a fast-flowing stream and little waterfalls, have attracted local walkers for decades. But recently residents have been driven to distraction by hordes of visitors descending on the place. Cars park everywhere, blocking access to homes; paths are being worn away, and ancient walls are being tumbled. The delights of this formerly almost unknown place had been highlighted on social media and 'went viral'. Things got even worse when things really did go viral during the Covid-19 lockdowns and Lumsdale Valley became the go-to venue for the permitted outdoor exercise. The valley had to be temporarily closed to visitors to prevent further damage.

The Covid-19 pandemic has reminded us how important access to the outdoors is for the wellbeing of society. It was at various times not possible, or not safe or convenient to go on holiday abroad, so people stayed at home. During the most severe lockdown restrictions, the government permitted and encouraged local exercise outdoors for a period each day. One enduring memory I will have of this officially sanctioned exercise time is the huge number of people out and about walking or cycling who had obviously been strangers to these activities before. They ranged from brand new 'all the gear but no idea' cyclists to people apparently without any appropriate outdoor clothing or footwear at all.

Time will tell if they keep up with their good intentions, but even before Covid-19, all the indications were that countryside-based leisure was increasing in popularity. There are indications too that the Covid-19 pandemic has not only increased interest in the English countryside and villages as a place to visit, but also as a place to live. This is the most recent episode in a long trend of swapping urban life and the 'rat race' for village life, or acquiring second home ownership that offers the best of both worlds.

BACK TO THE VILLAGE

A rail network at its peak and the increasing affordability of motor cars allowed aspirational mid-twentieth century families to escape from urban centres, not just for short annual holidays but permanently, or intermittently throughout the year as second home owners. The exodus to suburbs and commutable countryside in search of a better way of life was accelerated by grim town centre environments, ravaged by depression and industrial decline, war, the wrecking ball and some spectacularly poor town planning.

The populations of many of Britain's major urban centres started to stagnate or even shrink before the Second World War. Manchester's population stood at around 700,000 in the 1930s, but by the 1990s it was down to around 400,000. People back then were by no means 'mad for it' in the way they are for trendy Manchester now, but even London's population dropped by 1.5 million over the same period. Cities sprawled outwards to suburbs even as their core populations declined.

From the late 1960s to the 1980s, new town developments such as Milton Keynes and Peterborough New Town were planned and built to accommodate urban migrants. In both these places, formerly separate historic villages were incorporated into the newly urbanised areas. In many parts of the country, villages that were beyond the reach of commuters, or the desire of second home owners, also lost people and vitality to new suburbs and towns as employment patterns changed and the prospects for family life seemed better elsewhere.

As early as the 1970s, both the desertion of former working villages and the colonisation of villages by people who only wanted to live there in order to commute to somewhere else, or to live there for only a few days a year, was causing concern about the health of village life. 'Dormitory villages' became notorious for being utterly devoid of life during most of the day while their occupants worked elsewhere, and completely lacking in the sort of social interaction that follows from people meeting up regularly with others in their community.

In his 1977 book *Vanishing Britain*, Roy Christian despaired: 'There are villages in the Cotswolds and other beautiful areas of Britain where the locals have been banished to council houses on the fringe, to live like Red Indians in the reservations, while their old cottages are inhabited only at weekends in summer and during school holidays.'

Some indication of the changing balances between conservation, leisure and lifestyle choice in English villages and countryside is seen in the growing importance of the National Trust as a major landowner. In fact, the National Trust is now the fourth largest landowner in the UK, just behind the Crown Estate. The conservation organisation is also now the single largest farm owner, with 1500 tenant farmers. It owns fifty-six entire villages. Villagers in places such as Buttermere in Cumbria, Lacock in Wiltshire, Nether Alderley in Cheshire, Chiddingstone in Kent, and West Wycombe in Buckinghamshire, are tenants of a new, conservation-minded landlord. The National Trust is also a significant pub landlord, owning thirty-nine pubs.

VILLAGES OF LEISURE

Once, on the same day, I heard two very different perspectives on the subject of changing village character from two people of similar age concerning the village where they both grew up. This village in Cornwall is now extremely popular with visitors and second home owners. Holiday cottages alone are thought to comprise around sixty per cent of the total housing stock in the historic core of the village.

One person lamented that he no longer recognised the place, and that the maze of streets behind the area where the day visitors gathered, so full of life in his youth, were now all dead, because their occupants were absent for most of the year. The other recalled that a few short decades ago, local people could not wait to get out of those same old cottages (now each worth a fortune) and 'get up the hill' to new homes or further away as fast as possible. This man had actually let a large old house in the neighbourhood rent free for a year in the 1960s, because nobody was much interested in living there.

The consultation responses for the parish 'Neighbourhood Plan' (more of which later) reflect the two different personal perspectives I heard about the transformation of this village in modern times. Residents were asked for their opinions on the future of housing, employment and amenity development of this corner of Cornwall.

Here is a selection of respondents' comments that illustrate the depth of feeling these issues continue to provoke:

- Such development should be truly productive for the local community, not for the benefit of visitors or second home dwellers. I believe that encouragement of visitors to the area has been allowed to go far too far. What was a lovely place and community in which to live is now akin to living as a resident in a zoo. I object to thousands of rather sad lemming types wandering around looking for some ridiculous film set or so called celebrity. We all suffer because we are forced to pay far too much, whether it be for a pint of beer or everyday groceries. Tourists, like Game should have a season, preferably a short one.
- *Our Parish has the highest second home per cent in Cornwall. Public toilets are now being funded by full-time residents/local businesses for the benefit of visitors/staying in second home owners/second homes and contributing zero.*
- The income provided by second home owners is vital to this area.
- *It is tricky, without second homes the village wouldn't exist.*
- A small per cent of second homes is needed. They generate income for local people and Cornwall Council, having said that affordable housing is absolutely necessary.
- *Tourism is Cornwall's largest source of income by a considerable distance and second home owners more often than not almost invariably provide high quality rental accommodation to tourists who provide both income and employment for the county.*
- Sometimes you have to rely on distasteful sources of income and the parish has benefited from inward investment from

second home ownership and holiday home ownership in the past. You cannot just rely on local finance to achieve the lifestyle we all want to enjoy, so there has to be a balance.

- *Like many other local people, affording a house on the open market where I've grown up just simply wasn't going to happen. The grotesque and ever increasing ratios of second homes to year around residency ones continue to ghettoize the people that come from here. I absolutely wish that we could welcome anyone with a genuine intention to be a part of our unique communities but the playing field is not at all level and so local people MUST be prioritised.*

- The more second homes, the less of a community it becomes, the reason people love it becomes less and it becomes more of a toy town.

- *Houses should be affordable and for local people only – not second homes or buy-to-let holiday homes.*

And the utterly direct:

- Waste of f**king time, no one will be able to afford these houses and town people will come down and buy them and rent them out as holiday homes.

Second home owners are village people too, and bring their own experiences elsewhere to the debate:

I am responding as a second home owner, so in some ways feel a little hypocritical, however I do

Left: The terraced houses of North Street, Cromford, Derbyshire, were built by Richard Arkwright in 1776–77 to house his textile workers. Occupants who didn't work at Arkwright's factories were expected to work from home. Four light 'weavers' windows illuminate workshops on the second floor.

Right: A late fifteenth-century brick wall. The small bricks are laid in 'English bond' in thick mortar courses to compensate for their irregular shape. The colour variations are caused by uneven temperatures in the 'clamp' as they were fired.

Left: A nineteenth-century 'gault brick' wall in Flemish bond. Variations in colour suggest that these bricks were made in a local brick yard. From the end of the nineteenth century there were leaps forward in kiln technology and mass production increasingly concentrated in fewer, national centres. Bricks became far more uniform and less locally distinctive.

Two village towers, two distinctive building traditions. Buckden church tower (right) is early fifteenth century in date. It uses good limestone imported into the area for buttresses, string courses, door and window surrounds and tracery, but makes do with a local mix of fieldstone rubble and reused masonry for areas of walling. The Great Tower of the adjacent Bishop of Lincoln's Palace (background) dates to the late fifteenth century and uses newly fashionable brick with limestone dressings.

Lavenham in Suffolk retains many superb timber-framed buildings associated with its rise as a premier centre for woollen cloth production and trading. The Guildhall of Corpus Christi, shown here, fronts the market place. Built in the 1530s it displays the wealth and influence of its merchant patrons. The building at the far end of the row is a fifteenth-century shop. 'Close studding', which leaves only thin panels between vertical timbers, is a characteristic of timber-framing style in eastern England.

Left: The Moot Hall in the village of Steeple Bumpstead, Essex, was built as a market hall in the late sixteenth century. By the 1830s it housed a school 'for farmers' sons'.

Right: The National School in Steeple Bumpstead, Essex was built in 1848 to replace the 'Old School' in the nearby Moot Hall. A new village primary school was built in 1972 on another site. Many former village schools have found new uses. This one is now a pottery shop.

Left: The large windows and clock betray the origins of this house as a village schoolroom. Built in 1867 in traditional cottage style on land given by the local vicar. It closed in 1978 and the children then went to school in the neighbouring village.

Robin Hood's Bay (North Yorkshire), like many coastal villages, clings to the rocks and has lost houses to the sea throughout its history. A roofscape of orangey red pan tiles contributes to this village's distinctive character and attractiveness. Roofs like this can be seen throughout the eastern counties of England; an indication of connections with the Netherlands where pan tiles were widely used. A few grey Welsh slate roofs are also visible, showing the late nineteenth century spread of that popular roofing material as industrialisation and transport links developed across the country.

Clovelly in Devon has been a very popular tourist destination for more than a century. It is an estate village with a fishing heritage that is continued by the few boats that still gain protection in its small harbour. The structure with the arched entrance just right of centre on the waterfront is a limekiln, another reminder of the village's much grittier past. Limestone and coal for fuel was brought in by boat and burnt to create lime, an important fertiliser for arable land and building material. The village occupies a natural ravine and its main street is too narrow and steep for motor vehicles.

Siston near Bristol in South Gloucestershire typifies many of the smallest historic English villages. It has a church with Norman origins, a sixteenth-century mansion, and a handful of cottages and farmhouses grouped in a loose cluster. This looks like a deeply rural location, but industrialisation had direct and indirect effects everywhere in the countryside. The west side of Siston parish was most affected by Bristol's industrial and suburban growth. An important brass foundry was established there, a coal mine operated in the nineteenth century and a railway line was driven through the area.

RAF Alconbury's long Cold War runway is gradually disappearing as a new type of village is born. The United States Air Force still has an enclave here (top right) but a new private housing development, complete with schools, greens and a cricket pitch, is well under way (right of centre). An industrial park has been established (bottom right), while former bomb stores and hardened aircraft shelters (left) have found new business uses.

think there is a need to restrict all new homes to be full-time residency. I have been visiting [village X] for over 30 years, staying in holiday lets prior to purchasing property in 2009, and have seen many changes take place in the village over this time. Whilst the village is still as beautiful as ever, I think it is vital to protect the 'soul' of the village by preventing any new property built being snapped up by people wishing to buy as an 'investment' rather than with any 'heart' or need. I can see how this happens, as the area I live in is in the midst of that situation at the moment, with 'investors' snapping up property, and pushing up property prices to the detriment of local people trying to get a foot on the property ladder.

Whether second home owners and incomers are seen as part of the destruction of a village or its salvation, they undoubtedly bring in different expectations, outlooks, trades and professions and play a significant part in determining its future character and structure. Paradoxically, it often seems to be those who migrate to villages that are most vociferous and well equipped to protest against subsequent village growth. Perhaps they are particularly sensitised to becoming town dwellers by default. After all, urbanisation is not what they had chosen or paid for.

It is a real conundrum. Enabling all those who want to live a village life to do so, without destroying the very things that make village life so appealing, is an extremely tricky balancing act, and one that should not be determined by any universal decree. The needs and circumstances of each village and the views of its existing residents must be taken into account to come up with a bespoke solution for each village.

CHAPTER 10

VILLAGE PLANNING AND CONSERVATION

Throughout history some villages have been designed, founded and expanded by guiding authorities, such as a lord or industrialist with specific purposes and formats in mind. Others have grown in a series of individual developments without any single grand plan or end result ever being set out explicitly. More recently, national and local government planning legislation and policy, the conservation movement and local resident input have become major factors in guiding the future of English villages.

You might think that a rich history and legacy of regional and local diversity in the character of villages would provide natural inspiration and a starting point for anybody looking to add development to them. But no, many developers seemed determined to do anything but take any inspiration from a village or its past; they built without much constraint or obligation placed on them.

From the 1950s onwards, the national house builders and local developers simply responded to post-war recovery and baby boomer demand, building anywhere they could. There was little consultation and engagement with existing residents. There was not much concern with design that responded to local needs and character, not much thought about environmental cost, energy efficiency, sustainability, effect on local services, transport or anything else that might have a bearing on the long-term success or otherwise of the villages concerned.

Many villages continued to acquire successive accretions of characterless, ubiquitous, 'could be anywhere' type housing estates, whilst piecemeal back-land and infill development destroyed former orchards and gardens. Locals seemed to gain little and stood to lose a lot. The origins of village Nimbyism ('Not in my back yard') can be found in unsympathetic post-war planning, or rather the lack of it.

The positive aspects of village expansion, such as acquiring a greater critical mass of people to keep demand for local amenities thriving, more housing options to enable young families to stay within villages, and an injection of new blood bringing new ideas and capacity into village life, might have been more readily received if developers and planners had taken more trouble to understand village history, character and current needs, and built accordingly.

Developers of the late nineteenth century and twentieth century operated in the context of a brave new modern world that was busily rejecting and overcoming much of what the past had to offer. Poor sanitation, disease, poverty, illiteracy, rigid social and economic stratification all had to go. But too often old buildings were also thought to be part of the problem past. Many architects and developers seemed to view historic buildings as the built equivalent of cholera, which had to be eradicated.

They were not part of the infrastructure of a bright new future. Working with traditional building materials such as local stone, timber, slate, lime mortar, reeds, straw and earth was thought to be inconvenient and labour-intensive. Specialist skills, some of which were very localised, had to be carefully learnt and handed on; and a vicious spiral of decreasing availability of skills and materials and increasing expense, fuelled by decreasing interest and demand, developed during the 1950s and 1960s.

The story of Collyweston slate exemplifies the problems faced in many regions and with many other types of traditional building material. The slate takes its name from a small village in north-east Northamptonshire and for hundreds of years was the roofing material of choice for a wide area radiating out from the village into Northamptonshire, Cambridgeshire, Leicestershire, Rutland and Lincolnshire. Collyweston is situated within the limestone belt. In this locality the seams of the rock are bedded in thin layers that split. As far back as Roman times, somebody discovered that this made it a poor material for walls, columns and sculptures, but made it a very useful source of roof slates.

A considerable slating industry developed in the locality from medieval times onwards. The raw lumps of suitable limestone rock, or 'log', had to be quarried or mined in galleries that followed the suitable seams. The mined log was then laid out in the open in fields, where several seasons of rain, freeze and thaw would crack and weaken the bonds between the bedding planes. The log could then be split into thin plates of stone and dressed into a rectangular slate shape with special tools. A few more deft taps created a hole for a wooden fixing peg.

Collyweston slates are extremely durable. They can last several hundred years and, as time goes by, they weather to attractive buff and grey shades that complement the other local limestones used for walls. Collyweston slate roofs attract gradual moss and lichen growth, which then mellows them even more. The whole effect is of something attractive and natural that seems to grow from the landscape of the area, which in a sense it has. Collyweston slate utterly characterised the vernacular architecture of the region and its villages.

It wasn't only used for cottages and barns, Collyweston slate was used to roof stately homes, Cambridge University colleges, and churches. Unbelievably it was even shipped across the Atlantic to be used on a Long Island, New York mansion, Westbury House. However, things began to change as far back as the middle of the nineteenth century. The arrival of the railways and the Victorian building boom going on in the region's towns ensured that industrial quantities of Welsh slate and machine-made brick were more easily and cheaply available. The style of new buildings in the area changed with emerging fashions and to suit these mass-produced materials.

As the twentieth century progressed, demand for Collyweston slate fell dramatically. People skilled in slate production dwindled away, and fewer hard, frosty winters made the supply even more precarious. Eventually, no new Collyweston slate was being produced at all. For a while those who wanted to use it for their roofs could obtain it from the relatively abundant stocks salvaged from demolished buildings, but as this supply ran out, slates were quarried from the roofs of standing buildings.

Robbing the Church of St Peter to re-roof the Church of St Paul is not a sound conservation philosophy (even though it was mostly barn roofs being quarried for slates, not churches), and in any case, there was a drastically decreasing number of candidates to rob from. Substitute roofing materials of variable quality and appearance were increasingly used instead. A significant part of the character of the region began to disappear beneath roofs that were manufactured abroad, available from any builders' merchant, and could be seen on thousands of buildings anywhere in the country.

A few years ago I visited the last accessible Collyweston slate mine. The vertical access shaft to the mine was situated in the middle of a small industrial estate and unceremoniously covered with steel joists, old timbers and tin sheets. Climbing down the ladder into the mine was like descending into the past. The air got colder, modern sounds faded away, bright daylight disappeared, then from the dimly lit base of the shaft I could see low and narrow galleries leading away into the darkness.

Groping along them, I saw rusted iron props and columns of slate shoring up the gallery roofs from sudden collapse. Miners had lain on their backs in the galleries using picks, hammers and crowbars to hack and lever out thick slabs of limestone rock. They listened carefully for any slight cracking sound that might indicate an imminent rockfall.

I must admit, my first thoughts were archaeological rather than commercial. How could we make a thorough record of the mine for posterity? Perhaps a 3D laser scan, followed by tool mark analysis to see if we could distinguish the types used and whether we could relatively date the phases of mining? Maybe we could excavate infilled and collapsed galleries and find datable artefacts? I then thought about the mine as a heritage visitor experience. People love descending into the excavated Neolithic flint mines at Grimes Graves in Norfolk, and the caves of the Peak District have been popular for centuries. There is absolutely nothing else like the Collyweston mine in the region.

I gave a little thought to the prospect of this being a fully working mine and source of copious amounts of precious Collyweston slate, but quickly dismissed it as far too difficult. There was only room to use hand tools and even pneumatic drills and electric hoists would not vastly increase the possible flow of raw material to the surface. And what would happen when it got there? Who would make the enormous investment necessary to extract commercial quantities of the material? Who would then be prepared to hope that our generally warming, twenty-first-century winters would be punctuated by enough cool ones to ensure that the log would split?

Infuriatingly, open limestone quarries in the locality had also revealed a large seam of suitable Collyweston slate log, but with no means of guaranteeing its conversion to slate, it was being crushed up with all the other rock as hard core for general construction purposes. No, I thought sadly, the Collyweston slate industry is finished. It is history now.

At its worst, the modern building industry did not forgetfully fail to engage with conservation, unwittingly undermine traditional building materials and skills, and accidentally erode ancient village character, but actively sought to ensure that it would not be encumbered by any obligation to replicate, repair or reuse anything old. Most of the larger housing developers were quick to claim that it was simply too difficult and expensive to repair and restore old buildings, and anyway, the end result was not what the new market had been conditioned to crave. Better to pull it all down and start again.

Housing developers usually preferred to pursue new build schemes on green fields or sites swept entirely clear of problematic old buildings. As for responding to local character in new design, or using traditional materials in new buildings, why bother? Some horrible crimes against heritage and society were committed. It is often said that post-war planning and development did far more harm to England's stock of historic buildings in urban centres than anything the Luftwaffe's bombs had managed to achieve. Villages did not escape; even the smallest villages needlessly lost good, characterful historic buildings and gained badly designed, unattractive new ones in the name of progress.

WE ARE THE VILLAGE GREEN PRESERVATION SOCIETY

People often assume that comprehensive, protective legislation for historic villages and individual buildings must go back a long way, at least to early Victorian times, or perhaps even further, to the enlightened eighteenth century. It is true that Georgians were great collectors of classical architectural ideas and Victorians were busy restorers of medieval churches. However, the former were not especially enthused by saving the remains of the barbaric society that followed the fall of Rome; and looking at the work of Victorian architects, you get the impression that many of them thought they could do medieval architecture much better than medieval people. Most had few qualms about knocking down more original fabric than strictly necessary to achieve their desired, often theatrical, medieval effect.

The active preservation of buildings and built places may originate in the late nineteenth century, but it has taken a long while to formalise into a widespread conservation movement and a structured framework of national legislation and policy. Now, however, the conservation movement and the various systems through which conservation can be achieved are major factors in the way that English villages are managed and develop.

Until relatively recently, conservation happened mostly accidentally; the preservation of an old building was simply pragmatism or a lack of finance, having to mend and make do with what history had handed down. Rather than demolishing buildings entirely and expensively rebuilding from scratch, property owners large and small merely reclad facades in an up-to-date, fashionable style when finances allowed; putting a brave face on it. In really good times, perhaps the money stretched to adding a new extension. But often the ancient core of the building remained intact, enveloped in its new cloaking.

Over the years some amazing long-lost gems of buildings have been revealed when building works stripped back modern accretions. But I shudder to think how many valuable and irreplaceable historic buildings have been lost because they were hidden by later alterations, their real origins and significance not recognised until modifications and demolitions were well under way and it was too late to save them.

The Ancient Monuments Protection Act 1882 was the first piece of United Kingdom legislation whose purpose was the recognition and preservation of ancient structures and buildings for the sake of their archaeological and historical interest. The first things to be added to the 'schedule' were select prehistoric monuments, followed by things such as Roman villas and medieval castles. These were important monuments, but they were ruins that were unlikely to be too central to the operation of the estates on which they sat. Some landed gentry may still have occupied buildings constructed by their medieval ancestors, but not their prehistoric ancestors.

Nevertheless, there was still much opposition to the 1882 Act from landowners who did not want the state to interfere with their property, however ancient, or require them to look after it appropriately. The provisions of the 1882 Act when passed were much watered down from the initial proposals, and did not place any great burdens on the private owners of what was seen increasingly as national heritage. It was not illegal, for example, for owners to damage or demolish scheduled monuments.

The first convictions for offences against ancient monuments were for vandalism by members of the public. I like to think that Victorian graffiti artists were caught red-handed during the several hours they must have taken to 'tag' standing stones with etched copperplate handwriting.

The Ancient Monuments Protection Act 1882 was replaced by new versions throughout the twentieth century. The current Ancient Monuments and Archaeological Areas Act 1979 is more robust than its 1882 ancestor. It is now a criminal offence punishable by a fine, and even a prison sentence, to knowingly damage a scheduled monument without having first obtained consent. Scheduled Monument Consent applications are assessed and administered by Historic England on behalf of the Secretary of State (Department for Digital, Culture, Media & Sport). Consent will not be granted for unnecessary, unjustified, harmful work. People can no longer casually destroy scheduled monuments that help define the historic character of a village or that help tell the story of its past.

However, the 1979 Act retains important exemptions. Places of worship that are still in use as such cannot be designated as scheduled monuments, nor can houses that are still in use as homes. The 1979 Act was a leap forward in active conservation of heritage, but it was not the answer to the widespread non-scrutinised destruction of historic buildings in town and country.

The Town and Country Planning Act 1947 introduced the planning system that the UK has today. It gave local planning authorities (county, district and borough councils) the task of setting development plans for their areas and the responsibility for determining individual planning applications. It was no longer simply a matter of landowners and property developers building what they wanted, where they wanted. Instead would-be builders had to comply with development plans and frameworks set by their local authorities. Importantly, the 1947 Act also introduced recognition and planning control for historic buildings not covered by ancient monuments legislation. Buildings that were to benefit from this form of protection had to be 'listed'.

Listed buildings are historic buildings that the relevant Secretary of State of the day (currently the Secretary of State for Digital, Culture, Media & Sport) agrees meet the required level of architectural and historic significance. The current version of the primary legislation is the Planning (Listed Buildings and Conservation Areas) Act 1990. Terse list descriptions lead to an often repeated misconception that listing, and therefore listed building controls, only apply to the exterior of a building, when often it is the interior form and details that contribute a huge amount to its overall significance. Some owners don't seem to appreciate this and unwittingly harm the historic significance of their buildings through internal alterations.

Listing is an accolade, a recognition that a historic building meets a certain level of interest and importance. Many owners are quite happy with that, as research has shown that listed commercial properties usually generate higher returns on investment than non-listed properties. Listed homes also command higher prices. Estate agents, or at least eighty-two per cent of those surveyed, agreed that original features added to a property's value. Even homes near listed buildings accrue additional value; it is no coincidence that the most attractive and sought-after villages also tend to have the most listed buildings.

However, while owners of listed buildings are generally happy with the recognition of the historic value and financial value of their property, some are not happy with the additional controls that come with listed status. Demolitions, extensions and alterations to the fabric or appearance of a listed building cannot be carried out unless a specific Listed Building Consent has been granted. To fail to do so is a criminal offence.

Local planning authorities manage the listed building consent process and determine applications, as they do for planning applications. The national agency, Historic England, is a statutory consultee on certain types of listed building consent applications, mainly those affecting Grade I and Grade II* buildings. The various national 'amenity societies' (the Victorian Society, Georgian Society, Council for British Archaeology, etc.) are also consulted by local planning authorities on applications within their spheres of interest. Local authorities can also compile 'Local Lists' of historic buildings that may not meet the threshold of national significance, but are nevertheless important to the history and character of an area and whose protection will be recognised in local development policies.

Churches, though listed, are exempt from having to apply to local planning authorities for listed building consent, but only retain this exemption on condition that the relevant church authorities maintain a parallel system for assessing and determining proposals that could affect the historic fabric and character of their buildings. The Church of England does this through 'Faculty' jurisdiction, whereby proposed alterations, extensions or additions to churches have to be applied for in advance and determined by senior church officials drawing on specialist advisers.

The Civic Amenities Act 1967 allowed local authorities to designate 'conservation areas'. These are designed to recognise not just a special building or group of buildings, but a place that has a special architectural and historic character. The local authority can exert more than usual control over development and demolition in a conservation area, and it can implement additional measures (known as Article 4 directions) that provide control over types of alterations to non-listed buildings that normally fall outside the planning process (such as altering front doors or chopping down trees). The additional controls exerted by a planning authority under Article 4 directions are customised to the particular management needs of the conservation area in question.

There are now around 10,000 conservation areas in England, around sixty per cent of which are in rural areas. The historic cores of most villages are designated as conservation areas. Historic parkland, industrial, transport and military heritage sites, even nineteenth- and twentieth-century suburbs can be designated too. Homes in rural conservation areas usually command higher prices (currently twenty-three per cent higher on average) than equivalent homes outside conservation areas.

You could be forgiven for thinking that with all these layers of protection and with clear investment incentives, all historic English villages would be picture-perfect models of conservation excellence, but the reality is that there are many competing interests in a place that must be balanced alongside conservation. Much of the management of historic places and decision-making is left to owners, residents and local authorities, many of whom have limited conservation advice to draw upon. Experienced conservation officers are a disappearing breed in local government staff structures, and some local planning authorities do not seem adequately equipped to make informed decisions about heritage matters. Nevertheless, they all have the responsibility of setting out their development and conservation stalls in their Local Plans.

Local Plans set out the policies that a planning authority will use to make decisions about granting or refusing planning permission. The scope of what should be covered in Local Plans and how local planning authorities should determine individual planning permissions is defined in the National Planning Policy Framework. This stipulates how matters such as building design, transport and communications infrastructure, local economy, and the conservation of the historic and natural environment should be tackled. Individual planning applications are then scrutinised for their adherence to local plan and national planning policies (effects on highways, drainage, wildlife, heritage, views and so on) and are either determined by committees of elected councillors, or delegated to council officers.

The formation of a Local Plan is subject to layers of public consultation and ultimately is scrutinised by a government-appointed planning inspector, who must determine its 'sound-ness', the evidence underpinning its policies, and adherence to national legislation and policy. So a Local Plan policy that states, on a whim, that all new buildings must be rendered in a pretty shade of pink is unlikely to meet the required test. Though a similar policy, expressed and implemented in less clumsy and more nuanced wording, could well apply to villages in parts of Suffolk, where many historic buildings are rendered in mellow pinks, reds and yellows.

Local Plans should set out the development framework for a fifteen-year period, but they often take years to be defined, consulted upon, challenged and adopted, by which time they can be out of date. If a development meets Local Plan policy, the National Planning Policy Framework stip-ulates that local planning authorities should be approved 'without delay'. If the Local Plan is not in place, out of date or silent in respect of the specific matter in hand, the presump-tion is in favour of granting planning permission.

Often the most controversial element of local planning is the identification and allocation of land suitable for various forms of development, whether for new housing, industrial or business uses. Local authorities cannot get away with simply avoiding the issue of allocating land for new houses, or allocating as little as possible, they have to take their share of national housing targets based on projections of need.

Appleby Magna, a village situated just east of the M42 motorway in rural Leicestershire, right in the middle of England, has experienced something typical of many villages in recent years. A conservation area covers the historic core of the village, incorporating a Grade II* listed medieval church, several other listed buildings, and an extensive, scheduled monument manorial site. The village is surrounded by its fields of medieval earthwork ridge and furrow. In recent years Appleby Magna has been subjected to a barrage of proposals for large-scale developments from house builders to industrial developers.

The District Council did not have a new Local Plan in place and so developers effectively declared 'open season' on the village. Appleby Magna has grown considerably, but had all the proposed developments come to fruition, it would now have expanded well into the surrounding countryside to become a sizeable town, which perhaps could have been renamed Appleby-even-more-Magna. As it is, the Local Plan for 2011 to 2031 was finally adopted in 2017 and limits to the village's expansion have now been defined. However, the Local Plan will be reviewed periodically during its lifetime and the tussle over Appleby Magna's future, and the future of many other villages, will continue.

Neighbourhood Planning is a relatively new innovation in identifying what is special about a village and how it should develop in the future. The government description of Neighbourhood Planning states that it '. . . gives communities direct power to develop a shared vision for their neighbourhood and shape the development and growth of their local area', but it is not quite as simple or as self-determining as it sounds. Neighbourhood Plans can be drawn up by parish councils or town councils after comprehensive consultation and scrutiny. I quoted some responses to one Neighbourhood Plan consultation earlier. Neighbourhood Plans take a lot of work to get formally adopted and must align with or be accepted within Local Plans.

The response to proposed village growth is often emotive, angry and bitter, severely polarising opinion and setting neighbours against each other. There are vested interests and big financial gains and losses at stake; village land allocated for housing development is worth considerably more than agricultural land.

Emotive arguments about maintaining the peace and quiet of village life or not wanting to change the character of a village, however sincerely made, do not go very far in the planning process. The planning system requires objections to proposed development to be expressed in terms of variance from set policy, not the fact that people really don't like what is about to happen to their village. Of course, even the best-written planning policies and best-evidenced development proposals often leave plenty of wriggle room for interpretation and difference of opinion.

Planning appeals against refusal of planning permission can lead to hearings or public inquiries, presided over by a planning inspector. The latter are very formal with strict rules governing what evidence can by submitted by whom. Certain relevant interested parties can be permitted to speak, ask questions, or be cross-examined by specialist planning lawyers and barristers. Heartfelt entreaties and accusations of inconsiderate and underhand developer behaviour from members of the community may enliven proceedings, but they will not sway them.

It can get very messy indeed when planning barristers employed by developers get their teeth into well-meaning but not well-prepared citizens. It doesn't seem a very fair playing field, as major developers are used to fighting these cases and are very well equipped to do so. People sometimes are frustrated that planning inquiries often swing on some obscure, highly technical point of planning policy or law, rather than weight of objections, moral force or even apparently common sense.

I was once involved as an expert witness in a planning case that progressed through a public inquiry, to the High Court, then the Court of Appeal. A surreal moment came one morning in the Royal Courts of Justice when the determination of the whole case hinged upon case law involving Amnesty International (the human rights campaign group) and General Pinochet, one-time military dictator of Chile. The opposing barristers and presiding judge entered deep into their own world of near impenetrable legalese, citing and counter-citing case law and precedent, picking over the judgements of previous courts and judges.

I sat there (on an uncomfortable seat) wondering how on earth the refusal of planning permission concerning new development in an English shire county could escalate (or descend) to the point at which some very clever (and expensive) people at the top of their professions were ceremoniously and politely arguing over whether or not various judgements against a South American Junta might have been arrived at fairly.

Planning appeal and hearing judgements, by definition, always disappoint somebody. Only the barristers and paid experts are guaranteed any reward for their efforts. The overriding impression that some previously innocent and shell-shocked participants come away with is that there must be better ways of settling these things. Toss of a coin perhaps? Best of three? Sometimes homeowners themselves undermine the case for keeping a place special through their individual actions over a period of time.

Austin Village in Birmingham was founded to house workers for the Austin Motor Company's Longbridge factory during the First World War. Herbert Austin had 200 prefabricated bungalows shipped from America and quickly assembled them to form the basis of a new community. The unusual and distinctive development of red cedar wood bungalows, interspersed with brick-built houses to act as firebreaks, was designated as a Conservation Area in 1997 in recognition of its historical importance and special character.

However, unsympathetic alterations to individual buildings have diminished the character of the Conservation Area to such an extent that serious consideration has been given to de-designating it. The Austin Village Preservation Society, representing conservation-minded residents, is determined to fight this move and retain the village's conservation area status.

In another place, in a different part of England, newcomers to the pristine village of Milton Abbas in Dorset are given a welcome pack of information and advice about how to look after and present their property, and thereby protect the tidiness and uniformity that makes the village so distinctive. The message to new residents is clear: if you want to live somewhere really special, you have to do your bit to keep it special.

Conservation, preserving the character of a village, usually requires balance. Few people want to live in totally unmodernised homes, or accept complete stagnation in the development of a village. Many enjoy the special quality of living in lovely historic houses amid distinctive and picturesque settings, but this does come at the expense of what some consider to be an unhealthy degree of state intrusiveness. With regard to listed buildings that retain architecturally significant internal forms and features, the conservation battleground can extend into people's homes, their living rooms, bedrooms and bathrooms.

For some, like the Victorian opponents of the Ancient Monuments Protection Act 1882, this is state interference with private property and private lives gone way too far. For others, this level of control is in the public interest, proportionate and necessary to avoid the unfettered incremental loss of special historic buildings.

From far beyond parish and district council boundaries come much wider social, political and economic forces and pressures. Village growth versus conservation sometimes seems like a big political football that can be kicked around from time to time as the mood of the day swings between building more homes and increasing environmental protection. Developers habitually blame the convoluted planning process and local interference for stymying their developments and greatly increasing their costs. They continually lobby governments for less strict planning rules. But for strategic commercial reasons, many developers also land-bank sites that could be developed easily.

Some say they do this deliberately and cynically to ensure a slower supply, therefore maintaining higher demand and achieving higher asking prices. The Local Government Association calculates that over the last ten years planning permissions given for new housing schemes that have not been progressed by their developer applicants could provide a million new homes. The LGA points out that planning applications for new houses have doubled over the last decade, and that nine out of ten applications are now approved. Its message is that the planning system is not broken; it is not a barrier to building new homes and has not caused a national housing shortage, or a housing crisis in villages.

Nevertheless, the Covid-19 crisis is likely to provoke another reform of the planning process as economic recovery and ideas for different types of housing and working environments come even more to the fore. This matters because the detail of the formal planning and conservation process now shapes the present and future of villages just as profoundly as the lords of the manor, industrialists, speculative developers and social engineers of the past. The rules will be redrawn again and striving to achieve the balancing act between village conservation and growth will continue to be a source of much heated local and national argument and controversy.

FARMING FOR SURVIVAL

Most English villages, throughout their history, were inextricably connected to their surrounding farmland. What happened in the landscape around a village was either driven by the village, or affected the village. The direct relationships between villagers and farming is less strong in the twenty-first century than it has been at any point in village history, but farming still determines the environment, setting and a large part of the character of all rural villages.

Greater physical access to the countryside by greater numbers of people, more people choosing to live permanently in villages or acquire second homes, and even the continuing popularity of rural-themed virtual experiences (through TV and film, etc.) has meant that a considerable part of the nation's population has become exposed to countryside matters. Many people who don't actually live there, nevertheless, feel some connection to rural England. This undoubtedly helps to foster mutual understanding across society, but very often the history that helps provide the context for dialogue has been forgotten, and understanding and empathy suffer as a result.

The twentieth century saw another agricultural revolution. It was largely driven by international factors, to which government and the farming industry has had to respond, and it has had a profound effect on most English villages and their surroundings. The need for home-grown produce to counter the blockade of imports to Britain during two world wars saw hundreds of thousands of acres of hitherto difficult and neglected rural land thrashed into cultivation.

Often known simply as 'waste' land, vast areas of woodland, scrub, marsh and rough pasture, invariably rich in wildlife, were pressed into arable service. A national emergency and internal crisis demanded that the English rural landscape changed rapidly.

First established in the First World War, County War Agricultural Executive Committees were reconstituted in 1939 on the outbreak of the Second World War and tasked with vastly increasing farm productivity. The County Committees were supported by a tier of District Committees. The 'War Ags', as they were commonly known, comprised a smattering of a county's great and good along with active farmers and others with technical knowledge. With international trading partners under enemy occupation and the terrifyingly effective U-boat menace cutting off supply lines, the nation's survival depended on farmers' ability to feed soldiers and civilians alike. This was no time for committees simply to issue government advice and hope for the best.

The East Anglian Film Archive at the University of East Anglia has a fascinating thirty-five-minute wartime documentary recording the reclamation of some fen land in south-east Cambridgeshire. This land posed huge challenges. It had been drained and farmed in the nineteenth century and dug for peat, but it had subsequently become neglected and had reverted to swamp, reeds, bushes and trees. The opening shots of the film are of two ladies picking their way through this almost impenetrable wilderness.

The would-be farmer of this unpromising land, Alan Bloom, had bought the neighbouring run-down farm and wanted to acquire more land for arable production. The improbably named Bloom later set up one of the most famous horticultural centres in Britain at Bressingham in Norfolk, but in Cambridgeshire he was thwarted by a reluctant owner and the magnitude of the task. He called in the local War Ag and the Ministry of Agriculture and Fisheries for assistance. They responded by acquiring the land, installing Bloom as the tenant, and supplying manpower and machinery.

The film shows how the reeds and sedge were burnt off and the trees and scrub cleared. Standing water can be seen to cover huge areas, so long, straight drainage ditches were dug by hand and mechanical draglines. Then, as the cleared land was being prepared for cultivation, the workers came across the remains of an ancient fen environment: the preserved trunks, stumps and roots of trees from the prehistoric forest that once covered the area.

Always known locally as 'bog oaks', these are actually a variety of different tree species dating back 4000 to 6000 years, but they tend to have several things in common – they are massive, extremely heavy, and almost as hard as rock when first revealed. The trees died and keeled over due to rising water levels in the Neolithic and Bronze Age periods and were swamped and buried beneath the expanding marsh.

Bog oaks have fascinated me since childhood, when one day my dad snagged his plough on one. I helped in the laborious process of digging round and under the trunk so we could get chains around it and drag it out with a tractor. I remember the tractor wheels spinning and digging in ever deeper, as it strained with all its horsepower to prise the monster from the black earth. When we finally got it loose, we found two other iron shoes (detachable tips) from more ancient ploughs embedded in the venerable timber.

Alan Bloom brought in special ploughs to remove the remains of the modern trees and ancient forest alike. A 'stump jump' used to break the outback in Australia and a 'prairie buster' from Canada, however, were no match for the fenland bog oaks, one of which was said to be 90 feet long. The film shows two caterpillar tractors working together to pull out massive trunks, but the bog oaks were so many and so large that eventually more drastic measures were needed. A detachment of army Royal Engineers was called in to break them up with explosives. The film shows charges being laid and captures a series of explosions. Across the newly broken land, black earth leaps skywards and then showers back down in scenes reminiscent of footage from the battlefields of the First World War.

After the removal of hundreds of bog oaks, a lot of hard work was still required to prepare the land for drilling seed. The film shows a series of ploughs, harrows and rollers being deployed. The efforts finally bear fruit and we are shown members of the Women's Land Army feeding cattle, leafy sugar beet and potatoes, fields of waving wheat, followed by harvesting. Finally there is ploughing in preparation for next season's crops.

The documentary concludes with the statement: 'The bushes, the reeds, the turf pits and the oaks no longer hinder the work of food production. This black soil is fertile, and nothing will be left undone which can be done to make it yield its bounty.' Colossal effort had certainly gone into making these once forgotten acres of land fit to produce much-needed food.

Throughout the war, across England, the representatives of various War Ags visited and assessed the efficiency of farms and the capabilities of farmers. Arable production was favoured over pasture for milk, beef and wool production. The War Ags had the authority to insist that farmers plough up their pasture land to grow potatoes and other crops, even where none had ever previously been grown by any farmer. Their wide powers extended to dispossessing landowners and either putting their farms into new hands, or farming them directly themselves; more than 10,000 farmers are said to have lost their farms in this way.

The War Ags' relentless pursuit of greater yields was sometimes marred by accusations that they lacked understanding of particular local circumstances and agricultural methods. They were occasionally accused of dictatorial, partisan and downright vindictive behaviour. In one parliamentary debate in 1945, they were likened to the enemy's reviled Gestapo. This was a shocking observation at a time when everybody would have been well aware of the terror that the Nazi state's secret police had inflicted across Europe.

At least one forced eviction led to the ultimate tragedy. Ray Walden was the tenant of a small mixed farm in the picturesque Itchen Valley, east of Winchester. He had failed to engage or comply with a series of Hampshire War Agricultural Executives Committee directions, and so compulsory repossession proceedings were set in motion. Anticipating further non-cooperation, the local constabulary was called upon to assist. An eighteen-hour siege followed, gunfire was exchanged and policemen were wounded. Walden was shot and fatally injured during the final assault on his farmhouse. Justifiable homicide was the coroner's verdict.

It is incredible that during July 1940, when the Battle of Britain raged in the skies and a Nazi invasion was expected any day, a shoot-out between neighbours could take place in a corner of rural England. The small villages of Itchen Stoke, Ovington and Tichborne certainly could never have anticipated this particular consequence of war and the national drive to increase local arable productivity. This may have been the most dramatic and tragic result of the War Ags' many thousands of interventions, but angry clashes, bitterness, grief, hardship, and almost certainly illness, shortening of life and suicides, were experienced elsewhere.

These wartime interventions were yet one more episode in the long story about influence and control over the management of village farmland. They undoubtedly added to the suspicion with which some villagers and farmers met external official interference. Nevertheless, across England, the Ministry and the War Ags did the required job to great effect. Poor, old-fashioned, inefficient farming practices, which had stumbled on down the years and limped on through the Great Depression of the 1930s, were addressed. The productivity of the countryside was increased massively. The nation did not starve. This was 'Dig for Victory' on an epic level. Britain had much cause to be very grateful for its farms and villages.

Modern farming was born in the Second World War and its aftermath. Horses and steam traction engines were replaced by tractors, and farms became larger and more business-like. It was a trend that was set to continue throughout the following decades. The old mosaic of small livestock and arable mixed farms surrounding many villages gave way to much larger specialised farms that were far more effective in growing a narrower range of produce. As a result, villages themselves began to lose much of their former diversity and the character of village communities also started to change.

The varied mix of gentleman hobbyists, farming widows and spinsters, smallholders and labourers who lived and worked the local land began to homogenise. The war and post-war economics were the death knell for much of the old village squirearchy, many of whose country houses and estates had been requisitioned for war purposes. Maintaining massive historic houses and parkland proved too expensive in the modern era, and many were sold for new uses, such as hotels and schools, or found their way into the hands of the National Trust. Some burnt down or were demolished. Estate cottages and entire villages were sold off.

Market forces, government incentives and improvements in agricultural science, as well as confidence to invest in new machinery and to purchase land, ingenuity and sheer hard work, saw post-war farmers ramping up yields to levels that their ancestors could never have imagined. Ensuring food security, reducing trade deficits and keeping food prices low were the imperatives. Most farmers throughout history have known that they need to be good custodians of their land, if only to preserve its growing potential. Working so closely with nature meant that many also deeply appreciated the special qualities of their local environment.

In post-war England, however, conservation-led farming was not an indulgence that many farmers could afford, and it was certainly not what government agricultural and economic policy encouraged. There was a growing tension between villages and their surroundings as amenities for visitors and residents, as productive and viable workplaces, and the conservation of the natural environment.

GREEN AND PLEASANT LAND

Widening interest in environmental issues and recognition of the interconnectedness of different environments has encouraged people to think not only of melting polar ice caps and floods in Asia, but also about the environmental health of their own figurative backyards. In the last few decades, many more people have become interested in the environmental wellbeing of rural England. Even if this manifests itself as only a casual, passing armchair interest, or an opinion about where tax revenue is spent, considerable numbers of the population have become stakeholders in decisions about the future of the English countryside.

Sometimes this weight of numbers, sentiment and misplaced nostalgia, or narrow focus on one or two conservation issues, can be a distraction from seeing the bigger picture, when better understanding, dialogue and balance are really required. The UK still cannot afford for all its countryside to become an experimental wildlife sanctuary and leisure facility, even if that was remotely desirable. Neither do people wish to see nothing but aggressive, hyper-intensive, environmentally destructive farming, of the types carried out in other parts of the world. Those parts of the world, incidentally, from which much of the UK population seems quite content to buy very cheap food, and thereby encourage greater environmental damage. A balance has to be struck.

The widespread loss of hedgerows to create much larger single fields from multiple smaller fields is often used as one indicator of the environmental consequences of the inten-sification of post-war farming. People bemoan the vast, prairie-like, arable monoculture 'deserts' that their removal creates. Hedgerows provide important habitats for all sorts of wildlife and their loss has been keenly felt for that reason; but simply associating hedgerow loss with the erosion of historic landscape character is misplaced. Hedgerows only became a defining feature of parts of the English landscape during the systematic enclosure of farmland during the later eighteenth century and nineteenth century. Before then, most fields were not enclosed by any kind of physical barrier.

The thousands of miles of fences and new hedges laid to define farmland newly partitioned by private and parlia-mentary enclosure acts were seen by many at the time as the infrastructure of oppressive and distressing campaigns that dispossessed village folk of their ancient rights to use and enjoy the land around them. Without access to land for casual grazing and foraging, severe hardship for the poorest villagers often followed. Protests, violence, even murder, accompanied enclosure. It is strange to think that the loss of those same hated hedgerows have provoked despair, protest and protective legislation in modern times.

The Hedgerows Regulations 1997 were introduced under the Environmental Act 1995 to prevent the loss of naturally and historically significant hedgerows. Landowners have to apply to local planning authorities in order to remove all or part of a significant hedgerow, and consent will be refused if the hedgerow meets certain ecological and archaeological criteria. The Hedgerows Regulations 1997 are merely one mechanism in a gigantic body of legislation, policy and guidance that has been introduced to try to undo, or at least ameliorate, the effects of the drive for productivity that farmers were previously encouraged to pursue with vigour.

In recent years, various incentives have also been devised to improve the environment and offset the effects of intensive farming. Countryside stewardship schemes, paid from the public purse, are channelled through government funding streams and allow farmers to apply for a strictly defined selection of environmentally beneficial schemes and management options. The schemes, administered by Natural England and the Department for Environment, Food & Rural Affairs, offer payments to offset loss of production value and towards capital works to establish environmentally beneficial features, such as hedgerows and small woodlands.

Many of the options are for relatively short-term measures over an agreed period of a few years. These include leaving uncultivated margins along field edges, or leaving entire fields uncultivated, to encourage the presence of birds and wild flowers for the term of the agreement.

Today it is a common sight to see entire arable fields and parts of arable fields that look like they have been completely abandoned to weeds. These are sometimes misinterpreted as opening up corridors for free public access, habitat creation for walkers and campers, rather than wildlife. Some farmers, conscious of the colossal efforts they and their ancestors have made to improve productivity, are astounded that they are now encouraged to let good farmland go to what looks like ruin, though many accept their key role as custodians of nature in one form or another.

Participation in environmental stewardship schemes has always been voluntary, but there are signs that in the not too distant future adherence to a set level of enhanced environmental schemes will be required by each farm in order to draw on basic payments (subsidies), and to avoid financial penalties. Global influences and government policy are once again set to alter farmland and villages.

The wheel is turning again for the fenland whose reclamation was the subject of the wartime documentary film that I described earlier. This land, Adventurers Fen, belonged to the National Trust up to its acquisition during the war. It was attached to the very first English nature reserve that the National Trust founded back in 1899, called Wicken Fen. More recently, the National Trust has been buying up arable land in the neighbourhood of Wicken Fen with the aim of removing it from cultivation and vastly expanding wetland habitats in the area. Hard-won, productive arable land will disappear.

How will the character of the neighbouring villages of Wicken, Burwell and Reach, once solidly farming communities, change as a consequence?

CHAPTER 11

VILLAGES INTO THE FUTURE

Developments in agriculture, increasingly powerful and sophisticated agricultural machinery, much bigger fields and fewer farms have altered the character of village surroundings. They have also meant that ever fewer villagers have been involved in farming or supporting the agricultural industry.

In 1841, over twenty per cent of the population was employed in agriculture and fishing. This has declined to less than one per cent in the twenty-first century. Labour-intensive work, such as salad, vegetable, fruit and flower production, has come to rely on imported labour, not casual, seasonally employed local labour.

The farming industry estimates that it creates around 60,000 to 90,000 additional summer seasonal jobs, but even a national recruitment drive, when Covid-19 restrictions threatened the supply of workers from abroad, resulted in only eleven per cent of these jobs being taken by UK workers in 2020. In a normal year, it is nowhere near even this level. Villagers have long ago turned to other forms of work, especially where commuting to nearby towns and cities became feasible.

VILLAGE AMENITIES

For much of the twentieth century, villages retained a variety of businesses that primarily serviced the local agricultural industry and its workers. Local trade directories, the ancestor of local newspaper classified advertisements, Yellow Pages, and internet searches, are a mine of information about the businesses operating and services available in a village throughout time. A massive, digitised collection of these has been made available by the University of Leicester. Those now available online date from the 1790s to the 1910s and there is at least one historic directory covering every English county. The most well-known, long-running published series was *Kelly's Directory*, but several other brands were available.

Kelly's Directory comprised lots of useful local information arranged in various sections and indexes. The most useful section to village historians is the list of towns and villages in a county, each introduced with a bit of historical background and administrative information, followed by lists of residents with their house names, and proprietors of businesses with their premises.

In English villages at the start of the twentieth century, you will find farmers, nurserymen and market gardeners, carters and carriers, harness and saddle makers, wheelwrights, blacksmiths, builders, carpenters, plumbers, thatchers, millers, brewers, beer sellers and publicans, grocers, butchers, bakers, coal merchants, insurance agents and banks, tailors and a variety of retailers, even occasionally florists and fancy goods sellers. If one village didn't have it, the village down the road might. There was often no need to go much further. Only one hundred years ago, many villages appeared to be almost as self-sufficient and self-contained as they had been in early medieval times.

In the latter years of the twentieth century, changing working patterns, the loss of work opportunities within a village, the rise of commuting, a growing number of parents who both need to work, and the dominance of out-of-town, superstore shopping hit village facilities particularly hard. When most of the village workforce spent its working week elsewhere, then got into the habit of cramming its weekly shopping needs into a frantic three hours at supermarkets and shopping centres at the weekend, there was much less demand for a wide range of facilities in the village high street.

In addition, keeping increasingly specialised and sophisticated farm machinery running gradually became beyond the capabilities of village blacksmiths and local garage mechanics. Farmers had to seek technical support and maintenance from further afield.

The last few decades therefore have seen a drastic decline in formerly vital village facilities. Wander down many village high streets and this change is easy to trace. Even if it is difficult to read the relevant architectural changes in building fabric, homes with names such as 'The Old Post Office', 'Bank House', 'Rose and Crown Cottage' and 'The Smithy' indicate their former purposes. Using old trade directories, you can match these buildings to their proprietors over time, and speculate about where the other referenced businesses were located.

As time went on, village services found it ever more diffi-cult with the growing demand for shopping convenience, huge choice ranges and lower prices available elsewhere. However, some village businesses could probably have done more to compete and survive. One day many years ago, shortly after moving to a village, I found myself unexpect-edly working in a field not far away without having brought anything to eat and nothing much at home. Freezing cold, soaked through and very hungry, I went to the village shop at lunchtime, only to find the proprietor closing the door and turning the closed sign. She looked at me standing there, with the mixed look of disappointment and hope on my face, and said, 'We're closed.'

'But it's lunchtime,' I whimpered.

'Well, I have to eat my lunch too, you know,' she replied and closed the door in my face.

Perhaps it had been a hard morning for her, up at the crack of dawn to sort the papers, a stream of demanding customers, no time to sit down. Perhaps if I had been a familiar face or had not looked so bedraggled and caked in mud, she might have let me in to buy something with an admonishing, 'All right, just this time if you're quick, but I will need to lock the door.' Or something else that let me know this was my first and last friendly warning not to try buying anything for lunch at lunchtime in her shop.

Hers was the only shop in the village. The alternatives elsewhere were not reachable in what remained of my lunch hour. Had I been a real local, I would have known what the opening hours were on a Wednesday and would not have embarrassed myself or her. But I didn't, so I went hungry, and she lost a new customer, not only on that day but for a good while afterwards.

Of course, I fumed silently, she could open and close whenever she liked as there was no competition. Eventually my silent, and probably entirely unnoticed boycott had to be abandoned a week or two later when I needed something or other and couldn't get out of the village on that day to get it. By then I had memorised the whimsical patterns of the shop opening times, and was grateful of having that retail service on the doorstep.

My first encounter with that village shop had been a clash of expectations. I had lived in towns and become used to shopping whenever I wanted. The shop owner was having to balance making an income, maintaining a quality of life, and providing a service to the village. The particular shop I mentioned is owned by a convenience store chain now. There are also convenience-sized supermarkets belonging to national chains in the two neighbouring villages that are open all hours: as life has changed, so the shops have adapted to suit.

A school friend who lived in a very small village named its single shop 'The Sorry Shop', because every time he went in to ask for something, the answer was, 'Sorry, we don't have any of those . . .' The shop isn't there any more, but the villagers are keen to open a village hall that could support pop-up shops and other facilities. Across England there is a growing desire and trend to shop locally to support local producers and enterprise. More flexible and creative alternatives to opening new shops are being found by the major retailers, most of whom offer online shopping and delivery; but these don't replace the social aspect of village shopping.

Several other types of previously common village buildings and village high street activity have dwindled away or are under threat. Farmyards, barns and sheds constructed for horse-drawn farming may have survived the introduction of the first generations of small tractors, but they have become increasingly redundant as the size of farm machinery has grown. Inconvenient, disused farmyards situated right on or just off village main streets are often flattened and sold for far more profitable housing development. Their loss takes away a little bit more of a village's rural character and introduces a bit more commuter suburbia.

Across the country around thirty per cent of the farmsteads extant at the start of the twentieth century have now gone. The farmstead, comprising the main farmhouse and working farm buildings, is the nerve centre of a farm. Their loss indicates the decline of smaller family farming units and the assimilation of farmland into larger farming estates. The picture is even more stark, as only around a third of the surviving historic farmsteads are still in agricultural use, though this varies considerably from relatively high continuing use in upland areas of England to much more redundancy and conversion in lowland areas. Domestic conversions and alternative business uses are common.

Outfarms (farmyards and buildings detached from the main farmstead) and field barns have fared much worse.

Over seventy per cent have been lost since 1900. Many of the historic farm buildings that remain are effectively abandoned, not maintained and in serious states of decay. A shift to a greener type of farming in the future will not mean a return to horse-drawn implements, and therefore a new demand for disused historic farm buildings to be repaired and returned to agricultural use. The best chance of retaining historic farm buildings into the future, and thereby maintaining visible traditional character in village street scenes and surrounding countryside, is through sympathetic, respectful conversion and re-purposing to fulfil new roles.

Village churches and chapels are other character-defining classes of village building that are suffering from declining use and redundancy. Congregations for regular worship have declined and many villages, for historical reasons, find themselves with magnificent, huge churches and a range of Nonconformist chapels that neither they nor the religious authorities know what to do with any more. Increasingly vicars look after multiple congregations and churches in several different villages, which stretches them thinly and inevitably means their attention cannot be focused on all the issues across their portfolio at once.

Some churches have become 'festival churches', open for worship during the main events in the Christian calendar and not for regular worship. The Church of England process to close churches for worship formally can result in them being taken on by specialist national trusts, such as the Churches Conservation Trust, or Friends of Friendless Churches, or by local trusts set up for the purpose.

The steps towards formal closure and disposal also include the provision for churches to be marketed for private ownership. Some former churches and chapels have been sold and successfully converted for home and business use. However, it is extremely challenging to convert sympathetically a lavishly furnished and decorated, highly graded medieval church into a satisfactory home or office, without destroying much of its historical and architectural significance.

When the original use of a church or chapel is no longer possible, the next best options for its use are usually related to their original purpose as venues and community gathering places. Former churches host a wide range of arts, leisure and retail activities, harking back to their wider community use in medieval times. Uses have to be found for disused churches and other redundant historic village buildings, because as mere ornaments, without further purpose, they stand little chance of raising revenue to support themselves.

When a building ceases to host activities, maintenance is inevitably forgotten, problems with masonry, rainwater goods and drainage go unnoticed and unresolved, and they fall into a spiral of disrepair that will be catastrophic sooner or later. Worryingly, Church of England law and protocol even allows for the demolition of disused church buildings when all attempts to find a new use have failed.

Even when a church remains in use with an active congregation, the magnitude of the task of maintaining and repairing such a large and venerable building can often overwhelm the local vicar and parishioners on whom that responsibility largely falls. Addressing slow decay, promoted or accelerated by lack of regular maintenance, is a persistent issue.

Sadly, so too is the theft of lead from church roofs. Lead is expensive and easy to recycle, and all too often an easy target for especially cynical and thoughtless thieves, who leave vulnerable and precious church interiors soaking in the rain. Terne-coated steel is beginning to be employed as an alternative replacement for stolen lead. It is a shame, however, that a very good, historic roofing material is disappearing from the village scene after hundreds of years because of criminals.

Lead theft is especially expensive and disheartening for congregations to deal with since re-roofing costs are seldom now adequately covered by insurance. The national register of Heritage at Risk records that over 900 listed places of worship are at risk, which amounts to over six per cent of the total listed places of worship. Most of these are Church of England churches, and these figures do not include former places of worship that have been formally closed, sold on and are now in non-religious uses.

Churches are beacon buildings in the urban and village landscape of England, which are too important to lose. But is it reasonable to expect small numbers of villagers to look after them alone? Their care and rescue surely has to draw on a mix of local effort and national assistance, with a good deal of creativity and funding thrown in.

Village pubs have also played a key role in defining the characters of villages. Their state of health is a pretty good indicator of the health of a village as a whole, but they too have faced especially challenging times over the last few decades. Changing drinking habits, such as the increasing intolerance towards consuming any alcohol and driving, and the availability of a vast range of good quality and cheap supermarket alcohol, pose challenges to those traditional pubs that relied on beer and bar snacks.

The modern expectation that some reasonable food will be part of the offer has meant that for many rural pubs, coaxing people to take a long walk or get the car out means effectively becoming a restaurant. Offering only good beer, perhaps with some ancient pickled eggs from a jar and packets of crisps and nuts, may be enough for the connoisseurs, but generally does not pull in sufficient punters any more.

The publisher of the *Good Beer Guide* and authoritative surveyor of the public house scene, CAMRA (the Campaign for Real Ale), calculates that pub closures across the UK varied between an average of 14.5 and 20.2 per week each year from 2016 to 2019. In England alone a total of 339 pubs ceased trading temporarily or permanently in 2018. Other sources claim that 13,000 British pubs closed down between 2001 and 2018. There are reckoned to be around 47,000 pubs remaining in Britain, but a recent study commissioned by hospitality industry organisations suggests that almost a quarter of these will not survive the effects of the Covid-19 crisis.

Pubs often occupy prime sites in villages and include quite substantial car parks and gardens. They are great targets for house builders. Conversion or demolition for housing is by far the more profitable option for many marginally viable tied pubs (brewery owned) and free houses (independently owned). There are suspicions that some pubs that could maintain perfectly profitable trade have been deliberately run down in order to make lucrative housing appear the only viable option.

Villages often feel the loss of their last pub very keenly indeed. However, help is at hand. The planning system now specifically excludes all pubs (not just listed ones, or those in conservation areas) from automatic permitted development rights for change of use or demolition. Planning applications are now required to change the use of any pubs, and those applications can be challenged.

The National Planning Policy Framework (NPPF), which planning authorities must follow in determining planning decisions, explicitly mentions the importance of pubs as community facilities, along with shops, meeting places, sports venues, open space, cultural buildings and places of worship. The NPPF instructs planning authorities to 'guard against the unnecessary loss of valued facilities and services . . .' Local Plans too may contain specific policies preferring the retention of community facilities, such as pubs.

The Localism Act 2011 allows communities to nominate formally their pub as an Asset of Community Value. If the pub is put up for sale, the community has a six-month period to raise finance and make a bid to buy it. Village communities have rallied to save many pubs, organising committees to become landlords and forming not-for profit organisations, co-operatives or public limited companies.

There is hope too for other amenities that have suffered over the last few decades. In 2020, it was reported that there were around 360 community-run co-operative shops across rural England and their popularity is growing. Villagers have stepped up to the mark in similar ways to save post offices and village libraries, where local councils and private enterprise have not been able to find viable solutions.

NEW SOLUTIONS

Conservation of valued historic village buildings relies on maintaining active, sympathetic uses, or finding new ones. That in turn creates a demand for conservation know-how, and increased incentive to achieve creative conservation.

By the 2010s, the lack of Collyweston slate was reaching a crisis point. Local councils and planning inspectors were wavering in holding the line against inferior roof coverings being used on listed buildings in village conservation areas. Even major re-roofing and repair projects required at English Heritage and National Trust properties were in jeopardy. The problem was raised, almost incidentally, during a lunch-time retreat to a village pub to warm up after touring a senior figure around a few ongoing casework sites. In fact, it was a bit of a set-up. My colleague took a piece of slate from her pocket and explained that more funds were needed to investigate new ways of producing the much-needed material.

Funds were found, a partnership was established with local companies, and trials in artificial freeze-thawing began. The Collyweston stone log was soaked in tanks, left in the open and shipping containers were used as freezers. It was not all plain sailing. Only small batches could be produced at first, but eventually a commercially viable process was developed. Once it was possible to produce new slate, there was little excuse for not using it, and demand increased. Now there is a small but thriving Collyweston slate industry once more. The special character of the region's historic buildings can be maintained.

The Strategic Stone Study is a joint initiative between Historic England and the British Geological Survey, working in partnership with various stone specialists, to map sources of traditional building stone and their use in buildings across England. Identification of important sources will help to ensure that they are safeguarded where possible, and not built over or otherwise made inaccessible. Where it is simply not possible to use the original type of building stone, it may be feasible to find stone that serves as a good match. This is crucial, because unsympathetic repairs to historic stone and slate buildings with poorly matching materials can badly affect their appearance and their performance as structures. Much like the inappropriate use of concrete and cement, poorly matched stone can accelerate decay of adjacent good stone.

Similar challenges have faced the maintenance and repair of historic thatched buildings. Thatched buildings have defined the character of many English villages for centuries, but that has not meant the path to maintaining a sufficient supply of suitable water reed and straw has been easy. Not enough water reed is produced in this country to meet demand, so much of it is imported. Water reed was not used historically in many parts of the country in any case, and its use on buildings originally thatched with wheat straw can affect their appearance.

Old wheat varieties had much longer stems than modern varieties. The old harvesting method involved cutting the wheat straw at its base, tying it into bundles called sheaves, and then stacking the bundles upright in small conical arrangements called shocks (stooks or stacks). These were left in the field so that the wheat grains and straw dried out naturally over two or three weeks. The shocks were then taken away to be stacked together ready for threshing, which separated the grain from the straw. Even when the first machine harvesters appeared, pulled by horses or tractors, the wheat was still cut near its base so that long straw in sheaves remained to be set in shocks.

Combed wheat reed (actually wheat straw, confusingly) was produced by mechanically combing the wheat to remove the grain and waste leaves. This avoided crushing the straw, and every village in every wheat thatching district in the country used the local wheat straw for its buildings. Modern cereal straw is too short for thatching and in any case is shredded by modern combine harvesters in the field, so thatching straw now has to be specially grown for the purpose.

The National Thatching Straw Growers Association was formed in 2010 to act as a forum to share best practice, to promote the industry and to ensure a healthy supply of good thatching straw into the future. It has members across England who dedicate part of their farming business to this important specialist task. It is a pleasant surprise to come across shocks arranged in rows in a wheat field after harvest, when in recent times we have become so used to seeing only stubble.

This unexpected, delightful, encouraging sight transports you back in time by at least seventy or so harvests, and to scenes that would have been broadly similar around every village over many centuries before that. Like any other form of agriculture now and in the past, growing traditional thatching wheat straw is prone to having good years and bad years, but the supply has remained steady and the demand certainly persists.

Many rural villages have undoubtedly gone through rocky times during the last few decades, though the nature of the challenges they have faced varies enormously. Village health is not just about conservation of built fabric, but also about encouraging a balanced way of life. Some villages have almost been too successful in attracting visitors and new residents, to the disadvantage of existing communities.

Villages populated mainly by temporary residents can squeeze out normal village life to an unacceptable extent, and those that simply turn into commuter dormitories can be similarly unsatisfactory and unsustainable in the long term. Villages that stagnate, shedding amenities and accommodating only a narrow range of residents such as the retired or the unemployed, or that become too exclusive and available only to the very rich, are also problematic. Too many of these places polarise communities and perpetuate a divisive society.

Not all villages can, or should, grow and develop into something else. Some are far too precious and work perfectly well as they are. Others might benefit from significant shifts in direction. A mosaic of different village types is healthy.

Arguably, the most successful villages in the past have tended to be like little microcosms of wider society. Unlike major urban centres, however, villages place people from different social and economic groups in closer proximity to each other; they have to rub shoulders with each other and come together to make their village function. There are cliques in villages, like everywhere else, but generally an insufficient critical mass of people to enable these to form into clusters that seek to totally exclude others. There is generally very little potential for most villages to host exclusive gated communities or ghettos, whose mono-cultures never need to interact with each other.

The population of rural villages contrasts with towns and cities in other ways. Genetic and isotope studies are revealing a great deal about the ethnic composition of ancient populations, and how people moved around and settled their world. If archaeologists of the future analyse the skeletons of people buried in village cemeteries in the late twentieth century and compare them with those buried in urban cemeteries, they will see the contrast in the range and prevalence of ethnic diversity.

People from different countries have always migrated to English villages. Danes and Normans helped to shape English villages; Huguenots and Walloons came to weaving centres and newly drained farming areas; Scots came to east coast fishing villages, Irish to mining villages and Italians to brick-making areas. More recently, central and eastern European migrants have come to work in agriculture, horticulture and food processing industries. There has always been migration from within England as well. Nevertheless, archaeologists and historians of the future will correlate the patterns of post-war immigration with urban manufacturing centres, but perhaps not find too much to explain why there was not subsequently more movement of some ethnic groups out into the country.

The poet Benjamin Zephaniah grew up in Handsworth, Birmingham, and as a young man moved to London, but met with absolute incredulity from nearly all quarters when he moved from the capital to a small village in Lincoln-shire. Zephaniah has pointed out that many of the people of his parents' generation, who migrated to England from Jamaica, Barbados and other West Indies countries, came from villages; but they settled in urban areas and those communities are firmly associated with cities now. That is no reason why Zephaniah, or anybody else, should be met with bewilderment about their choice to live in a village in the provinces.

Somebody of South Asian heritage once gave me another perspective on the issue. Many people from those communi-ties had associated the countryside with backwardness and poverty, not aspiration and attainment. If you wanted to get ahead, you lived in a city. Perceptions like this are not confined to any particular community. I have met plenty of Londoners and others from large cities from all backgrounds, who are absolutely horrified at the thought of missing the opportunities that urban living and the twenty-four-hour bustle of a city provide. A Londoner once asked me, 'But what on earth do you do in the country if you suddenly fancy some Prosecco at 11.30 p.m.?' Perhaps new urban villages offer something of the best of both worlds?

The Olympic Village in Stratford, East London, built for the 2012 London Games, is working towards becoming a permanent urban village. The regeneration of this area of formerly derelict 'brownfield' land was always intended as a legacy of the London Olympics. From the outset it was envisaged that once the games were over, not only would the stadiums find new users, but the accommodation built for the athletes and supporting staff would be re-purposed as permanent housing. The hotel-like Olympic accommodation arranged in dozens of tower blocks was configured to be adapted to apartments, flats and 'town houses' after the games.

Around 3000 homes have been created in this way, just under half of which are designated as 'affordable', and the foyers of the tower blocks have plaques that record which national teams stayed in them. The former Olympic stadium and other venues such as the VeloPark are nearby and the development includes schools, a health centre, tree-lined boulevards and open 'green' areas and ponds, and free, high-speed Wi-Fi for residents. Various restaurants and shops have moved in as the new community has grown, and there are plans for further expansion.

One aspect of living in this village that differs from most in modern times is that the entire village is privately owned by one company, and the bulk of the homes are for rent only. 'East Village', as the place is now known, is creating its own identity and has drawn on the recent history of the site to do so. Only time will tell if this new model, urban village proves to be successful.

Building new urban villages on brownfield land in cities is one way to generate the villages of the future, but rural England must also look ahead. Creating opportunities for people to enjoy living in villages requires more than simply pointing out the potential lifestyle benefits. Active planning is needed to ensure that young people have options to stay in a village and are not forced to move away, and to ensure that new people are able to move in. Providing a wide range of social, economic and lifestyle choices in the countryside is key to avoiding these problems and ensuring that villages thrive into the future.

This means accepting sustainable development, and distributing it in the right way. However, expanding existing villages and re-purposing vacant, historic buildings can go only so far to meet necessary rural growth. Simply continuing to develop existing villages soon comes at too great a cost to their individual character and their surrounding open countryside, with its important agricultural and amenity land.

One day perhaps we will colonise the moon or Mars, hitherto uninhabitable deserts, or the bottom of the sea, and people will live in climatically controlled and environmentally sustainable new villages, towns and cities. Until then, already crowded places like England have to find ways to house and employ an expanding population by offering a range of different ways of sustainable living. Creating new settlements in the countryside is one answer. As we have seen in previous chapters, this has precedents throughout history. It is to a large degree inevitable, and has to be part of future planning. Redeveloping previously developed land offers exciting possibilities.

CHAPTER 12

VILLAGES FOR THE FUTURE

While the Reagan and Gorbachev regimes tentatively thawed the Cold War in the 1980s, and Berlin citizens euphorically smashed their way through the concrete wall that symbolised the ideological conflict that had threatened to destroy the world, you can bet that few people were thinking much about the consequences for English villages.

Some global drivers for changing the character of large parts of rural England and the fabric of villages are not immediately obvious, but can be far-reaching. The rapid post-war escalation and slower de-escalation of military force aimed across the Iron Curtain, for example, continues to have profound consequences, and offers one solution for creating new rural settlements. One of the many products of the so-called 'peace dividend' following the end of the Cold War has been the redundancy, mothballing and closure of many military facilities covering vast acres of country-side, not least Royal Air Force and United States Air Force stations. In fact, the story goes right back to the early years of the twentieth century.

MILITARY VILLAGES

The development of ever more capable aircraft and their increasing role in warfare during the twentieth century had a profound effect on large areas of rural England. For obvious reasons of flight safety and to limit potential harm to the public, early military airfields were located away from large centres of population. The permanent bases had to be easily accessible, however, so were located near rail lines and on major roads.

In the 1920s and 1930s, many of these followed the course of Roman roads. This is why if you follow the course of the old Roman road Ermine Street from Peterborough to just north of Lincoln, you pass close by (or pass through in some cases) the pre-war aerodromes of RAF Wittering, RAF Cottesmore, RAF Grantham, RAF Cranwell, RAF Wellingore, RAF Waddington, RAF Scampton, RAF Hemswell and RAF Kirton in Lindsey. Several more temporary aerodromes of the Great War and Second World War were built en route and nearby; all were named after their neighbouring villages. There is a similar pattern in Wiltshire around Salisbury.

By the end of the war in 1945, there were 720 military aerodromes in the United Kingdom, the vast majority in eastern and southern England. It is estimated that the amount of concrete poured to create runways, perimeter tracks and hard standings could have built a road 9000 miles long and 30 feet wide, comfortably enough to create a route to Beijing. With the arrival of the United States Army Air Forces from 1942 onwards, England effectively became a giant aircraft carrier.

Each aerodrome and its associated facilities took in a few hundred acres of land, which usually had to be requisitioned from several farms, dispossessing owners and tenants of land that had been farmed for centuries. Runways, perimeter tracks and roads severed lanes and roads between villages and destroyed hedges and woods. Each air force station included living quarters housing around 2500 personnel, the equivalent of a large village of the time, but these places usually dwarfed the historic villages amongst which they were built. This was a building campaign the like of which the countryside had never witnessed before. Life in many quiet and isolated English villages was utterly transformed almost overnight.

Around half a million American airmen were based in the UK in 1944. It came to be known as the 'friendly invasion'. Others from the Allied countries and across the Commonwealth came too: Polish airmen were prominent at the fighter aerodromes of southern England and at the bomber aerodromes of the Midlands; Elvington and surrounding villages in Yorkshire hosted Free French airmen. Many other places also welcomed hitherto unfamiliar cultures to the English rural scene. How many pre-war villagers in East Anglia would have anticipated bumping into a Maori in the local pub?

In many ways, apart from the very wide range of nationalities represented, the establishment of military settlements across rural England mirrored the earlier establishment of communities of migrant factory workers, quarry workers and miners, and canal and railway navvies, seen earlier in history.

The end of the Second World War saw the rapid closure of aerodromes and other military establishments, and the dispersal and repatriation of their personnel. This must have been a shock to rural communities that almost equalled their sudden arrival. The intensity of this shared wartime experience, which sometimes ran its course over less than two years as aerodromes were brought into service, fulfilled their operational role and were closed, is reflected by the strong ties between rural communities and service veterans that has continued down the decades.

However, the human bonds and physical changes brought about by military establishments in rural England has been even greater where the Cold War forced a much longer-lasting 'friendly invasion' of the countryside.

VILLAGES FROM THE BRINK OF OBLIVION

The ever-increasing sophistication, speed and power of aircraft, weapons, detection and surveillance technology saw aerodromes that had been established in the age of biplanes massively expanded. These post-war permanent stations became large military villages when family accommodation was added. Their communities drew on and contributed to the existing fabric of local society in many ways. Although Cold War air force stations were much fewer in number across the UK (declining from 270 in 1950 to 66 in 1991) they have had a very dramatic effect on rural England.

The shattering noise of military jet aircraft was the least of the disturbances felt in the countryside. Villages found themselves on the front line of the Cold War's precarious 'mutually assured destruction' stand-off. Villagers lived next door to horrifically destructive conventional and nuclear weapons; aircraft and missiles were primed at fifteen-minutes readiness, and loaded with bombs and warheads that could each easily destroy a city. The possibility of an accident, though ever present, had to be put aside in people's minds as they went about their daily business.

Hitherto obscure places such as Greenham Common in Berkshire and Molesworth in Cambridgeshire became internationally famous as focal points for demonstrations against nuclear weapons. Each attracted peace camps, which themselves became temporary but influential village-like communities with a lasting legacy in their own right, not least for female empowerment.

Other effects were less immediate, but even more significant. Though the bases were not easily accessible to locals, often shrouded in secrecy, fenced off and surrounded by security, there was nevertheless much permeability between the communities in other ways. Schools, shops, pubs, businesses of all kinds, clubs and societies, local entertainments and events adapted and developed to cater for and welcome the service personnel. Many service families decided to live off base and become more firmly part of local communities. Strong personal and familial relationships developed, and decades of symbiosis between base personnel and neighbouring villages changed the character of many of them.

The villages around the Suffolk American airbases of RAF Mildenhall and RAF Lakenheath have a curious Anglo-American feel. It is not only the liberal sprinkling of Star-Spangled Banners on business premises, lots of fast food outlets, huge pickup trucks and cars driven from the wrong side, snippets of drawl, and personnel milling about in the high streets in camouflaged fatigues and peaked caps. The modern architecture and distinctive local dry, sandy, pine-rich landscape seems to have been infused with American character.

When the timetable for the closure of RAF Mildenhall was announced recently, it sent shock waves through the region. The station has been part of the local fabric for eighty years, sixty of them in American hands. The enormity of the looming economic and social impact of closure was obvious.

New and exotic influences might be brought into a village, especially if the neighbouring base was an American one. American servicemen, some with families, lived in my village and our neighbouring villages when I was growing up. They represented much of the diversity of American society, ethnically and socially. Not only were we introduced to middle American music of both types (Country *and* Western, as the joke goes), but also to the quite different music preferred by the young black servicemen. We had visits to the American bases for air shows, Cub and Scout camps, barbeques and sports events. They were like trips to a little America.

I remember particularly chaotic cricket and softball matches that exposed how different countries that once shared a common language can become. The rules of the respective games were equally unfathomable to each side, as was the banter and swear words. In fact, we all got many interesting insights into aspects of each other's cultures.

The post-war and post-Cold War closure of military airfields and disappearance of their population from the community has left a similar void in village life in many places. It has also left some opportunities, which brings us back to the effects of outbreaks of peace, and Glasnost in the USSR, on the development of English villages.

Some former military airfields were almost entirely dismantled, their concrete chewed up and recycled as ballast for road construction. Many returned to agriculture, though the land was often mutilated by levelling and excavation. A few military buildings might serve as sheds and barns, the remainder crumbling away among the scrub, disintegrating concrete tracks now heading nowhere. These archaeological and architectural remnants and lone memorial plinths often comprise the only physical clues to their presence.

Many former airfields have been used, opportunistically, for a wide variety of new enterprises that have served the national and local rural economies very well indeed. Very few of these would have been developed deep in the country-side without the former military infrastructure as a starting point.

Post-war urban children played on bomb sites. Thousands of village kids have grown up playing on disused military sites. My friends and I spent many happy years exploring the old wartime airfield at the back of our village, the former RAF Mepal. We went up the narrow stairs of the watch office (or control tower as they are less accurately called), crept into various old huts and strange subterranean chambers, built dens out of piles of concrete rubble, dug out spent machine-gun rounds from the shooting range, and discovered unexploded bombs.

For some reason we were absolutely convinced these were practice bombs and merrily lobbed them around before storing them to impress other kids, whom we knew were busily assembling their own 'museums'. My sister discovered our stash, and when her history teacher invited the class to bring in some of their grandparents' wartime memorabilia, she took some of our bombs to school in a milk crate. I think he expected ration cards and gas masks. An army bomb disposal squad was called in, and later that day my parents were stunned to see camouflaged Land Rovers screech up to our house and soldiers combing the garden.

I crawled in and around the remains of the Thor ballistic missile emplacements, built on the disused airfield during the late 1950s, trying to work out how they functioned, and casually wondering whether they were radioactive. My parents recall the huge missiles being hauled along the local roads and anti-nuclear demonstrations. They told me about the missiles being raised to launch position and, worryingly, steaming during the Cuban Missile Crisis. I now think the steam was an effect of the liquid nitrogen used to pump fuel into the missiles at very high speed.

Any lessons we had learned about the dangers of the old airfield were negated by a fascination with the place; nothing could keep us away. We were not the first to discover its joys. Where my friends had lain down by a hedge watching the undercarriage of a crop-spraying aircraft pass repeatedly a few feet above us, my father, uncle and their friends had lain down on their backs to see Lancaster bomber wheels passing a few inches over them. They had also played with discarded ammunition, narrowly avoiding serious injuries.

There is a wider point to these reminiscences. Much of the airfield was returned to farming at the end of the war, but one of the wartime hangars became the nucleus of a cardboard box factory. Over time this has grown into a major packaging business, and the hangar is now submerged within the factory complex. The old watch office, other wartime buildings and missile emplacements were demolished to make way for an industrial estate, as this land, now considered a brownfield site, was ripe for redevelopment. The site now houses one of the largest straw-burning power stations in Europe. Here also can be found one of the largest used agricultural machinery auctions in the country. People come from all over the UK and Ireland on auction days.

Other parts of the old airfield were excavated for clay and used for landfill. A rifle club uses the old RAF shooting range, where air gunners once tested their aim. After the war, the airmen's billets were used to house displaced persons and refugees. Some people, who perhaps had very little to return to in Europe, stayed in the area, and several of my school-mates had central European surnames. The old airmen's quarters have nearly all gone, but brand-new housing devel-opment is now spreading onto the land where Stirling and Lancaster bombers previously taxied and parked.

The military purpose of RAF Mepal lasted for only a few short years. The somewhat dangerous, derelict play-ground of my father's and my youth has all but disappeared.

However, this place continues to play important new roles in the development of the village and region.

Some other former military aerodromes have retained an aviation function. Flying schools, private flying clubs, gliding clubs and aircraft maintenance businesses often use a mere fraction of the runways and other infrastructure required by the military, but are always proud to acknowledge the heritage of the places they occupy. Some developed into regional airports. However, the residents of Stansted Mountfitchet and surrounding Essex hamlets and villages could not have foreseen their temporary wartime airfield, which was hastily built by a United States Engineers battalion, becoming a major international airport.

The villagers around Heathrow and Gatwick saw their pre-war civil aerodromes adapt to wartime service, but the extraordinary post-war growth of commercial air transport has had massive implications for those formerly hidden-away parts of what was once rural England. It is not just the vast expansion of the airports themselves, but the incredible growth and development they have fed all around them.

Disused aerodromes were also well suited to motor sports. Karting circuits used concrete runways and perimeter tracks, and racing on a larger scale developed in several places. Snetterton Circuit (RAF Snetterton Heath/USAAF Station 13) in Norfolk, Santa Pod Raceway in Bedfordshire (former RAF Podington/ USAAF Station 109) and the internationally renowned Grand Prix circuit at Silverstone still retain evidence of their wartime origins. The latter has made the surrounding region a centre of excellence for automotive research and engineering. This would never have happened in this corner of Northamptonshire were it not for Air Ministry surveyors earmarking land for an entirely different purpose more than eighty years ago.

Villagers living near Bradwell Bay, in Essex, were probably horrified by the post-war development of a nuclear power station on the former RAF aerodrome there. The village of Aldermaston in Berkshire has on its doorstep the Atomic Weapons Establishment, the main centre for the manufacture of British nuclear weapons, because the wartime aerodrome there was deemed to be a suitable site for the development of Britain's main nuclear weapons research facility. The villagers of Chilton, East Hendred and Harwell in Oxfordshire lived alongside the national Atomic Energy Research Establishment for the same reason.

Elsewhere across England the various poultry farms, storage and haulage depots, factories, engineering workshops, industrial estates and business parks built on old airfields across the country have intensified and diversified rural economic activity and increased employment opportunities. It is amazing what you can find now taking place and being produced on old aerodrome sites. All of it is there only because it was convenient to reuse redundant military concrete hard standings and buildings.

If you are still not convinced of the magnitude of military development in the countryside, or its potential for redevelopment, consider this. Around twenty per cent of all land across the UK was under War Office control in 1945, and perhaps up to thirty per cent of all UK land has had some form of military use at some point. The Ministry of Defence is still the second largest single landowner in the United Kingdom. Old army barracks, battle-training grounds, firing ranges, depots, dockyards and a whole range of other facilities are now possibly open to new uses. When disused industrial land, such as that associated with mining, quarrying, steelworks and railway infrastructure, is added to the list, we can see that rural England has a huge capacity to accommodate new growth, without simply sacrificing green fields.

FROM OLD MESSES TO NEW VILLAGES

The enormous economic success of Cambridge in recent years, which has been partly driven by the symbiosis between the world-renowned university and high technology companies, has spread beyond the bounds of the city to the hitherto exclusively agricultural hinterland north of the city. This is now wryly known as 'Silicon Fen'. People have been drawn to the area from far and wide. But Cambridge is a small, historic city, with eye-watering house prices, and very little scope for further internal development. The solution to accommodating growth has been to promote the development of a number of satellite settlements, physically detached from the city by a few miles, but well connected for easy commuting.

All these new settlements make use of former RAF airfields. The former RAF Oakington, which later became an army barracks and finally an immigration detention centre, is being developed along with the surrounding area as part of 'Northstowe'. The new settlement of 'Cambourne', now well established, is continuing to spread over the former

RAF Bourn and the adjacent wartime relief landing ground at Caxton Gibbet.

The next development to get under way will be at the former RAF Waterbeach, which was also re-purposed as an army barracks when flying ceased. The company managing development there, Urban and Civic, is already overseeing extensive housing and mixed-use development on land that was formerly part of RAF Alconbury, about fifteen miles north of Cambridge. This new place has been named 'Alconbury Weald'. Significantly, this will also be the new home of Cambridgeshire County Council, who will vacate Shire Hall in the centre of Cambridge. South Cambridgeshire District Council left the city and built new headquarters in Cambourne several years ago.

Not far from Alconbury, the former RAF Brampton, a non-flying station built in the grounds of a country house, is being redeveloped. It is expanding historic Brampton village massively. New houses are going up alongside those originally built for officers and airmen. Interestingly, one or two of the brand-new executive homes are thatched, as is the former gate lodge, which was last used as an RAF chaplains' office.

In Rutland, the planned redevelopment of the former RAF North Luffenham, also later converted to Army use as St George's Barracks, exemplifies the issues faced in planning new settlements in the countryside. Even at the early masterplanning consultation stage, battle lines had been drawn between the development partnership, comprising Rutland County Council and the Ministry of Defence, and the neighbours of this proposed 'garden village' development.

Tension is now mounting: surrounding villages fear being swamped in a new, urbanised environment, and point out that local services and roads simply cannot cope with growth of the intended scale. Loss of wildlife habitat and destruction of heritage have also been raised, along with the wider environmental cost that building new homes entails. Rutland's motto, 'Multum in Parvo' ('much in little'), does not imply that this little county can cope with housing growth on this scale, they argue.

Surely there is a way to make sustainable new villages in the countryside? Perhaps there is a possibility of taking some inspiration from history, applying the best technology that the modern world can offer, and making these new places as self-sustaining as possible. Developers invariably consider sites like this as all brownfield land (i.e. previously developed), tending to forget that airfields incorporate huge expanses of grassland. They also prefer to start with a cleaned-up slate, finding it much easier to flatten existing buildings, construct new roads and amenity space, than working with the infra-structure that already exists.

The masterplan proposals for St George's Barracks/ RAF North Luffenham envisage retaining one or two espe-cially significant military buildings, but demolishing the remainder, including accommodation blocks, messes, tech-nical buildings and hangars. Apart from the unfortunate loss of rich and fast-disappearing, twentieth-century military heritage, this seems very short-sighted and wasteful of long paid-off carbon debt captured in buildings. Nothing is more environmentally responsible than reusing capable buildings, rather than flattening them and starting again. Surely here and in similar places there is an opportunity to re-purpose more of the existing buildings and work with the 'grain' of the existing site to create a characterful new place?

This is not as far-fetched as it might appear. Permanent pre-war aerodromes like RAF North Luffenham were designed on a campus-like basis, with a surprising amount of thought given to creating a pleasant environment for service personnel. Principal axial streets were lined with trees to create boulevards. There was plenty of open space, sports fields, parade grounds and so on. The layout and design of principal buildings was informed by the Royal Fine Art Commission. A conservative, stripped-down, but nevertheless elegant neo-Georgian style was preferred. These spacious brick buildings are readily convertible to modern uses and could cope with the introduction of many new energy-efficient measures.

New apartments, community meeting spaces, shops, offices, workshops, hotels and hostels, schools and colleges are not dissimilar from the range of building types and functions found on active military stations. Even huge aircraft hangars have found new uses as factories, sports halls, garages, storehouses, distribution centres and film studios.

WORKING FROM HOME

The Alconbury Weald development, though still in its early phases, integrates employment opportunities with the new housing, recognising the value of creating a well-rounded viable new place, rather than just a commuter dormitory village. Its Enterprise Campus includes some large-scale industrial development, but also business incubator facilities, offering smaller firms and start-up businesses desk and internet space. Alongside the incubators is the 'iMet' building, a centre for training, which will provide technical and professional courses for business. Shared meeting spaces, function rooms, a gym and a cafe have already been built to encourage a business community feel and networking.

The Second World War watch office has been restored and converted to offices and meeting space. It forms a poignant reminder of the place's history, among the new-build, and lends the development some special, distinctive character. It overlooks a new 'village green' and cricket pitch.

New synergies can be found by companies sharing facilities, ideas and projects. It is the concentration of companies on Cambridge's science parks, not far away, that has partly fuelled the phenomenal success of that city. Similar facilities could energise business growth on sites at St George's Barracks and elsewhere, further from the traditional urban centres of business and commerce.

Information and communications technology is finally catching up with the long-promised, *Tomorrow's World* dream of widespread, reliable, remote working, which avoids the daily commute to crowded cities to sit in crowded offices. It has long been recognised that the environmental cost, financial expense and harm to work–life balance caused by masses of people streaming into and out of cities every day is becoming totally unsustainable. The Covid-19 pandemic, in a few short weeks, demonstrated that much office work can be carried out at home.

Enforced home working has also prompted many people to think about their lifestyles in the long term. A national survey undertaken during the 2020 Covid-19 lockdown reported that sixty-eight per cent of workers who had been forced to work from home would like to do so permanently. Seventy per cent claimed they could be just as productive working at home as in their usual office.

The enthusiasm for home working that these findings indicated was subsequently tempered by a longer period of enforced home working. Concerns about separating work and home life, maintaining sufficient contact with colleagues, creating sufficient space for a home office set-up, and well-being issues associated with relative isolation emerged as time wore on. It is clear there are still some lessons to be learned, and of course much of the UK workforce simply cannot work from home.

Nevertheless, for many people, home working versus office working is not a binary choice. Working one or two days a week in a city centre office and the remainder at home or elsewhere nearby is the sort of flexible working that would give many people the best of both worlds. People might be prepared to live slightly further out of the established London, Birmingham, Manchester, Leeds, Liverpool, Newcastle, etc., commuter belts, if they faced the journey to work only once or twice per week.

It would also take some of the strain from the transport system, which across the country cannot really cope with the peak commute periods. There might even be more incentive to think about different transport options. It is notable that the growth of old and new communities north of Cambridge has not only prompted much-needed road upgrades, but has been accompanied by the introduction of something more innovative: a guided busway.

Buses, slightly adapted for the purpose with buffer wheels, run along a concrete trackway specially designed for their exclusive use. The course of the guided busway largely follows a former railway line (closed in the 1960s) that once served local villages, and is accompanied along its length by an elegant new cycleway. The guided busway was thought to be a cheaper option than reinstating the rail route, and it is a transport solution that could be adopted in many other places.

A greater percentage of people working from home has been shown to increase daily footfall and demand for local shops and amenities. Perversely, even as the centre of London became a virtual ghost town when workers and visitors stayed away during the Covid-19 pandemic, towns and villages in neighbouring regions reported more high street activity. New villages in the countryside could offer a range of services and amenities not currently available in those locations, and be confident of sufficient footfall to sustain them.

Easily accessible green space is also an important part of the mix for quality of life in new villages, and a considerable incentive for moving from cities. At St George's Barracks, prompted by the need to exploit important mineral reserves, the development partnership is proposing to quarry and then reinstate a large part of the airfield to create a wildlife and amenity area. Part of this area, coincidentally, includes the country's best-preserved Thor missile complex, now designated as a Grade II* listed building, like the one I played around during my youth. There is plenty of scope at St George's Barracks to enhance the existing campus character of the place, create new amenity and wildlife areas, and integrate new green infrastructure throughout the development.

Allotments, introduced early in the twentieth century to give urban families some working garden and then used mainly as retreats for grandfathers, have become trendy. Young people have discovered them, and long waiting lists to take on allotments are now common. Modern housing developments do not tend to feature substantial private gardens, preferring smaller yards and higher housing density. However, new village settlements could easily incorporate allotment areas, and offer residents something in the spirit of the pioneering countryside settlers of history.

The redevelopment of the massive former Cold War airfield at Upper Heyford, in Oxfordshire, includes green infrastructure to accompany over 1000 houses, businesses, schools, leisure facilities, and the retention and re-purposing of some military buildings. It also includes provision for an energy generation plant. Many former airfields have already been developed as wind farms and solar farms. Most have acres of land where ground source heat pumps could be buried. At St George's Barracks and elsewhere, new energy-efficient villages, perhaps even energy self-sufficient villages could be created.

Modern housing developers have tended to be risk-averse and usually promote only tried and tested development formulas. Creating the villages of the future will require investment beyond the current commercial models, experimentation, and some inspiration drawn from the past.

A BRIGHT FUTURE

The conservation of historic villages, the successful growth of existing villages and the creation of new villages relies on understanding village pasts, and applying a balance of traditional techniques and modern innovation to guide their futures. Nostalgic books written about English villages over the last few decades tend to emphasise and lament that something precious and long-established is being lost forever. However, it is wrong to think of village history as static, or villages as only passive victims of a changing world, having things done to them in the name of progress. Today, more than at any time in history, village communities have opportunities to help shape the places where they want to live.

This is not to say that economic circumstances are always favourable, that sufficient skills and desire reside among the population, or that the planning system is always good at delivering fairness and good quality development. Villagers themselves may not hold all the cards, but arguably they are better equipped than ever to marshal resources from within and without their own community than their predecessors.

Government and the various authorities with relevant roles will have to do their bit. To a large extent, England will get the villages it deserves.

Undoubtedly there will be exciting new chapters in the history of many long-established English villages. New villages will begin to write their own histories. Villages undoubtedly will change and adapt in many interesting ways in future years. But they are here to stay. Since prehistory, village life has been through highs and lows, boom and bust, disasters and triumphs, in and out of fashion, but it has persisted and thrived.

There are no signs that the role of the village has ended. In fact, the reverse is true. English villages have proved their resilience, and they are more popular and varied than ever. A new golden age for villages might well be dawning.

INDEX

INDEX

ACKNOWLEDGEMENTS

Thank you to Elly James at HHB Agency for prompting me to embark on this project and for her faith and guidance throughout. To all at Blink and Bonnier Books, especially editors Susannah Otter and Madiya Altaf, thank you for your encouragement and help, and also to Barry Johnston for his editorial skill. Jitesh Patel, Stephen Millership and Emily Rough have illuminated the book wonderfully.

Diana Hare, Tony Parker, the former regional *Inside Out* teams and others involved in the BBC villages programmes have given me the opportunity to explore places I didn't know well and to revisit villages I thought I knew. I am indebted to you all.